THE KEYNESIAN
RECOVERY

THE KEYNESIAN RECOVERY
And Other Essays

Peter Howitt

PHILIP ALLAN
New York London Toronto Sydney Tokyo Singapore

First published 1990 by
Philip Allan
66 Wood Lane End, Hemel Hempstead
Hertfordshire HP2 4RG
A division of
Simon & Schuster International Group

Typeset in 10/12 pt Times by
Best-set Typesetter Ltd, Hong Kong

Printed and bound in Great Britain by
BPCC Wheatons Ltd, Exeter

British Library Cataloguing in Publication Data

Howitt, Peter, 1946–
   The Keynesian recovery and other essays.
   1. Economics. Theories
   I. Title
   330.1

   ISBN 0-86003-081-4
   ISBN 0-86003-189-6 pbk

---

1 2 3 4 5   94 93 92 91 90

To my Mother

CONTENTS

PREFACE AND ACKNOWLEDGEMENTS

All the essays below except for the introduction have been published before, over the period from 1974 to 1988, as indicated on the first page of each. They are reprinted with minor corrections and with alterations to give uniformity of style, update references, and facilitate cross-references.

For permission to reprint the essays I am grateful to the American Economic Association (Chapters 2 and 10); the Western Economic Association International (Chapter 3); Elsevier Science Publishers (Chapter 4); the editors of the *Canadian Journal of Economics* (Chapter 5); the University of Chicago Press (Chapters 6 and 8); Messrs. Basil Blackwell (Chapter 7); the Eastern Economic Association (Chapter 9); the editors of the *International Economic Review* (Chapter 11); R. Preston McAfee (Chapters 11 and 13); and MIT Press Journals (Chapters 12 and 13).

I am indebted to the many people whose help is acknowledged in separate notes attached to each essay, but especially to Robert Clower, for his encouragement and advice, as well as for having written the works that inspired most of the essays. I would also especially like to thank my colleagues Joel Fried and David Laidler for having contributed so much to the development of the ideas in the essays.

1 · INTRODUCTION: PRICES AND COORDINATION IN KEYNESIAN ECONOMICS

1.1 INTRODUCTION

The coordination of economic activities involves many dimensions. To achieve a high level of economic development people must be guided somehow into making complementary production, consumption, investment, saving, occupation, labor-force participation, advertising, technique of production, and many other decisions. Yet macroeconomists have tended to reduce the problem to a single dimension, that of getting prices right. Classical or New Classical Economics, which embodies the view that coordination is best left to the market, is distinguished formally from Keynesian economics, which depicts an economy in need of central guidance, almost entirely by its assumption that wages and prices are perfectly flexible.

This reduction of the coordination problem to sticky prices is at the root of the decline of Keynesian economics. Not only does it raise problems of logical coherence that Keynesians have not succeeded in addressing, but, more fundamentally, it is not very plausible. Although there is plenty of evidence that wages and prices are indeed less than fully flexible, there is no good reason to attribute major coordination failures to that lack of flexibility. The massive downturn at the beginning of the Great Depression in the United States was accompanied by an unprecedented fall in wages and prices, and did not end until the deflation stopped. And there is no evidence that the reduction of price flexibility that has taken place since World War II has made the US economy less stable.[1]

The irony of this situation is that Keynes's main purpose in writing the *General Theory* was to refute the idea that unemployment, the

I am grateful to David Laidler for comments on an earlier draft, and to Joel Fried for extensive conversations.

archetypical coordination problem, was attributable to sticky wages. That idea was at the heart of 'classical' economics:

> Thus writers in the classical tradition...have been driven inevitably to the conclusion...that apparent unemployment (apart from the admitted exceptions) must be due at bottom to a refusal by the unemployed factors to accept a reward which corresponds to their marginal productivity.... But when we have thrown over the second postulate, a decline in employment, although necessarily associated with labour's *receiving* a wage equal in value to a larger quantity of wage-goods, is not necessarily due to labour's *demanding* a larger quantity of wage-goods; and a willingness on the part of labour to accept lower money-wages is not necessarily a remedy for unemployment. (1936: 16, 18)

In short, the classical theory that Keynes set out to refute is the one to which Keynesian economics has since tied its fate.

The present introductory essay tries to put the rest of the collection into some perspective by tracing this distortion of the coordination problem to the logical appeal of the Walrasian parable of perfect coordination, and to the failure of Keynesian economics to provide a coherent alternative parable. It argues that this failure was not remedied by the reappraisal of Keynesian economics started by Patinkin (1956) and Clower (1965), or by the new version of Keynesianism that has developed since the rational-expectations revolution. It also discusses some recent developments in the theory of transactions externalities which, together with some theory of adaptive learning behavior, may succeed finally in remedying that failure, in building a coherent theory of macroeconomic coordination problems freed from the dependency on price stickiness. These developments are helping to create what I have elsewhere (Chapter 5) called a Keynesian recovery.

1.2 THE COORDINATION PROBLEM

A formal distinction can usefully be made between two different aspects of the coordination problem: equilibrium coordination and disequilibrium coordination. The former refers to the efficiency properties of a system's equilibrium. It is the achievement of a coherent collective outcome when people are basing their individual decisions on mutually consistent beliefs. Equilibrium coordination requires providing people with the incentives to act in the social interest even when they are fully appraised of the consequences for their self-interest. I use 'equilibrium' in the game-theoretic sense that people's beliefs are coordinated; they have agreed upon a common set of priors, and hence would all form identical expectations if faced with the same information. There is no disagreement about the correct model of the economy. Disequilibrium coordination is the ability of the system to arrive expeditiously at an equilibrium; to harmonize people's beliefs. In Walrasian theory, disequilibrium coordination is achieved by the auctioneer's tâtonnement. In more general contexts it requires learning on the part of individuals, combined with the collection and dissemination of information. As the authors in Frydman and Phelps (1983) have shown, the convergence of learning to an equilibrium is not guaranteed by the consistency arguments of statistical theory, because the relationships being estimated will generally be affected by the process of estimation itself.

To discuss coordination intelligibly we must have in mind a concrete example. I would say we have to build a model, except that what is required is not a mathematical description of behavior but a conceptually coherent description of a paradigmatic economy,[2] one that exemplifies the key features of the coordination problem but abstracts from much else. Such an example is provided by the parable of Walrasian general equilibrium theory; the story that underlies the equations of Walrasian theory and provides, in Lakatosian terms, the theory's positive heuristic.

Imagine an initial state in which claims to society's resources have somehow been allocated among people. Each person cares only about his or her own consumption. Each can transform resources into consumption through the private activities of production and storage, or through the social activity of exchange. The economic problem is to arrange a post-exchange allocation not too far from the economy's Pareto frontier.

The problem requires coordination, partly because no one is concerned with the social objective of achieving efficiency, just with pursuing personal gain, and partly because the exchange opportunities available to any single person will depend upon others' decisions. That is, when a is negotiating with b, b's willingness and ability to trade will depend upon what trades b has already conducted with others, and upon b's expectations of what kinds of exchanges can be negotiated with future trading partners. Furthermore, the willingness of anyone to enter the exchange process in the first place, and to spend resources trying to contact trading partners, will depend upon expectations of others' willingness to do the same. On the realistic assumption that no one knows the economy's exact configuration of tastes and endowments, the names of all future trading partners, and their detailed trading plans, then there is a nontrivial problem of ensuring collective compatibility of plans.

1.3 THE WALRASIAN PARABLE

According to the parable of general equilibrium theory the people congregate in a single location, where they negotiate at no cost, under the direction of the infamous auctioneer, who cries out prices, adjusting them in response to excess demands until all markets clear, and allows trade to take place only when the adjustment is over. At that point the auctioneer also provides a clearing-house in which everyone deposits excess supplies and withdraws excess demands.[3]

According to this parable, the economy achieves a perfect solution to the coordination problem, for two reasons. First, the plans made at equilibrium prices constitute a Pareto-optimal allocation, and second, all trades take place at equilibrium prices. The first part assures perfect equilibrium coordination; the second perfect disequilibrium coordination. Both are important.

Perfect equilibrium coordination – the optimality of competitive equilibria – comes from the fact that all social interactions are mediated by prices which each person takes as given. The only social constraint on anyone's choices is the single lifetime budget constraint with parametric prices. If someone decides to buy more x, other buyers of x will generally be harmed, and sellers will benefit. But the benefits and costs are bestowed exclusively by price changes. If interactions were not so mediated, optimality would be lost; in short, any nonpecuniary externality will impair equilibrium coordination.

Perfect disequilibrium coordination – the fact that all trades occur at equilibrium prices – reflects two basic sets of assumptions. The first is the set of technical assumptions guaranteeing existence. The second is the set guaranteeing that everyone knows the equilibrium prices. If they didn't, and had to plan on the basis of imperfect guesses, there would be unsold goods and frustrated buyers; the resulting allocation would not be Pareto optimal.

The auctioneer in this story performs two essential services. The first is that of coordinating people's beliefs. The tâtonnement ensures that everyone is informed of equilibrium prices. In the case of more than one equilibrium it also ensures that everyone is taking the same equilibrium prices as given. Furthermore, when excess-demand functions are not single valued in equilibrium the auctioneer informs everyone which among their various preference-maximizing plans to implement. The process of gathering and disseminating this information is costless. Thus perfect disequilibrium coordination is accomplished.

Most commentators focus on this first service of the auctioneer. But there is a second, equally important one. Specifically, the auctioneer matches buyers and sellers at no cost. There are no costs of contacting trading partners. All trades are impersonal exchanges with the market. The clearing-house arrangement ensures that as long as total acquisitions and disposals are equal for each good there are no unmatched buyers or sellers left over at the end of the day.

The auctioneer's second service is important for achieving equilibrium coordination, because costs of contacting trading partners generally create nonpecuniary externalities. When someone puts more resources into the contacting process with a view to buying x, for example, sellers of x typically find their selling costs reduced, as when extra recruiting effort makes it easier to find a job, or when a rise in the demand for housing makes it easier to sell a house at its maximum realizable price. At the same time, other buyers of x find it more costly to buy, as when an increase in demand causes longer lineups or when a tight labor market makes it difficult to fill vacancies.

As we shall see, these two kinds of transaction externalities are important in the Keynesian recovery. The first is a 'thin-market' externality, and the second a congestion externality. They correspond to the sort of externalities that arise in almost any communication network. For example, my acquiring a phone confers an external benefit on people that might want to contact me and an external cost on people that might want to contact the people that I will be trying to contact. By making contacting costless, the auctioneer avoids these externalities and thus assures perfect equilibrium coordination.

1.4 THE ROLE OF PRICES

It is easy to be misled by the Walrasian parable into thinking that the coordination problem for macroeconomics is equivalent to getting prices right. The parable derives much of its logical appeal from the artful separation between individual decision problems, in which prices are given by the market, and the market process that determines those prices. Coordination is the job of the market process. If prices are set at their equilibrium values, then the job is done, except for problems of imperfect competition and externalities that have not until recently played a central role in macroeconomics.

This division between private decision problems with parametric prices and the impersonal market process that determines the prices has a ring of truth to it. It appeals to the everyday observation of market institutions that post prices and allow customers to buy at those prices; retail and wholesale distributors, trade unions, etc. The story is so congruous in many respects that someone who has fallen under the Walrasian spell finds it difficult to think that there could be anything more to coordination than allowing the auctioneer, or his real-world analog, to get on with the job of adjusting prices. It is easy to forget that in real life there are many other problems which these market institutions deal with (inventory management, quality verification, advertising, etc.), and which constitute an important part of their role in the coordination mechanism, but which have been assumed out of existence by Walrasian theory.[4]

Of course, the pervasiveness of price-quoting institutions in most economies of record is evidence that getting prices right is an important aspect of the coordination problem. But it is misleading to focus exclusively on that one aspect, because the fundamental coordination problem of society is not to get prices right. Rather it is to get people's beliefs harmonized, and to induce them to carry out collectively rational actions once their beliefs are harmonized; that is, to achieve disequilibrium and equilibrium coordination. Only in Walrasian theory do both aspects amount to getting prices right.

The reason why getting prices right appears all-important in the Walrasian parable is that the auctioneer's matching service is even less explicit than the price-adjustment service. In standard accounts of the parable no mention is even made of the matching problem. The coordination problem is posed as that of finding the solution to the simultaneous equations of excess demand. This problem being difficult enough to formulate and solve, it is natural to forget other problems that might impede coordination.

However, the few authors who have explicitly recognized the auctioneer's second service have shown that when it is no longer provided costlessly then perfect coordination is no longer guaranteed by getting prices right. Ostroy (1973) has shown, for example, that even if everyone knew the Walrasian prices in a pure exchange economy, there would remain a serious problem of disequilibrium coordination, because people also generally need a full description of the trading plans of all traders in the system and their schedule of meetings. Without this information there would be no incentive-compatible way of ensuring that people all finish a round of trading with their desired allocations, unless some coordination device like money were introduced. Walrasian theory has no room for money. And as Jones (1976) and others have shown, money gives rise to coordination problems of its own.

Likewise, as Diamond (1987) has pointed out, even if no communication channel is needed to ensure disequilibrium coordination, serious problems of equilibrium coordination can arise from externalities in the matching process. Friedman (1968) defined the 'natural rate of unemployment' as the rate that would be 'ground out by the Walrasian system' if it were amended to include the appropriate frictions. Those frictions imply a nontrivial matching problem. Given the likelihood of thin-market and congestion externalities, such amendments of Walrasian theory generally produce an inefficient amount of unemployment. Thus the nonoptimality of the natural rate is another coordination problem that could not be solved by getting prices right, because its cause is external effects that will persist even after prices have adjusted all the way to their equilibrium values.

1.5 KEYNES AND THE KEYNESIANS

Whatever was the 'classical economics' from which Keynes was struggling to escape, it was not that of Walras. The Marshallian economics that he was raised on had little to say about the economy as a whole. Nevertheless, the Marshallian system was also built upon a parable in which all interactions were mediated by prices. Indeed, the Walrasian parable can be interpreted as the multi-market version of the Marshallian scissors, with the addition of some non-Marshallian formality and explicitness. More to the point for present purposes, the 'classical' view that Keynes was trying to refute with his *General Theory* was essentially the same as that embodied in the Walrasian parable described above: that unemployment was attributable to a failure of wages to adjust to their market-clearing levels, and that the remedy was to make wages and prices more flexible.

In the *General Theory* Keynes set out to develop a theory in which unemployment did not depend upon wage or price stickiness. His reasons for doing so were not the theoretical ones stated above. Instead they were largely empirical. Unemployment in the United States had continued to rise during the early part of the Depression, while wages and prices fell precipitously. The deflation had appeared to do nothing to cure the problem. Indeed, unemployment started to fall only when wages and prices stopped falling, in 1933. It was hard to reconcile this evidence with the idea that unemployment is caused by the failure of wages and prices to respond to excess supply in the economy.[5]

Keynes was a great success in many respects. But in his main objective, that of freeing the theoretical explanation of unemployment from depending upon sticky wages and prices, he was a failure. The Keynesian revolution soon settled on the conclusion that Keynes's system made sense, and resulted in unemployment, only under the assumption of a sticky money wage rate (Modigliani, 1944). Since no one was inclined to dispute the realism of assuming that wages were less than perfectly flexible, the Keynesian revolution proceeded on the classical basis of sticky wages. Keynes's original concern that making unemployment depend upon sticky wages was inconsistent with the historical record was conveniently forgotten.[6] His struggle to escape from classical economics ended with a reaffirmation of the classical diagnosis of unemployment.

This is not to say that Keynesian economics misinterpreted Keynes, or that there is in the *General Theory* a theory of coordination failure that no one has yet managed to find; just that Keynes was a failure. He failed not just to get his message across; more fundamentally he failed to propose a coherent alternative to the classical explanation of unemployment. The IS-LM system that Hicks and Hansen drew out of the *General Theory* was a marvelously useful tool for analyzing the interaction of real and monetary factors in the determination of the level of unemployment, but only under the classical assumption that unemployment is attributable to sticky wages, the very assumption that Keynes had set out to challenge in the *General Theory*.

In general terms, Keynes's failure was in not specifying an alternative parable of how society solves the coordination problem, an alternative as simple and compelling as the classical parable with its distorted picture of the role of prices. Therefore he provided no reason why there should be non-price interactions in equilibrium; no reason for equilibrium coordination problems. In terms of disequilibrium coordination, chapter 19 of the *General Theory* had some fascinating and sensible stability analysis, but it was not compelling. This was partly because it was a verbal analysis of a complicated but incompletely specified dynamical system, but also because it was not based on a coherent account of the economy's communication channels. His attempt to explain why a free-market system 'seems capable of remaining in a chronic condition of subnormal activity for a considerable period' (1936: 249) fell short of the mark.

1.6 THE KEYNESIAN REAPPRAISAL

In the absence of any alternative parable, sympathetic interpreters of Keynes tried to analyze his ideas in terms of the most coherent account available, namely that of Walras.[7] Thus Patinkin (1948) argued that Keynes should be understood as referring to what happens in Walrasian theory when price adjustment takes place in real time, and expectations and distributional effects are allowed to feed back to the adjustment. In chapter 13 of Patinkin (1956) he furthered that interpretation by noting that when there was an excess supply of output, the demand-for-labor schedule would no longer be given by marginal product schedule, because firms would face sales constraints, and that this might help to rationalize Keynes's views on the inability of labor to solve unemployment by agreeing to wage reductions.

Patinkin's contributions became famous not for these positive contributions to Keynesian theory, but for having reaffirmed classical theory; for showing that the real balance effect, which Keynes did not fully take into account, would guarantee the existence of a full employment equilibrium, and would make involuntary unemployment incompatible with equilibrium. His attempts to integrate Keynesian ideas into a coherent account of the market mechanism were ignored for many years while Keynesian economics developed by focusing mainly on the components of aggregate demand. However, his analysis of labor demand contained the seeds of a reappraisal of Keynes, because the sales constraints he analyzed were the kind of non-price interactions needed to get less than perfect equilibrium coordination.

The reappraisal began with Clower (1965), who showed that the Keynesian consumption function was inconsistent with the Walrasian parable unless trading occurred out of equilibrium, because it involved a non-price interaction, specifically the effect of realized sales of labor on the demand for consumption goods. He proposed a modification of the parable that allowed the non-price interaction; the famous 'dual decision hypothesis.' He also argued that the system's adjustment would be weaker under the dual decision hypothesis than in Walrasian theory, because in a situation of unemployment the constrained demands of the dual decision hypothesis would not be as strong as the notional demands of Walrasian theory, and thus firms would have less inducement to hire back the unemployed.[8] Leijonhufvud (1968) argued forcefully that these insights of Clower could be used as the starting point for a wholesale re-examination and reconstruction of Keynesian economics.[9]

The reappraisal reached its culmination with Barro and Grossman (1971), who integrated the separate contributions of Patinkin and Clower. In the Barro–Grossman analysis, when there is excess supply in both goods and labor markets, the demand for goods depends upon the demand for labor, through Clower's consumption function, and the demand for labor depends upon the demand for goods, through Patinkin's mechanism. In a 'fixed-price' equilibrium both these equations are solved; the expectations of demanders of labor and goods are coordinated by quantities, not prices.

The equilibrium concept of Barro and Grossman was important because of its affinity with Keynes's concept of effective demand. The sales constraints taken as given by firms and households were the non-price interactions that Keynes had postulated,[10] but now they were derived from a coherent conceptual framework. The fact that people's plans and beliefs were harmonized by quantity interactions rather than prices embodied what Patinkin (1976) later identified as the central message of the *General Theory*.

For a brief period in the early 1970s, this reappraisal was the hottest topic in macroeconomics. It became identified with the search for a microfoundation for (Keynesian) macroeconomics. However, that situation soon changed dramatically, and fixed-price analysis disappeared from most journals, at least in North America. The reasons for this sudden disappearance are no doubt varied and complex. But it is clear in retrospect that the research program set out by Leijonhufvud, and exemplified by Barro and Grossman, was flawed from the beginning.

First, although this analysis succeeded in deriving non-price interactions from an underlying account of the market mechanism, the interactions were completely dependent upon the failure of prices to adjust. In a Barro–Grossman analysis, if prices are Walrasian then so are quantities. The multiplier process requires sticky prices. Thus the reappraisal was unable to explain equilibrium coordination failure. The analysis was just as dependent as traditional Keynesianism on the classical explanation of unemployment: sticky wages and prices. Indeed, it went beyond the classical analysis by supposing that prices would remain fixed for so long that quantities would adjust all the way to their fixed-price equilibrium values.

Second, in terms of disequilibrium coordination, the attempts to show how Clower's dual-decision hypothesis would change the stability properties of the system, thereby perhaps rationalizing some of the analysis of Keynes's chapter 19, were based upon the weakest part of classical analysis, its theory of price adjustment. In Walrasian theory the tâtonnement is just an observationally irrelevant device for rationalizing equilibrium analysis; the vagueness of its theoretical foundations is of little importance.[11] But to someone who believes that disequilibrium coordination is a serious problem, there could hardly be an intellectually less satisfying way of explaining how society achieves it than to invoke a mysterious auctioneer who uses no resources, whose motivation is left unexplained, and whose very existence even in classical theory is predicated on the belief that disequilibrium coordination is not a serious problem.

In short, the reappraisal never got much beyond Walras. It did not model the various aspects of the coordination problem assumed away by Walras. Thus it had no way of answering such fundamental questions as why prices change the way they do, why workers who remain unemployed for long periods of time do not succeed in underbidding the workers who have jobs, thus passing the unemployment like a hot potato among all workers, and why firms unable to sell all they want cannot find willing buyers by lowering their relative prices rather than taking as given an absolute sales constraint.[12]

Perhaps the most embarrassing aspect of this failure was the demonstration by Barro and Grossman (1971) that recessions are as likely to be caused by increases in aggregate demand as by decreases. Start at the Walrasian equilibrium and raise aggregate demand. Shortages emerge on the goods market. Frustrated households supply less labor, because quantity rationing reduces the real value of their wages. The withdrawal of labor forces a further reduction of goods supply, thus starting off a new round of shortages and withdrawal of labor. After this 'supply-multiplier' process has converged, output and employment have fallen as a result of what experience suggests should have been an expansionary shock.

When one searches for a way out of such embarrassments it becomes clear that the same market institutions that give the Walrasian theory its verisimilitude also minimize the extent of the demand rationing at the heart of the supply multiplier; wholesalers, retailers, brokers, shop-keepers, middlemen, and so on, typically quote prices and allow buyers to choose quantities, at least as long as inventories and order books are reasonably under control. But none of these institutions are in Walrasian theory. They need to be included, or a new parable needs to be developed that embodies the institutions in some simplified form.

Having tied itself to the mast of sticky wages and prices, without building any such alternative parable, Keynesians were defenseless when Barro (1977b) showed in terms of a parable of his own choosing that wage/price stickiness was compatible with the absence of a serious coordination problem. Barro invoked the institution of implicit contracts between firms and workers with rational expectations, which would freeze wages but specify the Walrasian quantity of labor. Barro's institutional setup assumed away as many coordination problems as Walrasian theory. But Keynesians had no alternative setup, and thus no intellectually defensible argument for taking coordination problems seriously.

In retrospect, the Keynesian reappraisal was too much influenced by the Walrasian parable. This influence was not entirely bad, because the Walrasian parable had the virtue of conceptual coherence that was badly needed by Keynesian economics. But within that framework it is hard to avoid the conclusion that the coordination problem amounts to getting prices right, and that in the end was the conclusion reached by the reappraisal. Again Keynesian economics found itself supporting the classical theory that Keynes had tried, for good reason, to refute.

1.7 RATIONAL EXPECTATIONS

The search for a microfoundation for Keynesian macroeconomics reached its pinnacle with the Phelps *et al.*, (1970) volume. In the introduction to that volume, Phelps sketched what seemed like a new parable of exchange that would rationalize Keynesian economics. The parable involved people trading on informationally separate islands. Changes in aggregate demand, neutral in a Walrasian setting, would affect real activity, not because the auctioneer adjusted prices slowly, but because the typical seller would read the decline in prices, at least with some probability, as a decline in his relative selling price.

The Phelps island parable dealt with some of the coordination problems that Walrasian theory assumed away. It incorporated an explicit matching technology with costs of contacting potential trading partners, those on separate islands. But instead of rationalizing Keynesian economics it became the theoretical basis of a classical revival once Lucas (1972) formalized it and added rational expectations.

The Phelps–Lucas model accomplished two major objectives. First, it put the auctioneer out of the picture. On each island an auctioneer functioned as in Walrasian theory, as an observationally neutral computational device. Thus nothing depended upon this *ad hoc* device, provided it could be assumed *a priori* to converge in meta-time. Second, it replaced the mechanical expectational assumptions characteristic of most macroeconomics at the time with the assumption of Muthian rational expectations, which produced the famous policy-ineffectiveness proposition.

The Lucas paper was heralded by many as having finally provided macroeconomics with proper microfoundations. And it did, in the sense that it was a model of equilibrium interactions between explicit maximizers with optimal expectations. But it dealt only superficially with the coordination problem. Equilibrium coordination was a problem in the Lucas model only to the extent that monetary policy could interfere with rational decision-making by adding noise to the price system. The fact that no one could be on more than one island at a time meant that there were costs of matching. But the peculiar setup, in which all costs of matching were either zero or infinite, and not subject to individual choice, ruled out any non-price interactions through this channel.

Disequilibrium coordination was no problem at all in the Lucas model. The tâtonnement on each island was infinitely fast. More fundamentally, the assumption of Muthian rational expectations rules out all problems of coordinating people's beliefs. It says that no one tries to play Keynes's beauty contest. No one makes systematic errors in guessing the values of variables that depend in turn upon others' guesses.

The success of new classical economics was important for the development of Keynesian economics because it forced Keynesians to incorporate rational expectations, in order to eliminate at least some of their most obvious loose ends. The immediate result was the contract models of Fischer (1977) and Taylor (1979), in which wages were set before all information concerning aggregate demand and supply of goods was available, and employment was determined later by demand.

These new Keynesian models had the advantage of building on salient aspects of actual labor markets, and providing needed counterexamples to the policy-ineffectiveness proposition of new classical economics. But they did not provide Keynesian economics with a useful parable of coordination. They reaffirmed the dependency of Keynesian economics on the classical diagnosis of unemployment, without providing a coherent explanation. Nor did they solve the embarrassing problem of the Barro–Grossman supply multiplier. Instead, they merely assumed, with no coherent justification, that quantities would be demand determined.

Furthermore, by adopting the fashionable assumption of rational expectations, Keynesians conceded to their opponents that disequilibrium coordination was not a serious social problem. The price stickiness of new Keynesian models was now equilibrium price stickiness. Prices were set not by people trying to cope with an unknown system, but by people trying to anticipate the outcome of exogenous random variables, with well-defined probability distributions about which everyone had perfect information.

The more recent vintage of sticky-price Keynesian models, exemplified by Blanchard and Kiyotaki (1987), based upon menu costs of price adjustment and the Akerlof–Yellen (1985a) analysis of near-rationality, has made some progress toward a new parable. It incorporates some long-neglected aspects of imperfect competition into Keynesian economics, it provides a more coherent explanation of the motivation of wage/price setters, it rationalizes the assumption that quantities are normally demand determined, and it provides a reason for equilibrium coordination failure, by deriving an 'aggregate-demand externality.' Furthermore, as Blanchard (1986) has shown, the analysis yields valuable insights into the dynamics of inflation.

Nevertheless, this analysis shares most of the fundamental shortcomings of the earlier Fischer–Taylor models. It too reverts to the pre-Keynesian diagnosis of unemployment (sticky wages and/or prices), it provides no alternative parable that could accommodate the many real-world institutions involved in the coordination process, and by adopting the assumption of rational expectations it too rules out any problem of disequilibrium coordination. Because of this superficial treatment of the coordination problem it is no surprise that it is just as reliant as new classical economics upon unrealistic labor-supply assumptions for explaining employment fluctuations (Blanchard and Kiyotaki, 1987), that the coordination problems that it can explain turn out to be second-order small (Rowe, 1987), and that even sympathetic economists, frustrated at the ability of mainstream Keynesian economics to explain the rising unemployment problems of Europe in the 1980s, are beginning to see the mainstream as a degenerating research program (Summers, 1988).

1.8 THE KEYNESIAN RECOVERY

In my opinion, the main reason why Keynesian ideas are about to make a recovery is that a new parable is finally starting to be developed in which costs of contacting trading partners are explicit, and in which the resulting transaction externalities create a serious problem of equilibrium coordination. Not only are equilibria inefficient because of the externalities, but there may be multiple, Pareto-ranked equilibria. This parable, which starts with the seminal contribution of Diamond (1982b), at last offers a coherent explanation of why unemployment can persist for long periods without invoking an unrealistic degree of wage or price stickiness. An economy can simply get stuck in a bad equilibrium, with a lot of unemployment.

The reason for multiple equilibria is the thin-market externality arising from the transactions technology. If people expect a lot of aggregate demand, then they expect selling costs to be relatively low. This will encourage high production levels, which in equilibrium will result in high aggregate demand, thereby fulfilling the original expectation. By the same token, the expectation of low activity can also be self-fulfilling, because the associated prospect of thin markets and high selling costs will discourage activity.

The parable also provides a deeper explanation of the Keynesian multiplier process. More demand on the part of one group of traders will induce others to demand more. The reason is that, as in the Keynesian consumption function, there is a 'strategic complementarity' (Cooper and John, 1988) arising from a non-price interaction; specifically, the thin-market externality. When some people begin to trade more, that reduces the thinness of markets and induces a further round of increased trade.

The following sketch may help to illustrate the new parable. Consider a world with a continuum of people, indexed along the unit interval, with unit mass. Each can produce output, but wishes to consume only goods produced by others. Time is discrete. The technology has an indivisibility; in each period each individual must produce either zero or one unit. Goods are not storable across periods.

Trading is costly. The probability of any given individual finding a trading partner who has produced, and hence with whom trade is possible, equals $P(N)$, where N is the number of people who have entered the market.[13] That is, when N people enter the process with goods to trade, the total number of matches formed will be $NP(N)$. The function P describes the matching technology. To capture the idea of a thin-market externality suppose that P is an increasing function. Doubling the number of people looking for a partner will more than double the number that succeed.

The function P is plotted in Figure 1.1. It passes through the origin because when there is no one to find it is impossible to find anyone. Its slope is first increasing and then decreasing because at first, as the market begins to be filled up, it takes some critical mass to generate a significant probability of finding someone, but eventually the marginal contribution of more people must diminish because P cannot exceed unity. Assume that the curve intersects the 45-degree line exactly three times, as illustrated.

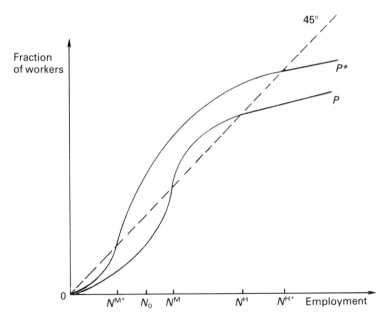

Figure 1.1 Multiple equilibria with thin-market externalities.

Each person is identical, except for the cost of producing and entering the market, c, which is uniformly distributed on the unit interval. Each person that produces will receive the payoff $1 - c$ if a trading partner is found, in which case there will be a one-for-one trade and the proceeds will be consumed, or $-c$ if not. Thus the expected payoff from producing and entering the market is the probability of making a match minus c.

All people have the same subjective probability p of finding a trading partner. This will equal the actual probability P only in equilibrium. The actual number who will enter will be the number for whom c is less than or equal to p. Given the uniform distribution of c, this implies that $N = p$ each period. The market is in equilibrium when everyone's expectations are fulfilled. Thus an equilibrium occurs whenever $p = P(N)$. Given that $N = p$, this means that an equilibrium will occur whenever N solves the equilibrium condition: $N = P(N)$; that is, whenever the P function intersects the 45-degree line in Figure 1.1.

This is a model with an equilibrium coordination problem, because of the thin-market externality. People interact not through prices but through the probability of finding a trading partner. Thus the equilibria are Pareto-ranked, with more N being Pareto-superior.[14] Furthermore, even the highest equilibrium yields less than the maximum social welfare, defined as the sum of individual expected utilities.[15]

We might think of the people who choose not to participate as unemployed. Thus N is the employment level, and the model has multiple natural rates of unemployment, all higher than optimal. The model also has a multiplier process, in the following sense. Suppose that P depends positively upon a parameter g, which might be government purchases if the model were modified appropriately. An increase in g would shift the curve in Figure 1.1, and the usual geometric argument would show that employment in the high-level equilibrium would increase by more than the shift in P.

Thus it is possible to develop some of the central ideas of Keynes in a formal model based on this parable, without invoking any wage or price stickiness. The example we have sketched is so simple that it does not even have prices in it. It is based just as firmly as new classical economics on the microeconomic principles of equilibrium and rationality, but it has a nondegenerate matching technology that creates problems of equilibrium coordination.

1.9 BEYOND RATIONAL EXPECTATIONS

Models like this have gone at least part way toward putting a serious coordination problem into macroeconomics. But they deal only with equilibrium coordination. Like current Keynesian models based on wage/price stickiness, they assume that the economy is always in a rational expectations equilibrium. They do not deal with how the economy arrives at this equilibrium, with the coordination problems that can arise when people's beliefs are mutually incompatible.

It is a mistake to focus upon one aspect of the coordination problem to the neglect of the other. This is true in general, but it is doubly true in models with multiple equilibria. For in such models the assumption that the economy is in a rational-expectations equilibrium is not enough to make empirical predictions. And without some explicit adjustment assumptions that describe how people behave and interact when they are not in an equilibrium, we have no way of knowing which equilibrium they will go to, if any, or how fast, or by what route.

Thus for example, to model the Great Depression as a low-level equilibrium may help in understanding why the slump persisted, but it begs the question of why it happened then. And the argument that mobilization for World War II shocked the economy out of that equilibrium is unconvincing without some systematic way of analyzing how an economy can converge upon a new equilibrium after a shock.

Also, if the middle equilibria in Figure 1.1 were always observed, the model would have a negative multiplier: increases in g would reduce employment. Furthermore, even if the economy was always observed in either the high-level equilibrium or the low-level (shutdown) equilibrium, there would still be a problem in using the model to explain the existence of a positive multiplier process, because what would stop the economy from going from the high equilibrium to shutdown in response to an increase in g?

Thus if the Keynesian recovery is to persist, it will need to attack the coordination problem on both fronts. There is at least some hope that this can be done with the new theory of disequilibrium dynamics being developed by such authors as Marcet and Sargent (1986), Woodford (1987), Evans (1985), and the contributors to Frydman and Phelps (1983). These authors have been concerned with the question of the convergence properties of self-referential adaptive systems. Observed outcomes depend upon expectations, and expectations in turn depend, through a learning process, upon past observations.

Thus consider the following example. Suppose that at any date t, people have available a history of observations: $\{P_0, \ldots, P_{t-1}\}$ on what fraction of participants have actually succeeded. They believe that this series has been drawn from an unchanging distribution, and that P_t will be drawn from the same distribution. Thus P_t will equal their estimate of the mean of that distribution. As dictated by any statistics book, their estimate is the observed sample mean:

$$p_t = (1/t)(P_0 + \ldots + P_{t-1})$$

Since $N_t = p_t$ and $P_t = P(N_t)$:

$$N_t = (1/t)(P(N_0) + \ldots + P(N_{t-1}))$$

which implies the difference equation:

$$N_t = N_{t-1} + (1/t)(P(N_{t-1}) - N_{t-1})$$

At the initial date 0 people make their participation decisions arbitrarily, since they have no experience. These initial decisions determine an arbitrary starting value N_0. Given N_0, the above difference equation determines the future course of employment.

In terms of Figure 1.1, the difference equation asserts simply that employment will always increase (decrease) when the P function lies above (below) the 45-degree line. Therefore employment will converge asymptotically on either the high-level equilibrium or the low-level equilibrium, depending upon whether N_0 is greater or less than the middle equilibrium, N^M. It will converge on N^M only if it starts there. Thus N^M is indeed unstable, and the other two equilibria are locally stable.

A multiplier process would be observed in this economy, in two senses. Suppose $N_0 \neq N^M$. Let g increase permanently. The P function shifts up to P^* (Figure 1.1). If employment was converging on N^H it will now converge on N^{H*}, according to the usual multiplier story. If instead it was converging on shutdown, then either it will continue to do so, in which case the multiplier is zero, or else, if the jolt is large enough, it will converge upon N^{H*}, in which case the multiplier is even bigger than in the usual story. The necessary and sufficient condition for the latter to occur is that $N_0 > N^{M*}$, as illustrated.

Furthermore, if the economy were in a slump, with employment falling toward zero, then the slump could be reversed permanently by a temporary jolt. This is the old idea of pump-priming. If P^* remains in place until $N > N^M$, then g can be returned to its previous value, and the economy will continue to recover, with employment converging asymptotically on N^H.

The learning mechanism in this story is subject to the criticism that it is based upon a false hypothesis, namely that P_t is drawn from an unchanged distribution. There are three responses to this criticism. First, it applies to any story that does not involve rational expectations, and hence that does not assume away the problem of disequilibrium coordination. Second, the false hypothesis will be true asymptotically, since P_t will converge asymptotically on 0 or N^H. Third, the mechanism could be adopted by someone with no prior idea about the macroeconomic structure of the economy; it is the kind of atheoretic prediction scheme that econometricians such as Sims have been arguing is a reasonable way to cope with our profession's vast ignorance. The mechanism breaks down in the event that shifts in g are recurrent. For then even if someone had no idea about the structure of the economy he would want to take into account the possibility that P_t would depend upon g, as it would in an equilibrium. However, if changes in g were rare events, the scheme could be amended with little change to allow people to take this dependency into account. Specifically, they could proceed as nonparametric econometricians under the assumption that the distribution of P_t depended only upon g_t, as again it would in equilibrium. They would form the estimate P_t as a weighted average of past observations on P_s, with weights that depend upon the difference $g_t - g_s$. Once enough observations had been gathered for a given value of g, the prediction could place all its weight on observations of P_s corresponding to that same value of g. In that case, the first time that g changed it would affect employment in qualitatively the same way as analyzed above.

Of course this exercise is far too simple and special to form a general theory of macroeconomic coordination. But it illustrates at least that the Keynesian recovery that has been created by developments in the theory of coordination failures may be kept alive by the theory of adaptive self-referential systems. It offers some hope that we may eventually go beyond our fixation with getting prices right and shed some light on the fundamental question that Keynes struggled with, of why the same economic system that is capable of coordinating economic activities at the level required for an advanced stage of industrial development can also produce coordination failures on the scope of the Great Depression.

This is no more than a tiny first step. Further progress will depend upon supplying the institutional detail from which the story has abstracted, including the inventory-holding, advertising, negotiating, inspection, and even price-quoting services of intermediaries and other market-making institutions of real life.

1.10 THE PRESENT COLLECTION

The rest of the essays all relate to the ideas just outlined. They reflect the gradual evolution and changing of positions that occur when one wrestles with ideas over a long period. But they all deal with the coordination problems raised by Keynesian economics and the difficulty of modeling them in a way that meets the standards of rigor and coherence set by Walrasian general equilibrium theory.

The essays fall into three categories. Part I contains critical essays discussing the evolution of Keynesian ideas. Chapter 2 is an appraisal of the Barro–Grossman reappraisal model. It points out the problem of the supply multiplier, and argues that paying attention to the behaviour of inventory-holding middlemen in coordinating the other traders in output markets would help rationalize what is worthwhile in the approach. In this paper I did not yet have a clear notion of the importance of non-price interactions in the coordination process, and I argued that it was not important whether the dynamics of adjustment were modeled as an equilibrium or a disequilibrium phenomenon.

Chapter 3 is a review essay stimulated by reading Axel Leijonhufvud (1981b). It applauds Leijonhufvud for treating the coordination question seriously, for refusing to accept the pat answers given by the popular macro-paradigms, and for offering many stimulating suggestions. Although it criticizes Leijonhufvud on several points, it makes clear that he has gone well beyond the Barro–Grossman reappraisal model in analyzing the details of market organization and interaction. It also compares Leijonhufvud's research program favorably with that spelled out by Lucas (1980a), particularly because of the latter's unwillingness to address the question of disequilibrium coordination. (More recently Lucas (1986) has argued that disequilibrium learning is crucial for understanding market interactions, for reasons related to those of the previous section.)

Chapter 4 discusses New Classical Economics. It consists of a review of Klamer (1984). I agree with Klamer that much of the success of New Classical Economics has little to do with its scientific merits relative to those of Keynesian economics, but argue that there is more than style at issue between Keynesians and New Classicals. I suggest that the New Classical insistence on attention to equilibrium and rationality may prove to be its undoing, as technical progress in economics makes it increasingly easy to model Keynesian ideas in accordance with this precept. Chapter 5 continues with this theme. It reflects on the position and likely future importance of the central message of Keynes's *General Theory*, and argues that a Keynesian recovery may be on its way. Most of the themes of this chapter have been touched upon above.

The essays in Part II focus on the implications of price adjustment for Keynesian ideas. The first two deal with the stability of competitive equilibrium, the issue raised by Keynes's chapter 19. The focus of Chapter 6 is on the disequilibrium dynamics of a trading system in which both prices and quantities adjusted simultaneously. The paper does not accomplish a great deal, but it is one of the few formal attempts in the literature to model the role of trading institutions such as inventory-holding middlemen in the economy's coordination mechanism.

Chapter 7 explores Leijonhufvud's notion of 'the corridor' – a full-employment equilibrium might be stable in the presence of small shocks but not large ones. It discusses formal aspects of the idea, including the notion of short-run stability, and constructs some examples based on a Barro–Grossman style macro analysis. In one the deviation-counteracting feedback effects of price adjustment are overtaken by the deviation-amplifying feedback effects of the revision of income expectations when the shock is large. In the second, a large shock can put enough firms on the brink of bankruptcy to make price adjustment itself deviation-amplifying through a Fisherian debt-deflation process.

The next two chapters model price setting as part of equilibrium coordination. Chapter 8 constructs a rational-expectations equilibrium argument for an activist monetary policy, by showing that competing price-setters may choose not to become as well informed as the monetary authority, even though it would be socially worthwhile to do so. The argument goes beyond Fischer and Taylor by endogenizing the monitoring of information. The chapter also presages the multiple equilibrium analysis of the Keynesian recovery by showing that there will often be multiple monitoring equilibria; there may be one equilibrium in which all price-setters monitor, and another in which none monitor.

Chapter 9 returns for a third time to the stability issue, but this time looking more directly at the specific issue raised by Keynes: the effects of wage flexibility on the stability of employment. The analysis differs from that of Chapters 6 and 7 by interpreting stability as lack of statistical variance rather than as convergence, and by assuming that the economy is always in a rational-expectations equilibrium.

The essays in Part III deal with equilibrium coordination problems arising from transaction externalities. Chapter 10 shows how multiple equilibria can emerge in the Barro–Grossman reappraisal model once transaction externalities are introduced, and relates the analysis to themes in the Keynesian literature. Chapter 11 does the same for an explicit model of the labor market with costly search and recruiting. This chapter shows that the same transaction costs that produce multiplicity also induce an indeterminacy of the wage bargain, and hence result in equilibria that come in closed loops in the space of wages and recruiting intensities.

Chapters 12 and 13 examine the equilibrium dynamics of models with trading externalities. The first develops a simple model of the business cycle from a stochastically disturbed model with a unique equilibrium. The positive results are very much like those of New Classical Economics, except for the labor market, where unemployment exists, and where no unrealistically elastic supply of labor schedule need be invoked. The welfare properties of equilibria reflect the conflicting influences of thin-market and congestion externalities; thus the natural rate of unemployment may be too large or too small.

Chapter 13 explores the perfect-foresight dynamics of a model like that of Chapter 11 with multiple stationary equilibria. It turns out that the stability of intermediate stationary equilibria like N^M in Figure 1.1 depends upon the strength of the congestion externality relative to the rate of interest. If the externality is strong enough or the rate of interest low enough, then there will exist a continuum of perfect foresight trajectories starting at any point in the neighborhood of the intermediate stationary equilibrium and converging to it.

NOTES

1. This argument has been made at length by DeLong and Summers (1986a).
2. On conceptual coherence, see Clower (1984: 264ff).
3. For a detailed description of the parable, and a historical account of its development, see Newman (1965).
4. A similar remark can be made about money (and has been made, by Clower, 1969). Like prices, money is so common that it is hard not to see it in a parable of organized exchange. But as many have now observed, money has no place at all in the Walrasian story. The social role of money in actual economies is that of enforcing budget constraints. To the individual, the role is that of buffer stock. However, neither of these roles applies in the Walrasian world, where the auctioneer enforces budget constraints costlessly, and the individual, able to choose all transactions *ex ante*, has no need of a buffer against unanticipated transactions. Laidler (1988) has argued that the Walrasian influence on much of modern macroeconomic theory has rendered it incapable of analyzing monetary issues seriously.
5. Patinkin (1988) has a more detailed account of why the unemployment of the 1930s constituted an anomaly, in Kuhn's sense, for classical theory.
6. As Samuelson (1983: 216) observed, 'The fiction that Keynes assumed rigid wages was found to be a useful fiction.'
7. Clower (1975) has described the interweaving of the Keynesian revolution with the development of Walrasian theory, pointing out in particular the key role of Hicks.
8. Clower made the last point by arguing that Walras' law was invalid. The terminological issues raised by this argument (see Patinkin, 1987) are not relevant for the substantive stability issues.
9. Leijonhufvud also argued that there was another important unexplored dimension to Keynes's thinking about the coordination problem, the intertemporal problem of coordinating investment and saving. I argue in Chapter 3 below that he failed to make the case that these coordination problems would have serious consequences for unemployment in the

absence of sticky wages. However, as Woodford (1988) and others have now made clear, once there is a basis of imperfect equilibrium coordination and there is also money and capital in the economy, there is also scope for 'rational sunspot equilibria' that produce extraneous fluctuations in savings and investment reminiscent of Keynes's remarks concerning animal spirits. In Chapter 5, I cite these developments in modeling animal spirits as another of the mainsprings of the Keynesian recovery.

10 At least he postulated them for households. On this, see Grossman (1972a).

11. Indeed one might regard vagueness as a virtue. The auctioneer is just one of many hypothetical ways in which equilibrium might be established, all observationally equivalent (except for cases of nonunique equilibrium) because all imply that the outside observer will never see the system out of equilibrium. If one assumes *a priori* that the economy will go directly to equilibrium, then it is a waste of time listing all the possible ways it might happen. This seems to be the attitude adopted by devotees of Walrasian theory in response to Scarf's (1960) demonstration that the tâtonnement is nonconvergent in a large class of economies. Instead of finding their belief undermined, they gave up stability analysis.

12. The latter problem was first identified by Patinkin (1956, ch. 13).

13. Assume that no one can relocate trading partners from previous periods, so that lasting trade relationships cannot be formed.

14. To see this, take two equilibria, N_1 and N_2, with $N_1 < N_2$. Those individuals who participate in both equilibria will have a higher expected payoff in the second, by the amount $P(N_2) - P(N_1)$. Those who participate in neither will have the same payoff, 0. Those who participate only in the second will have a payoff of $P(N_2) - c > 0$ in the second and 0 in the first.

15. Social welfare is defined as:

$$W = W(N) = \int_0^N [P(N) - c]dc = NP(N) - N^2/2$$

Therefore:

$$W'(N) = P(N) - N + NP'(N)$$

If N is an equilibrium, then $P(N) = N$. Also, by assumption, $P'(N) > 0$. Therefore if N is an equilibrium $W'(N) > 0$; social welfare could be raised by increasing participation.

PART I

THE EVOLUTION OF MACROECONOMIC THEORY

2 · EVALUATING THE NON-MARKET-CLEARING APPROACH

This chapter is concerned with evaluating the non-market-clearing (NMC) approach of Barro and Grossman (1976) and others from a purely positive point of view. That is, it deals with the broad question of the extent to which the approach provides a theoretically satisfactory explanation of certain stylized facts characterizing the dynamic behavior of aggregate output and the price level. It does not deal with the important and difficult normative questions involving stabilization policy that are often associated with the approach.

From this viewpoint the main strength of the NMC approach is its compatibility with the evidence that (1) fluctuations in aggregate output are closely (positively) correlated with fluctuations in aggregate demand; (2) output appears to respond with a much shorter lag than does the price level to changes in aggregate demand; and (3) changes in output are serially correlated from quarter to quarter.

The main weakness of the approach is its failure to provide any satisfactory account of how markets are organized. For example, it offers no explanation of how prices are formed, beyond the crude hypothesis that they move in the direction of excess demands, despite the fact that the assumption that prices fail to respond quickly enough to clear markets lies at the heart of the approach. Nor does it explain why agents should be constrained to trade at these prices, even though these constraints are what ultimately produce the multiplier process of the approach. This inattention to the details of market organization also appears to be responsible for the curious 'supply multiplier,' according

I am indebted to David Laidler for helpful conversations on the topic of this paper, to Robert Solow for his critical comments, and to the Humanities and Social Sciences Research Council of Canada for financial support.

Reprinted from *American Economic Review Papers and Proceedings* (1979), **69**, May, 60–3.

to which an increase in aggregate demand, from an initial position of generalized excess demand or even of full employment equilibrium, causes a decrease in output – a prediction that threatens to undermine the compatibility of the approach with the positive correlation between aggregate demand and output unless some reason can be found why excess demand should be less common than excess supply.

This shortcoming does not imply that the NMC approach is not useful for many purposes, nor that its predictions are inconsistent with the evidence (except for the predictions of the supply multiplier). But to be consistent with the evidence is not to explain it. What the approach lacks is a satisfactory theoretical underpinning that would at least make it consistent with the same notions of rational self-interest that underlie the rest of economic theory.

This leaves us with the question of whether a satisfactory underpinning can be provided to the approach. In other words, can the approach be revised or replaced in such a way that the resulting theory contains a more satisfactory account of market organization, and explains the above-mentioned stylized facts in a way that closely resembles the NMC approach?

This question cannot now be answered with a great deal of confidence because no one has yet developed a satisfactory theory of market organization. However, I think that an affirmative answer is likely, and that the key to developing the answer lies in recognizing that different markets are organized in different ways. In particular, some markets, such as those for many labor services, personal credit, and heavy capital goods, are organized on a highly personal basis with individually negotiated contracts, whereas other markets, such as those for widely traded financial assets and for most consumer durables, are organized on a less personal basis by trading specialists like retailers, wholesalers, jobbers, brokers, and stock-market specialists. The rest of this chapter attempts to shed some light on the question of providing a satisfactory theoretical underpinning for the NMC approach by investigating how a market organized by such specialist traders would behave following a reduction in aggregate demand.

In such a market all trading activity is typically arranged by inventory holding traders who quote prices at which they stand willing to sell to demanders at dates and in quantities that may be chosen by the buyer. Some traders also quote prices at which they likewise stand willing to buy from suppliers at the suppliers' discretion, as in the case of stock-market specialists, although this arrangement is less common. These traders may be separate middlemen who neither produce nor directly consume the good being traded; or they may be identical with the producers of the good, as in the case of the sales departments of large manufacturing companies that produce to stock. In order to back up their willingness to trade, specialist traders allow their inventories to act as buffer stocks so as to absorb unanticipated fluctuations in excess demand, except in cases where the fluctuations are large enough to exhaust either the trader's inventories or his storage capacity. Thus under normal circumstances they allow other traders (at least buyers) to make their notional plans effective, even when full general equilibrium prices have not yet been established.

The existence of such specialist traders can be rationalized by supposing that there are costs of transacting, which the specialists reduce by being available for trading at known locations and at announced prices, and by their willingness to refrain from quantity rationing. Because there is a large setup component to the cost of transacting, a fixed cost paid at each transaction date regardless of the amount traded, agents will choose to trade at discrete dates rather than continuously in time. This means that some device is needed to coordinate their timing decisions. Specialists partly fulfill this role by standing open continuously for business, thereby permitting others to make independent timing decisions. Thus the specialists' inventories absorb not only the unanticipated fluctuations in excess demand that will eventually call for a price change, but also the transitory fluctuations due to differences in arrival times of buyers and sellers (see Clower and Howitt, 1978).

How such a market would react to a decline in aggregate demand obviously depends upon what kind of pricing policy is pursued by the specialists. The theory of optimal price-setting behavior is only beginning to be worked out. Meanwhile an intuitive and simple working hypothesis is to suppose that prices are always set at their expected market-clearing values. That is, each specialist's selling price is one such that over any interval of time the specialist expects to sell the quantity that he would prefer to sell if in fact he could choose the volume of his sales at that price.

Suppose that prices are set at their expected market-clearing values. When aggregate demand falls, if this is anticipated in all markets and if each specialist is able to anticipate its effects on all other prices, then all prices will fall immediately so as to offset the expected effects of the shock. But generally it will not be fully anticipated. At first it is more likely to be interpreted at least partly as a temporary change in demand. If so, then the price level at first will not respond to the shock, for the same reason that in any speculative market the price is unlikely to respond to a temporary shock in demand or supply. Instead, the specialists, like speculators, will allow their inventories to accumulate to absorb the shock. At first the rate of output may also remain unchanged, but as the level of inventories increases, the rate of output is likely to decrease. How this happens is most easily seen in markets where producers are their own specialist traders. As the level of inventories increases, the relative shadow price attached by a firm to its inventories is likely to decline, thereby inducing a lower rate of production. Thus right away there is a strong resemblance to the NMC approach in the sense that output will move in sympathy with aggregate demand, except when there is perfect price flexibility (which occurs when the shock is fully anticipated). It is unlike most versions of the NMC approach, however, in that the connection between aggregate demand and output involves the same sort of inventory change that is a common feature of textbook accounts of the Keynesian cross diagram.

An important feature of the NMC approach is the multiplier process, according to which the ultimate decline in output may exceed the initial decline in aggregate demand, provided that the deviation-counteracting feedback effects of price reductions on aggregate demand are not large enough to offset the deviation-amplifying effects of quantity rationing. This too is likely to be consistent with an aggregate model in which output markets are assumed to be organized by specialists. Indeed the multiplier process is one that does not depend, as is often supposed, upon the failure of markets to clear. All it requires is that the reduction in output and employment be associated with a reduction in the typical household's expected lifetime wealth, causing a secondary reduction in aggregate demand that is not fully anticipated by all price setters. In the NMC approach this shift occurs as a result of the quantity rationing of sellers. But even in a market-clearing approach in which the connection between aggregate demand and output arises from the inability of individuals to distinguish a change in aggregate demand from a change in relative demand, the same perceived change in relative demand that induces quantity reductions will also induce a reduction in the typical household's expected lifetime wealth. The same is true of models in which the labor market is organized around long-term contracts. The worker who is laid off by a firm that partly interprets the decline in aggregate demand as a decline in relative demand does not himself have to suffer from any such confusion to reduce his estimate of his lifetime wealth.

An important sense in which the present approach differs from the NMC approach is that it does not rely in any essential way upon the notion of quantity rationing. In labor markets employment will respond to a balanced reduction in aggregate demand if and only if it is at least partly interpreted in some markets as a reduction in relative demands. Whether separations in the labor market take the form of quits or layoffs does not matter for any aggregate predictions.

On the other hand, in output markets the price-setting behavior of the specialists appears to be consistent with the market-clearing (MC) approach of Lucas and others. The situation of a specialist and a customer who has just appeared in his store may be treated as a 'Phelpsian island' informationally isolated from other such islands. According to the MC approach the price on such an island should equal the temporary equilibrium price that clears the market, given each side's expectations of the market-clearing price on the next island. It seems reasonable to suppose that the specialist's supply curve in such a temporary equilibrium situation would be horizontal, or nearly so, at a price equal to the expected equilibrium price, for this represents the expected opportunity cost of selling on this island rather than the next. If this were true then the MC approach would result in exactly the same behavior as the present revised version of the NMC approach, and the inventory accumulation that appears as 'involuntary' to the textbook Keynesian accounts of the NMC approach can be regarded as 'voluntary' speculation in the present approach.

The point of all this is not to argue that what Keynesians regard as involuntary is really voluntary, but rather to argue that the NMC approach does not depend in any essential way upon a violation of the basic assumption of rational self-interest in the form of a failure to exploit perceived gains from trade. Indeed the above discussion suggests that the distinction between voluntary and involuntary behavior is not a useful one for macroeconomic theory. The misery of unemployment is as great if it is voluntary or involuntary, the behavior of the unemployed does not depend upon whether they quit or were fired, and the reaction of a firm to an accumulation of inventories does not depend upon whether the accumulation was involuntary or whether it is a result of voluntary speculation. If progress is to be made in unifying the micro and macro branches of economic theory it is vital that we be able to base macro theory upon principles of voluntary behavior. I think this is possible without substantially altering the character of orthodox macro theory. But if I am right it is probably simpler in most applications of macro theory to assume stickiness of prices and to assume that markets fail to clear than to both specifying the entire set of assumptions that would make this consistent with rational self-interest.

3 · INFORMATION AND COORDINATION: A REVIEW ARTICLE

3.1 INTRODUCTION

The seminal work begun in the late 1960s' on the micro-foundations of macro theory (e.g., Phelps *et al.*, 1970) altered the course of macroeconomic research in ways that few could have predicted at the time. It started as a reaction to the then prevailing 'Keynesian' orthodoxy, as an attempt to replace the illusions and rigidities which the orthodoxy took as given and which appeared to constitute *ad hoc* violations of basic microeconomic principles, with the fundamental informational imperfections of which it was believed they were a manifestation. Just what kind of macro theory these authors saw their work providing a foundation for was not always clear, but the papers of the Phelps volume leave the impression that it should not differ greatly from that of Keynes's *General Theory*, except perhaps that Keynesian 'disequilibrium' results ought to be limited to the short run. Indeed Axel Leijonhufvud, in his influential book, *On Keynesian Economics and the Economics of Keynes* (1968), argued that combining this new economics of information with Clower's (1965) analysis of effective demand was the way to understand the real message of the *General Theory*, which he argued was about the type of communication problems which might arise if the auctioneer was removed from general equilibrium theory.

Of course, that is not how it turned out. The economics of information may have taken over the professional journals in macroeconomics, which now are filled with the analysis of private forecasting behavior, signal extraction problems, and the distinction between anti-

---

The author is indebted to Robert Clower, Meir Kohn, David Laidler and Tom Kompas for helpful discussions, and to Axel Leijonhufvud, whose contribution to the ideas expressed in the paper goes well beyond having written the book under review. A stronger than usual disclaimer of responsibility is warranted.

Reprinted from *Economic Inquiry* (1984) **22**, July, 429–46.

cipated and unanticipated changes without which no analysis of macro-economic policy is taken seriously any longer. But the macro theory being built upon these foundations appears in many respects antithetical not only to Keynesian economics but to Leijonhufvud's 'Economics of Keynes,' for it is characterized by such 'classical' propositions as the ineffectiveness of stabilization policies, the optimality of business cycle fluctuations, the rationality of expectations, the perfect flexibility of all prices, and the absence of involuntary unemployment.

The recent publication of Leijonhufvud's essays, *Information and Coordination* (1981b), thus provides an opportunity to re-examine some of the themes and issues in current macroeconomic research from the point of view of someone who led the escape from the Keynesian orthodoxy but whose work clearly was pointing in a direction other than the one that macroeconomics has followed. These twelve essays constitute the bulk of what Leijonhufvud has written other than his earlier book. Four of them summarize the contents of that book, and the rest, of which all but two have been published before, deal with such diverse topics as inflation, the interest-rate mechanism, the stability of full-employment equilibrium, Say's law, methodology, the history of monetary theory, and the sociology of economics. Although their style is informal, non-mathematical, and more critical than constructive, they reveal a unique, compelling vision of macroeconomics, whose import-ance is heightened by the scarcity of good 'non-classical' analysis in macroeconomics today.

3.2 BASICS

What unifies the essays is primarily the concern that accounts for the title. According to Leijonhufvud the central issue of macroeconomics is how, under what circumstances, and to what extent the economic system *coordinates* the activities of different agents. The job of coordination requires, above all, a great deal of *information*, and Leijonhufvud argues that the logical way to address the question is to study the processes by which agents acquire, communicate, interpret, and respond to information in large complex economic systems. He argues that both general equilibrium theory and the Neoclassical Synthesis, while capable of great subtlely and complexity in other dimensions, address this central issue in too simple a fashion. One says that coordination (general market clearing) is achieved at no cost, through the notorious 'tâtonnement' process. The other says not at any cost (at least in the short run) because of the 'spanner-in-the-works' of sticky wages and prices.

Leijonhufvud makes frequent use of the benchmark of *full information*; a hypothetical equilibrium state of full coordination, in which all exogenous variables and parameters assume their actual values but 'agents have managed to *learn* all that can be (profitably) learned about their environment and about each others' behavior' (p. 136). He argues that serious departures from full information are usually the result of one group of agents forming beliefs which are inconsistent with those of other agents. With mutually inconsistent beliefs, their plans will be incompatible, and this he calls a state of diseqilibrium (p. 140).

To understand any state of disequilibrium, Leijonhufvud sensibly recommends to begin by asking what has gone wrong. That is, whose belief or action in the actual situation differs radically from what it would be in full information? To proceed from diagnosis to prognosis the key is to discover and analyze the homeostatic, or deviation-counteracting processes generating messages that can re-equilibrate beliefs, and the deviation-amplifying processes that tend to prolong or worsen the communication failure. If the latter dominate, or if market adjustments are slow, then:

> Faced with a diagnosis that pinpoints the 'wrong' value of one variable as the source of the disequilibrium of the entire system, the natural impulse is to look around for some policy instrument that would impinge as directly as possible on this variable while, ideally, leaving alone those which are already 'right.' (p. 74)

He claims that by and large this is the key to understanding Keynes's policy prescriptions. It is also the key to understanding much of what Leijonhufvud has to say.

Another key is his use of the concept of liquidity, in the sense of saleability at low transaction cost rather than absence of risk. 'The price obtainable for the services of a resource which has become 'unemployed' will depend upon the costs expended in searching for the highest bidder. In this sense the resource is illiquid.' (p. 6) The lines of communication in a market economy are governed largely by the pattern of transactions. Transaction costs impose impediments not only to buying and selling goods but to communicating one's willingness to buy or sell. If, as Clower (1967) showed to be the case in standard general equilibrium theory, all goods are assumed to be perfectly liquid, then the main impediments to communication have been removed, and it becomes a genuine puzzle how to account for such phenomena as involuntary unemployment, where people are obviously forgoing mutually advantageous opportunities to trade, without resorting to *ad hoc* rigidities. Such puzzles do not arise for Leijonhufvud, in whose theories the illiquidity of human capital and of most non-human capital plays a central role.

3.3 IS THE ECONOMIC SYSTEM SELF-ADJUSTING?

This is the Big Question that Leijonhufvud wants his readers to take seriously, rather than giving the simplistic implicit answers of the Keynesian and classical traditions. Needless to say he does not answer it, but his general approach is ideally suited to address the issue in as undogmatic a way as possible, and he offers a characteristically sensible conjecture, backed with some tantalizing fragments of analysis.

His conjecture is that the economic system is probably like most other control systems that have either been designed intelligently or survived some test of time; it works well under a range of normal circumstances but there are limits to the size and nature of disturbance it is capable of handling. The area inside these limits he conceives of as a 'corridor' around the full information growth path.

His analysis is clearest with respect to a decline in aggregate demand. Within the corridor the decline is dampened by wage and price adjustment. The potential deviation-amplifying multiplier process is held in check by buffer stocks of liquid assets which insulate consumption demand from transitory income fluctuations, by the inelasticity of permanent income expectations, and by the willingness of employers to accumulate inventories of finished goods and to hoard labor rather than have declines in demand feed through one-for-one to employment.

But a large and prolonged decline will alter the balance between these forces. It will cause dysfunctional revision of permanent income estimates, more employers will reach the end of their patience and/or financial means to keep output and employment at normal levels, and household buffer-stocks of liquid assets will start to disappear, either because bond-market speculators, anticipating a return of high interest rates, begin hoarding liquidity, or because a monetary collapse leads to a contraction in financial intermediation. When this happens not only does the multiplier process gather strength, as the links between current income, spending, output, and employment become tighter, but the normal homeostatic properties of price adjustment become impaired. In Clower's (1965) terminology, sellers, instead of receiving the notional demands of full information, receive the lower effective demands constrained by current incomes. Likewise the message that savers are willing to supply more loanable funds, which ought to be sent to investors in the form of lower interest rates, at first may be intercepted by bond-market speculators, and later will be eliminated entirely by the fall in incomes. When such 'effective demand failures' occur,

> Price-incentives may be effective in all markets and all prices perfectly 'flexible', and a market system may still go haywire in its groping for the co-ordinated solution. ...some prices may show no tendency to change

> although desires to sell and buy do not coincide in the respective markets. . . . Prices may be at their 'right' (general equilibrium) levels, but amounts transacted differ persistently from the desired rates of sale and purchase in some markets. . . . Prices that were at their GE values may tend to move away from those values so that the information disseminated by price changes is 'false' and makes the coordination failure confusion worse. (pp. 111–12)

Of course, this does not constitute a demonstration of global asymptotic instability. In particular, the fact that not all variables in an interdependent dynamic system are monotonically approaching their equilibrium values says nothing about stability, for the existence of dynamic interdependencies guarantees that such monotonicity will be rare. What the argument does suggest is that important indicators of the state of the system, such as the level of output or employment, which a well-designed system might be expected to make monotonically convergent from a wide variety of commonly experienced initial positions, will, if the system is displaced far enough or in an unusual enough direction from equilibrium, show persistent deterioration (deviation amplification) in the short run, whether or not convergence may be ensured in the long run. To make these ideas more precise and manageable it is necessary to give a definition of short-run stability. In Chapter 7 I propose several such definitions and show how this type of argument may be made more formally,[1] in terms of a much simpler model than Leijonhufvud has in mind. However, much work remains to be done on this important issue.

3.4 STICKY PRICES VERSUS MISPERCEPTIONS

It is widely believed that the major analytical issue in macroeconomics today is whether aggregate demand causes output to fluctuate because sticky prices prevent markets from clearing, as in the analysis of Barro and Grossman (1971), and in the overlapping contracts approach of Phelps and Taylor (1977), or because the failure of sellers to recognize that the attendant changes in their selling prices are purely nominal, not real, fools them into supplying more, as in the island parable of Phelps (Phelps et al., 1970, pp. 1–23) or Lucas (1972), which assumes instantaneous market clearing on each informationally isolated island. With his emphasis on quantity rather than price adjustment, the multiplier process, and removing the auctioneer, Leijonhufvud often is seen as a guiding spirit of the former approach.

In fact, Leijonhufvud rejects the 'spanner-in-the-works' of wage and price rigidities, which he thinks obscure the serious informational problems that arise even in their absence (see, especially, p. 111, fn. 14), and thinks the fix-price approach grossly understates the homeostatic capabilities of the system within the corridor. He points out the irony of using a rigid-wage theory to crystalize the experience of the Great Depression – a time of one of history's most dramatic wage deflations. His own story of how output fluctuates is quite explicitly an island story, with perhaps more emphasis than is currently fashionable on workers being fooled into and out of search rather than leisure (pp. 6, 199, fn. 109).

The fact that Leijonhufvud is able to develop Keynesian ideas using the 'island' approach of new classical economics suggests that something is amiss with the common view on this issue. Indeed the differences between the two approaches have more to do with their respective advocates' states of mind than with any inherent substantive differences in analysis. From an operational viewpoint the two approaches offer almost identical predictions. Both imply that the short-run effects of unanticipated demand changes will be reflected primarily in quantities with relatively little effect on price and that the effects on price and quantity of anticipated changes will be reversed. There is some implied disagreement about the length of time necessary for a change to become anticipated, but even Lucas (1975) assumes that some time is taken for new information to be reflected in expectations.

None of the popular island stories have multiplier processes, but that is primarily because they typically do not include permanent income as an argument of aggregate demand functions. If they did, and if the typical seller misread a nominal drop in aggregate demand as, with some probability, a permanent drop in his relative selling price, then a multiplier process obviously could result for as long as that misperception remained. The misperception would cause a drop in the typical household's estimated permanent income, causing a secondary decline in aggregate demand, which could not be fully anticipated by the typical seller, since it results from a shock that he himself is misinterpreting as specific to his own market. Of course these dynamics would be intertwined in a rational-expectations model with some optimal adjustment of forecasts, which might be made to converge stochastically on the equilibrium, but only eventually.

The reason for this strong similarity between the two supposedly different approaches is that in fact neither has market clearing in the usual Walrasian sense of one centralized auction market for the entire economy, yet both retain the auctioneer in modified form. One has him operating with a split personality in different localities simultaneously; the other has him working gradually (prices eventually adjust according to some kind of Phillips relation) but unable to prevent trading at disequilibrium prices.

It must be admitted that the sticky-price story suggests a more realistic description of the manner in which job separations occur in recessions. Quit rates definitely do not behave anti-cyclically, but layoffs do. But if that were the only difference it would not be much ground for preferring one approach over the other, for it is surely not an important primary task of macroeconomic theory to account for these fine details concerning which side of the market makes proximate quantity decisions.

An important primary task is to explain not how unemployment arises, but rather why it persists. The misperceptions approach is recognized widely to be deficient because it may account for persistence only if workers fail persistently to perceive the increase in their real wages resulting from a falling (or decelerating) price level, if their preference for leisure increases, if their marginal products fall, or if firms misperceive their marginal products to have fallen. None of this bears the remotest resemblance to the experience of the 1930s or the 1980s.

The explanation offered by the sticky-price approach is hardly more credible. It asserts that the unemployed worker remains in that state because he does not offer to work for less than the going wage. Either he cannot, because unions have the market cornered, in obvious contradiction with the facts, or he will not, in which case his predicament is really voluntary.

Leijonhufvud points out that this reliance of 'Keynesian' macro models upon sticky wages is a return to the pre-Keynesian idea that unemployment is always the result of workers asking too much for their services. Indeed the effort to refute this idea was one of the major themes of Keynes's *General Theory*. Although the first eighteen chapters of the *General Theory* were written on the premise of a given money wage, Keynes stressed that this was only a provisional simplifying assumption. Once the analysis had been worked out on this premise, the crucial chapter 19 was supposed to show that having wages adjust in response to unemployment makes no essential difference to the level of unemployment, which is determined by the demand for producible goods. Variations in the money wage have uncertain and offsetting effects on the demand for goods, and thus cannot be assured to have any significant effect on the level of employment. Although Keynes gave several reasons for thinking that wages are less than fully flexible, this was not, in his view, an obstacle to full employment. Indeed he emphasized that if wages were more flexible the problem of unemployment would probably be even worse.

This theme of the *General Theory* has always been an awkward aspect of Keynesian exegesis. Even those who take a dynamic, 'flexible wage' interpretation of Keynes have argued that his analysis of wage flexibility was in error by its failure to take proper account of the real balance effect (e.g., Patinkin, 1948). For the most part, Keynesian macroeconomics has ignored the theme, and has relied upon historically given, slowly adjusting wages as a crucial part of the explanation of the emergence and persistence of unemployment.

Leijonhufvud's insistence upon reinstating this theme to the center of macroeconomics reveals why it has been such a troublesome one. He argues that the effects of wage reductions cannot be studied independently of the 'benchmark' diagnosis, and that the only case where wage deflation will cure unemployment is that of workers' reservation wages being higher than in full information, a case which he suggests ought to be fairly rare.

He analyzes in great detail the case where the expectations of bond-market speculators are wrong because they overestimate the natural rate of interest. He argues that this was Keynes's diagnosis of the UK in the early 1920s, with bear speculators unrealistically expecting interest rates to remain at historical levels despite a drop in the natural rate of interest which they had failed adequately to take into account. These mistaken expectations supported a speculative demand for money that prevented the market rate from falling with the natural rate, and thus were causing a deficiency of aggregate demand. In this situation, Leijonhufvud argues that 'the willingness of labor to reduce the money wage will not help...the response of price to excess supply of labor does not bring about a meshing of quantities in that market.' (p. 167)

Several critics found Leijonhufvud in error on this point in his earlier book (e.g., Bliss, 1975), and the same problem persists in the present volume (1981b) (a fact that has also been brought out by Kohn, 1981). Leijonhufvud's argument is restricted to within the corridor (p. 183, n. 87), where stability problems would not prevent the attainment of full employment. Nor is he invoking either a liquidity trap or an interest-inelasticity of investment demand, two of his pet hates. He argues that a 'horrendous all-round deflation' (p. 193) that brought the Pigou effect into play would leave the system 'more disorganized than ever' (p. 194) if it failed to cure the basic underlying problem. But the text of the long essay in which this argument appears lacks any explanation of why a less horrendous deflation might not restore full employment through the usual Keynes effect. Thus his argument invokes a nonexistence result – the absence of a vector of prices that would generate an equilibrium for the system with full employment of labor as long as bond-market speculators persist in their erroneous beliefs. Yet no reason is given why the usual continuity and boundedness assumptions should not guarantee existence despite those beliefs. The kind of price expectations which usually create existence problems arise from a too elastic response to current prices (e.g., Grandmont, 1977). In this case Leijonhufvud is dealing with just the opposite extreme of inelastic bond-price expectations.

The problems with Leijonhufvud's arguments on this point reveal a weakness with his 'benchmark method,' namely that it obscures the fact that many of the effects of disequilibrium arising from one source can be offset indirectly by adjustments that do not directly address the basic disequilibrium. In this case the rate of interest may be too high because of erroneous expectations. But the 'compensating error' of a money wage that is too low (again in relation to its full information value) nevertheless may bring about the coincidence between market and natural rates of interest required to restore full employment. It may violate common sense to require an adjustment of wages to compensate for erroneous interest-rate expectations, and there is, of course, a presumption that a full-employment equilibrium with correct expectations has better welfare properties than one with erroneous expectations, but in a highly interdependent system it seems quite possible that such indirect methods may deal effectively with the most serious manifestations of a problem (in this case unemployment). Just as any reasonably well-functioning control system ought to exhibit corridor phenomena, so ought it contain backup mechanisms to keep it performing tolerably well when the usual homeostats malfunction.

These problems also reveal a huge gap in macroeconomic theory, namely the lack of any coherent explanation of persistent unemployment. Leijonhufvud is one of the few writers on the subject to recognize the implausibility of relying upon sticky wages and to insist upon finding an explanation that will hold up even in the face of wage flexibility. But his attempt to build such an explanation upon the observation that what has 'gone wrong' may be something other than the reservation wages of workers is not fully convincing.

Nevertheless there may be elements of a coherent explanation in Leijonhufvud's insistence upon the illiquidity of human capital. Both the island approach and the sticky-wage approach neglect the cost of making effective offers to trade in the labor market. The unemployed worker may have an accurate perception of the existing real wage for his services, yet be unable to locate the prospective employer willing to pay it. Once the appropriate contact has been made, both sides must be willing to pay all the other transaction costs – costs of bargaining, screening, documenting, relocating, and so forth. The labor market is a notoriously difficult one in which to do all this, because of the problems of heterogeneity, indivisibility, inalienability, and moral hazard. Surely it is this difficulty in effecting transactions, especially the difficulty of contacting potential trading partners, rather than unrealistic wage demands of the unemployed, which accounts for the persistence of large-scale unemployment, as well as for its obviously involuntary character.

In other words, once a worker has become unemployed, he must do more than show a willingness to work for less than the going wage to become re-employed. He must also find a new trading partner. New transaction costs must be paid, and partly in the form of extra search time. Reducing reservation wages below the value appropriate for re-establishing equilibrium would permit all the displaced workers to regain employment more readily, but at wages below their potential marginal value product in the best match. If everyone settled on the spot for the best available offer, then measured unemployment might be eliminated, but with professors selling apples and so forth, involuntary unemployment would still persist, in the very real sense of people not finding employment at the wage 'going' for their services. More generally, as long as labor has not been reallocated so that society is on its intertemporal production frontier, involuntary unemployment by this criterion will persist. Attaining the frontier is a coordination problem that takes more than the willingness to work for less. It involves the communication of more than just price information.

This Leijonhufvudian perspective also reveals an important aspect of labor-market contracts. They exist in part for the purpose of eliminating the transaction costs that would arise if hiring had to be done afresh every day, and thus they serve to increase the liquidity of the human capital employed. But by the same token they greatly increase those costs, and reduce liquidity, for the unemployed. For part of most contracts, even the implicit ones, is an understanding that employers will not replace existing employees at the drop of a hat whenever someone shows up willing to work for less. These understandings also limit the willingness of firms to undertake the observationally equivalent transaction of hiring a cheap new worker when previous employees are being laid off. They thus reduce the opportunities for the unemployed to make effective offers to work for less than the going wage, especially during a recession.

Now it might be argued that this is precisely what fix-price theorists have in mind when they refer to contracts as keeping prices sticky and hence accounting for involuntary unemployment. (See, for example, Solow's (1980) lucid and penetrating account of the labor market.) But it is not in their theories.[2] By the same argument it might be what Lucas (1973) has in mind with the *ad hoc* persistence terms in his aggregate supply function, but it is not in his theory either. What is called for is an explicit account of the limited opportunities available to transactors in all markets, not just those for labor services, to contact potential trading partners and to make effective proposals for exchange, of how those opportunities are affected by the presence of many other people looking for the same potential partners, and how they are affected by the sales dificulties in other markets experienced by those potential partners during a recession. For an initial, very limited attempt to provide such an account, see Chapter 10 below.

This discussion also highlights the importance of the 'benchmark' diagnosis, and helps to account for Leijonhufvud's stress on the role of relative prices and their absence from IS-LM (e.g., p. 14; p. 72, n. 22; pp. 191–4). Suppose the reservation wages of workers has 'gone wrong.' During the period of unemployment some workers will have lost contact with their former employers, some false trades will have been made that require a rearrangement of job matches, and some employers will have been driven bankrupt by the downturn. But before much of this has happened a speedy reduction in reservation wages would permit the re-establishment of former trading relations, and thus a return to the neighborhood of full information. The faster the speed of wage adjustment, the quicker the return. The more serious problems arise when someone's beliefs prevent a relative price from assuming its full-information value, in which case the effective demands for labor in different employments will not guide workers into their full-information jobs. It is easy to imagine how this confused state of demand for labor can greatly increase the difficulty of making effective contacts in the labor market.

3.5 THE INTEREST RATE MECHANISM AND IS-LM

According to Leijonhufvud, the return of Keynesians to the pre-Keynesian diagnosis of sticky wages has gone along with a neglect, and misunderstanding, of the interest-rate mechanism. When large-scale unemployment arises, he argues that the problem is usually to be found not in labor markets but in capital markets. Early stages of a recession are usually characterized by a reduction in confidence, which increases the demand for liquidity to provide flexibility,[3] and simultaneously reduces the demand for capital goods. The problem worrying Keynes in the early 1920s was referred to in the previous section: a drop in the natural rate of interest imperfectly perceived by bond-market speculators. Deep depressions, he argues, are characterized by a collapse of entrepreneurial sales forecasts underlying the marginal efficiency of capital, which as a result of the experience of a prolonged decline fail to reflect the sales opportunities that would prevail in full information.

He argues, based on his benchmark method, that these different diagnoses require different policy prescriptions. In the deep depression case the market rate of interest will be below the natural rate – i.e., the rate that would prevail in full information where entrepreneurial and speculative expectations were not systematically mistaken – because of the depressed level of investment demand. His prescription in this case is for fiscal policy, which will serve directly to correct the problem – namely entrepreneurial expectations. The extra demand generated by government purchases will 'belie the expectations that demand will continue unchanged at its depressed level and thus set in motion a process of upward revision of demand forecasts.' (p. 74)

The efficacy of his benchmark method is revealed by his argument against using monetary policy in this case. By assumption, bond-market speculators are right, i.e., their forecasts of the long-term rate of interest are equal to the full-information natural rate. Thus very large-scale open-market operations would be required in order to have a noticeable effect on aggregate demand, for the market rate would have to be driven even further below the expected long-term rate, and as this happened the interest elasticity of the speculative demand for cash would become large. But Leijonhufvud does not invoke a liquidity trap. He argues that monetary policy actually would do the job. Instead, he invokes a long-run consideration typically ignored in Keynesian expositions of IS-LM.

Specifically, he argues that if such a massive policy were used, inevitably it would induce some speculators to 'go along' and lower their expectations. But if the policy were successful the interest rate eventually would rise to its natural rate, the speculators would suffer capital losses as 'punishment' for having gone along, and 'this learning experience would make the Central Bank's task harder the next time a monetary policy à outrance is tried.' (p. 35) A policy that alters the expectations of those who were not mistaken in the first place is thus likely to waste credibility, depriving future monetary policy of its much needed 'announcement effect.'

In the case of a decline in the natural rate, the early 1920s diagnosis where entrepreneurs are right but speculators wrong, the market rate will lie above the natural rate, held up by a speculative demand for cash. In this case the benchmark method calls for monetary policy that will correct directly the mistaken expectations at the root of the problem, through its announcement effect. Again the argument goes beyond the usual textbook IS-LM analysis in focusing upon the expectational effect of the policy and, indeed, contradicts the usual argument in this case. For, as in the deep-depression case, there ought to be a relatively high interest elasticity of demand for cash, since the market rate is below the expected long-term rate, and the usual textbook argument would imply a preference for fiscal over monetary policy under these circumstances.

Leijonhufvud's argument against fiscal policy in this case is also revealing. If it were to work it would confirm the wrong expectations of the speculators by raising the rate of interest. It might restore full employment, but it would have to be a permanent policy, since as long as speculators persist in their expectations of high interest rates any attempt to remove the fiscal stimulus will re-create the original problem. This is in sharp contrast to the deep-depression case, where fiscal policy can be used as a temporary 'pump-primer' – once entrepreneurial expectations have been revived the fiscal stimulus may be removed, since full information has been restored. Thus the argument against fiscal policy in the early 1920s case, like the argument against monetary policy in the deep-depression case, relies upon long-term considerations and expectational effects, both of which receive little attention in the usual textbook IS-LM expositions. Indeed the very possibility that the relative merits of monetary and fiscal policy could vary systematically with the state of information in capital markets is rarely entertained in expositions of IS-LM.

How the neglect of expectational factors causes IS-LM to misrepresent the interest-rate mechanism is also shown by Leijonhufvud's analysis of the 'Paradox of Thrift.' Starting from full information, an increase in the propensity to save will reduce the natural rate of interest. Full information would require a shift of resources from consumption goods to capital goods industries, but according to IS-LM, this reallocation of resources will be delayed by the increase in the demand for money induced by the fall in the market rate of interest, which forces the system through a costly deflation unless counteracting policy measures are taken.

According to Leijonhufvud the only reason for supposing an interest elasticity of demand for money large enough to cause such problems is the speculative demand that arises when the market rate falls below the rate forecast by speculators. But this will occur only if speculators do not perceive the fall in the natural rate, or if they get caught up in Keynes's beauty contest. Consistently with his corridor hypothesis, he argues that speculators normally spend their forecasting efforts trying to guess the natural rate, not trying to guess each other's guesses. A decline in the natural rate will normally cause no adjustment problems, for if it is perceived by speculators, the fall in interest rates will induce no increase in the demand for money, and full employment can prevail at the historically given level of prices.

Thus Leijonhufvud's main critique of IS-LM is that by ignoring the state of expectations in capital markets, and by neglecting the effects of disturbances, whether policy shocks or changes in tastes and technology, upon these expectations, the apparatus builds in a 'communication failure' of dubious general validity. In essence his argument is the same as the 'Lucas critique' of econometric policy evaluation. The IS-LM approach treats as 'structural' certain coefficients (e.g., the reaction of the demand for money to changes in the money supply or to changes in thrift) which in fact critically depend upon whether the exogenous changes are anticipated or not. Furthermore, the question of whether they will be anticipated must be seen in a broader context than that of a single isolated disturbance. The strength of the announcement effect will depend upon what people have learned about the operation of policy. To what extent changes in tastes or technology will be anticipated in the market depend upon the familiarity of the disturbances, and upon the freedom of markets from policy-induced noise that obscures the signals of market prices. Leijonhufvud's treatment of this noise-signal problem will be discussed in section 3.7 below. In this sense, Leijonhufvud has been one of the founders of the modern tendency in macroeconomics to promote expectations and signal-extraction problems to the forefront, to take a longer-run perspective on policy, and to denounce the pessimism inherent in IS-LM concerning the efficacy of market-adjustment processes.

Leijonhufvud goes beyond this emphasis on informational aspects of the interest–rate mechanism, and argues that to correct the problems of IS-LM it is necessary to replace its liquidity-preference theory of interest with a loanable funds theory. The difference between the two he sees not in terms of which equation determines which unknown, but which excess demand governs the out-of-equilibrium adjustment of the rate of interest. He argues that only by reinstating loanable funds into macro theory can it be made clear that (a) what normally governs the rate of interest are the basic forces of productivity and thrift ('the denial of the (loanable funds) mechanism makes nonsense of the very notion of a 'natural rate' of interest' (p. 135)), and (b) most macroeconomic maladjustments are attributable to various factors which interfere with the unfettered operation of these basic forces upon the rate of interest, factors such as perverse monetary policies, poor judgment by commercial bankers, and wrong-headed speculation.

There is much to be said in favor of Leijonhufvud's call for a return to loanable funds. It would certainly be an improvement from the textbook assumption that the rate of interest responds to the excess demand for money. After all, the rate of interest is defined by the price of bonds, and the signals to which bond quotations respond are surely more closely represented by the excess demand function for bonds than for money (see, e.g., Patinkin, 1958). It is common to argue that in a short-run two-asset macro model the two excess demands are linked through a

'Walras' law for stocks,' so that it makes no difference which is used. But this argument becomes invalid in the face of transaction costs which prevent the separation of portfolio allocation decisions from consumption-saving decisions (see, e.g., Purvis, 1978). Likewise, once Clower's dichotomized budget constraint is taken into account, current expenditures and the holding of liquid assets become inextricably linked and commeasurable (Kohn, 1981). Excess demands for both money and bonds can coexist, along with an excess supply of goods or labor, and in this situation it obviously makes a difference to which excess demand the interest rate responds (see Laidler, 1984).

Another advantage of the loanable-funds approach is that in order to define their supply and demand precisely several details of the circular flow of money must be considered which otherwise appear unimportant, but which matter greatly for understanding the role of money in economic activity. As Kohn (1981) has argued, the detailed sequence analysis required to comprehend financial flows can easily lead to a fog of dynamical complications without any apparent general results. One of the appeals of Keynes's short-run equilibrium method was its apparent ability to cut through this fog to a relatively simple set of static relationships. But Kohn has shown that the fog can also be avoided by a more elegant and technically parsimonious treatment of loanable funds than Robertson was able to give, without losing track of the circular flow and its importance in constraining people's expenditures, and in such a way as to shed new light upon such issues as the superneutrality of money, the importance to the transmission mechanism of how money is injected, and the role of monetary factors in influencing the rate of interest and the level of output.

Despite these arguments in favor of loanable funds, it is difficult to agree with Leijonhufvud's argument that most of the major macroeconomic confusions are directly attributable to neglect of loanable funds. It is a fairly elementary exercise to construct an IS-LM model in which the roles of entrepreneurial sales expectations and speculators' interest expectations are made explicit, in which the demand for money depends not upon the rate of interest *per se* but upon its difference from the rate expected by speculators, and in which (as originally argued by Hicks, 1937) the interest elasticity of money demand becames zero when the rate is higher than expected and the speculative demand disappears, but increases as the rate falls below the expected rate. Such a model may be used in a routine fashion to illustrate and make precise the arguments outlined above with respect to monetary and fiscal policy under different circumstances. It may also be used to illustrate Leijonhufvud's point about the paradox of thrift – an increase in thrift whose consequences are perceived perfectly by speculators will shift the IS and

LM curves down by equal amounts, with no change in output. The point of this exercise is not that IS-LM is free of defects, but that without any loanable-funds mechanism the apparatus may be made to exhibit those propositions for which Leijonhufvud has argued that loanable funds is indispensible.

Whether most macroeconomic maladjustments may be traced to the faulty working of the interest-rate mechanism is arguable. But Leijonhufvud certainly has an important point when he argues that in recent years too much emphasis has been shifted away from credit markets, toward labor markets. He argues that this is what led Keynesians (e.g., Solow, 1969; Tobin, 1972) into the untenable position of maintaining the existence of a stable Phillips curve in response to the accelerationist challenge of Friedman. He argues that the proper Keynesian response should have been to assert 'that unemployment will not converge to its natural rate *unless* the interest rate goes to its natural level – and that the latter condition will not always be fulfilled.' (p. 135).

The discussion of the previous section implies agreement with the criticism in the above quotation of Keynesians' reliance upon the Phillips curve to explain macroeconomic problems. But as argued in that section, Leijonhufvud has not succeeded in showing how they could dispense with that reliance and base their analysis upon a maladjustment in the interest-rate mechanism. Specifically, he has not shown how loanable-funds theory can help in this respect. Indeed Kohn's loanable-funds analysis bears out the necessity of rigid wages to account for equilibrium unemployment even in the presence of various interferences with the forces of productivity and thrift.

Nor is the neglect of the interest-rate mechanism by Keynesian economics as pervasive as Leijonhufvud seems to imply. Despite its ultimate reliance upon rigid wages, the IS-LM analysis does, after all, focus upon the rate of interest as one of the two variables to be given explicit graphical representation. The whole approach is designed to show how changes in employment are determined in the markets for goods and financial assets, not labor, and how various interest elasticities play a crucial role in comparative-statics results. Furthermore, for the purpose of these results the assumption of wage rigidity is not as crucial as it is for the more fundamental question of explaining the persistence of unemployment. For what difference would it make whether the assumption is made that wages did not change or that wages decreases caused, say, a decrease in confidence which offset the shift in LM (compare the *General Theory*, pp. 263–4).

Indeed, one of the best attempts in the literature to show how unemployment may persist despite wage flexibility was presented by the arch-Keynesian Tobin. In a paper (1975) directly addressed to

Friedman's accelerationist challenge he took almost exactly the line that Leijonhufvud says he should have taken. He posited a model in which the real rate of interest in the short run is affected inversely by expected inflation. When the adjustment of expectations interacts with the expectations-augmented Phillips curve, dynamic instability can result. He does not refer to the natural rate of interest but it may (naturally) be defined as the real rate when full-employment saving equals intended investment. Thus his conclusion 'the adjustment mechanism of the economy may be too weak to eliminate persistent unemployment' (p. 202) is exactly Leijonhufvud's recommended response.

3.6 INFLATION

One of the longer essays is on the institutional, legal, and social costs and consequences of changes in the value of money. Leijonhufvud believes that money should be treated as an institution, for in all its aspects each person's choices about how much to use, hold, etc., depend crucially upon convention – upon the confidence that others will play by the same rules.

> If we construct our explanation of the Social Contrivance of Money from the usual building blocks of the theory of individual choice alone, some aspects of the social institution will escape us in a way that can, embarrassingly, only be covered up by resort to brute tautologies – 'Money is accepted because it is accepted,' and so forth. (p. 220)

From this point of view he reveals at least three novel economic aspects of the effects of inflation. First, inflation is necessarily a ragged process, with different prices rising by discrete jumps at different times, in a way that price-setters will find impossible to coordinate because money is the conventional unit for quoting prices and striking contracts, and because there are discrete costs of renegotiating contracts and of changing prices. It has been recognized in the literature (e.g., Sheshinski and Weiss, 1977) that this will cause the dispersion of relative prices to increase with inflation. Leijonhufvud stresses the related proposition that inflation will reduce the ability of the price system to convey important messages concerning resource allocation, as agents find it difficult to distinguish between permanent changes in relative prices that call for long-run adjustments and transitory changes that arise from the jerkiness of inflation. This is, of course, to some extent the message of Lucas (1972), but in the Lucas model the problem arises only if monetary policy is unpredictable; smooth, neutral, steady inflation causes no problems. For Leijonhufvud there is no such thing as a smooth, neutral, steady inflation.

The second novel aspect has to do with capital market distortions. It is commonly understood that these arise with inflation because of its unpredictability, which makes real interest-rate calculations increasingly difficult. Again, it is commonly supposed that steady, perfectly foreseen inflation would cause no such problems, trivial Tobin–Mundell effects excepted. Leijonhufvud observes that perfectly foreseen inflation is no more possible than smooth, neutral inflation, because a commitment to stable money is the only possible anchor to people's expectations. Once that commitment has been abandoned:

> Observed inflation rates are not 'drawn' from a probability distribution generated by a law-abiding mechanism. The appropriate metaphor for this case, I suggest, is that of playing 'chess' in the presence of an official who has *and* uses the power arbitrarily to change the rules – i.e., a man who may interrupt at move 14 with the announcement: 'From now on bishops move like rooks and *vice versa*...and I'll be back with more later.' (p. 264)

In such a world he argues that people agreeing to a nominal rate of interest for debt contracts (another convention hard to account for with the logic of choice) cannot hope to be agreeing on a real rate, as efficiency would require.

The third aspect has to do with the demand for flexibility, which increases with inflation and its attendant uncertainty. Not only do people seek to avoid long-term contractual commitments, but, contrary to normal presumption, they may substitute into *nominal* assets. The institutions of a monetary economy make the portfolios with the most short-term nominal assets the most flexible ones. Inflation raises the expected cost of flexible positions but Leijonhufvud points out that it also raises the expected gain.

3.7 RATIONAL EXPECTATIONS: LEIJONHUFVUD AND LUCAS

Leijonhufvud's approach shares a great deal with modern rational-expectations theory in its focus upon signal-extraction problems, its view of policy as a process rather than as a series of isolated actions, its implication that textbook Keynesianism deals inadequately with expectations, and its insistence that the self-regulating capacity of the economic system is grossly underestimated by textbook Keynesianism. But there are two important differences, both of which are revealing in the light they shed on the two approaches.

The first concerns the stability assumptions embedded in the rational-expectations approach. Lucas (1980a) is not concerned with the process by which people learn about the stochastic relationships between what they can observe and what they wish to predict. Instead, he proceeds as if it has somehow managed to converge upon a set of consistent beliefs; and not just any consistent beliefs. He makes no use of speculative bubbles, self-fulfilling prophecies, and Keynes's beauty contests, all of which may be described as consistent, equilibrium patterns (see, for example, Brock, 1975; Azariadis, 1981; Townsend, 1983). Instead, learning is assumed to have converged upon fundamentalist beliefs according to which all that is expected to influence the behavior of a price at any date are the underlying factors of tastes and technology which influence supply and demand at that date independently of expectations.

Much of the interest of Leijonhufvud's work comes from his insightful remarks about the learning process and about the degree to which fundamentalists will prevail in the marketplace. His policy recommendations generally are aimed at aiding the learning process when it gets away from fundamentals, as in the case of the bear speculators who need to be kept in check by the Central Bank. This sort of thing will make little sense to the believer in stable fundamentalist expectations, for whom 'what's wrong' is typically nothing that governments will learn about any faster than the market.

Like the fundamentalists, Leijonhufvud stresses the corrective losses that people with wildly wrong expectations will incur. 'Normally,' he argues that they give a presumption to stability. But here again there is a corridor effect. It is too much to suppose that the market weeds out even those with erroneous conjectures about circumstances which have never been experienced. When large and unusual displacements occur, much previous knowledge becomes obsolete, and learning has to start again. Whether or not it converges, and how rapidly, is an extremely difficult question to model, as recent attempts (for example, Frydman and Phelps, 1983) have demonstrated. Unlike the Bayesian learning of econometric theory, which may usually be shown to converge upon 'the truth,' macroeconomic learning interacts with market adjustment in complicated ways. The relationships about which one person is trying to learn are affected by the attempts of others to do the same, in ways that can make it impossible to identify the relationships. Although nothing much may be said in general, it is clear that unusual events may cause prolonged deviation-amplification, as people fumble about trying as best they can to cope with a changing environment.[4]

The other crucial difference between Leijonhufvud and Lucas is revealed in the latter's (1980a) lucid account of the main methodological advantage of his research strategy; namely that deriving everything from the logic of choice is the best way to impose empirical discipline upon the investigations. Most of the accumulated stock of knowledge, both theoretical and empirical, concerns individual decision-making. If economic time series are modeled as if they were chosen by representative households and business firms, intermediated as smoothly as possible through perfectly competitive markets, it is necessary to limit what may be taken as exogenous (in the methodological, not the econometric sense) to tastes, technology, and endowments, and ensure against both making *ad hoc* departures from what is known and using too many degrees of freedom in the form of unexplained 'market adjustment' parameters.

Nothing could be further from Leijonhufvud's approach, which is to regard 'market adjustment' as the principal phenomenon to be explained. For Leijonhufvud the 'logic of choice' is not to be ignored, but in many cases must take a back seat to the 'rules of interaction.' It is evident in his treatment of money as an institution, his focus on 'liquidity' as an essential ingredient to communication in a monetary economy, the importance he assigns to the question of whether market processes will bring different agents' beliefs into harmony, and his insistence that real-world market institutions function very differently from the centralized Walrasian auction house.

What is at issue is whether institutions fall into place according to the dictates of efficiency or whether they place independent limits upon the ability to cooperate. No doubt there is an element of truth in both points of view, and there are reasons for thinking that in the long run efficiency prevails. But in the here and now we have no choice about the institutions with which history has endowed us. Our ability to cooperate in developing more efficient ones when circumstances change is limited by their existence, and outmoded conventions are notoriously hard to break. Their evolution is not well understood. Still, recognition of our ignorance does not imply that any theory based upon institutional constraints must be rejected as *ad hoc*. The choice in macroeconomics is often the uncomfortable one between 'ad hocery' and the foolishness of assuming away obvious, and obviously important, facts of life.

Lucas and many others may not easily be convicted of such foolishness. Not only is Lucas well aware of the limitations of any policy implications that follow from very special models, and of the empirical limitations of his theories; but in the class of models he uses to account for the business cycle, institutions do play a crucial role – specifically the institutional requirement that prevents agents from acquiring information on other 'islands.' Without this exogenous rule of interaction, or something like it, these models would have no way of accounting for the effects even of unperceived and unanticipated monetary disturbances.[5]

Thus the point is not that these models ought to be abandoned for their lack of institutional content; indeed they are likely to constitute a valuable, lasting contribution to the science. Rather the attempt to purge them of such content to get down to the hard core of tastes and technology will push us in the wrong direction and will inevitably prove to be self-defeating. Exogenously specified rules of interaction are as necessary to macroeconomics as exogenously specified 'rules of the game' are to game theory.

The research agenda suggested by Leijonhufvud's analysis is thus a highly ambitious one, for it involves many of the complicating factors of rational-expectations theory without two of that theory's key simplifications: the assumption that learning has worked its way out to an equilibrium, and the absence of exogenous 'market adjustment' factors. These simplifications serve not only to avoid ad hocery, but to make the theory tractable.

Thus new simplifications will have to be found before this research agenda can begin to claim any concrete success. As with any empirical science these simplifications will have to originate in careful observation. If it is not possible to rely exclusively upon the stock of data concerning individual choice, then new institutional data must be gathered, concerning the rules of interaction. What forms of market organization predominate for what kinds of commodities? What are the implicit rules of contract in different markets? How are prices set? Whose inventories typically are used to buffer shocks in demand and supply? Which groups of agents tend naturally, because of their position in the organizational structure of exchange, to acquire specialized knowledge about what kinds of activities? What are the limits upon agents' abilities to contact potential trading partners and to make effective offers to buy and sell in various markets? By what rules do markets ration credit when uncertainty and moral hazard make an equilibrium based upon rational choice difficult to conceive of (see Hellwig, 1977)?

The task of pursuing this research agenda may seem hopelessly ambitious, and suspiciously lacking in detail. But two recent papers by Peter Diamond (1982b, 1984a) offer hope that the agenda is indeed workable. In the context of extremely special models of costly search he shows how low-level equilibria arise where production is depressed because the cost of search is high, because there are few trading partners available, because no one else bothers to produce more; all with perfectly flexible prices and no misperceptions. These low-level equilibria arise because of a coordination problem that might or might not be solved under existing trading arrangements, depending upon initial conditions. They also illustrate how the lines of communication are affected by the pattern of transactions, how it takes more than the willingness of the unemployed to work at the going wage for the system to achieve a high level of employment, and many other 'Leijonhufvudian' themes.

If this agenda can indeed be transformed into a successful research program, the potential gains are enormous. The extent to which the economic mechanism is self-regulating has for too long been put aside as too loaded with ideology, or else given an implicit and unbelievable, simple answer in the initial setup of a model. As Leijonhufvud stresses, it is hardly a satisfactory state of affairs concerning one of the most important central issues in the history of economics. His approach suggests a way of bringing that question back into the realm of science. It suggests a way to account not only for the successes of the system upon which Keynesian theory sheds so little light, but also the obvious failures, such as those of the 1930s, which modern classicists like Friedman and Meiselman (1963) and Lucas (1980a) have had to recognize as 'outliers' to their theories. At the very least it shows that the question of where the economics of information leads in macroeconomics is still wide open.

NOTES

1. Most of the ingredients of that argument were already presented by Tobin (1975, esp. p. 201) whose paper is referred to in section 3.5 below.
2. One exception is the insightful discussion by Okun (1981).
3. On the connections between these concepts, see Jones and Ostroy (1984).
4. For an example of how this might cause a cumulative decline in output when monetary policy switches from a long-expected inflationary regime to a cold-turkey zero-inflation regime when people are not sure how firm the authority's resolve will be, see Howitt (1982).
5. In this respect it is also worth noting that Lucas (1980b) and the others have now adopted the institutional feature of Clower's dichotomized budget constraint as a way of introducing money into their models.

4 · CONVERSATIONS WITH ECONOMISTS: A REVIEW ESSAY

4.1 INTRODUCTION

In the past decade the frontiers of macroeconomics have been transformed radically by the rise of New Classical Economics (hereafter NCE). As recently as 1968 Leijonhufvud was writing of the reigning orthodoxy of Keynesian economics. The monetarist controversy of the late 1960s and early 1970s damaged the authority of Keynesianism, but did not touch its theoretical core. The only serious attacks on that core came from writers (e.g., Phelps *et al.*, 1970; Barro and Grossman, 1971) who were trying not to overthrow the orthodoxy but to give it a better micro foundation.[1] Until some time in the 1970s almost everyone seemed to accept one version or another of the neoclassical synthesis, according to which general equilibrium theory describes long-run trends, Keynesian theory describes short-run fluctuations, and a Phillips curve, possibly augmented by mechanically formed expectations, describes the transition between the two runs.

Within a few years consensus over the neoclassical synthesis had disappeared. The work on micro foundations produced a theory according to which even short-run fluctuations were describable in terms of general equilibrium. The journals were soon filled with articles containing such un-Keynesian notions as ineffectiveness of stabilization policy, nonexistence of involuntary unemployment, perfect flexibility of wages and prices, rationality of expectations, and even optimality of

This paper was written partly while I was visiting professor of economics at Université Laval. I am grateful to Russell Boyer, Joel Fried, Herschel Grossman, David Laidler, Lloyd Paquin and Don Patinkin for helpful comments and criticisms.

Reprinted from *Journal of Monetary Economics* (1986), **18**, July, 103–18. © 1986, Elsevier Science Publishers B.V. (North-Holland).

business cycle fluctuations. Although Keynesian economics is still the main approach of policy-oriented macroeconomists, it has clearly been displaced as the main approach in academic discourse.

Klamer's *Conversations with Economists* (1984) is an innovative attempt to describe this change in macroeconomics through transcripts of tape-recorded interviews with eleven economists,[2] including some of the leading Keynesians and New Classicals. The book consists of these transcripts, together with Klamer's preface, his introductory essay on macroeconomics for non-economists, and his concluding essay.

The book is aimed at least partly at non-economists, and economists may read it chiefly for its entertainment value. Klamer is obviously a skilled interviewer and has managed to get his subjects to say some interesting and provocative things about their work, and about other economists. But it deserves to be taken more seriously. The spontaneous reactions of the leaders of our profession yield insights into their work that cannot be gleaned from the work itself. Furthermore, Klamer advances two propositions about the rise of NCE that deserve to be taken very seriously indeed.

The first of Klamer's propositions is that the success of NCE is not attributable solely, or even substantially, to its objective scientific merits, that there are no conclusive theoretical or empirical arguments that one can point to as explaining its widespread adoption according to the methodology of economics as a positive science, that instead the New Classicals have used a vast array of rhetorical devices to persuade others of their point of view, of which the appeal to logic and fact is only one of many, and not necessarily the most important.

Klamer uses NCE as a case for viewing economics as an 'art of persuasion' rather than a positive science:

> Economists do not only construct models and conduct empirical tests, they also argue on what a good model should look like. Moreover, they philosophize, appeal to common sense, and talk about other economists and their work. Economics involves the art of persuasion. In the absence of uniform standards and clearcut empirical tests, economists have to rely on judgements, and they argue to render their judgements persuasive. This process leaves room for nonrational elements, such as personal commitment and style, and social discipline. (p. 238)

In particular, when assessing the theoretical and empirical arguments adduced in support of NCE he concludes that 'theoretical arguments are uncertain and their acceptability relies on a judgement which is made plausible with a variety of arguments' (p. 243) and 'just as there is no definitive theoretical argument, there is no definitive empirical argument' (p. 244).

The second important proposition advanced by Klamer is that the theoretical core of NCE has nothing to do with issues like price stickiness versus misinformation, how people form expectations, the effects of monetary policy, or the explanation of employment fluctuations, that the writings of NCE have dealt with, or indeed about any substantive issue at all. Instead, he argues that the main issue raised by the New Classicals is merely their style of argument, that the 'core claim' of NCE is 'to use a new language that dictates precision of expression, in strict adherence to the principles of microeconomics.... The issue, then, is the style of argument.' (pp. 239–40)

Klamer advances this second proposition in a fairly matter-of-fact way, as almost a restatement of what Lucas and Sargent say in their interviews. His main objective is not so much to uncover the essence of NCE as to advance his claim that economics should be viewed as an art of persuasion rather than a positive science. Nevertheless the proposition obviously suits his main objective. One can hardly view the recent transformation of macroeconomics as part of Popper's process of conjecture and refutation if there is no substantive issue involved.

Both of these propositions ought to be taken seriously because they suggest that a radically different perspective is needed to understand the recent transformation in macroeconomics, and because they can be supported by a considerable amount of evidence. But I shall argue that although the propositions contain some important truth, they are also seriously incomplete, because they neglect the historical context in which NCE has developed. A more complete understanding of the essence of NCE and of the reasons for its success can be gained by viewing NCE as a continuation of what Friedman (1970a) called the monetarist counter-revolution.[3]

4.2 STYLE OR SUBSTANCE?

It is convenient to deal first with what I call Klamer's second proposition. But before I can address either proposition, some operational definition of the term NCE is needed. Like any other such label in economics, NCE is most clearly and usefully defined as the distinctive common elements in the writings of some subset of writers. In the present case we want to choose those writers whose works have figured prominently in the transformation described above. For the sake of definiteness it is helpful to choose a relatively small subset.

Klamer implicitly defines NCE (pp. 12–13) using the subset consisting of Lucas, Sargent, Townsend, Wallace, Barro, Prescott and McCallum, the first three of whom are the representative New Classicals among his subjects. But in his interview Townsend resists being labeled this way, and rightfully so. It is hard to imagine that when people argue over NCE they typically have his writings in mind. I propose to define NCE in terms of the writings of Lucas and Sargent. These two are arguably the most prominent leaders of the transformation in macroeconomics. They are also, conveniently, two of Klamer's subjects. Furthermore, in a joint paper (Lucas and Sargent, 1978) they have adopted the label themselves. One could make a case for including various other writers, but in my opinion it is most useful to stick with these two.

With this definition it is easy to see how Klamer could arrive at his conclusion that NCE is defined by its style of argument. In his interview Lucas characterizes the models he uses in the following terms: 'The decision problems faced by individual agents in the models are clear, and the rules by which they interact are clear. You've got to spell out individual preferences and technology and you've got to spell out the rules of the game.' (p. 38) Likewise Sargent says: 'I think the key thing about new classical economics is a commitment to some notion of general equilibrium and some notion of optimizing behaviour, strategic behavior.' (p. 70) This insistence upon clear and precise adherence to the dual principles of rationality and equilibrium is made explicit also in the more reflective writings of Lucas (1980a) and Lucas and Sargent (1978). Furthermore, their writings since the early 1970s show that by and large they practice what they preach. More importantly for my purposes, this style of argument has characterized the above-mentioned transformation. Thus the insistence that this is the only legitimate style of argument can reasonably be described as the NCE methodology.

Of course the principles of equilibrium and rationality in themselves have no substantive implications, even if the principles are restricted to admit only perfectly competitive equilibria, and Lucas and Sargent recognize this. How then could Klamer conclude that this methodology, with no substantive content, is the only salient core claim of NCE?

The answer is partly that many of the substantive propositions commonly associated with NCE are also associated with monetarists like Karl Brunner, one of Klamer's subjects, who on methodological grounds are obviously not New Classical economists.

But curiously enough Klamer's main grounds consist of what Lucas and Sargent themselves say in their interviews. Both are reluctant to endorse any of the more controversial substantive claims that one might ascribe to them, such as the policy-ineffectiveness proposition. Both assert that this proposition should be seen more as a counterexample to Keynesian models rather than as an important proposition in its own right.

Indeed, Klamer is right that in their interviews Lucas and Sargent sound so open-minded on substantive issues that they might even 'accept neo-Keynesian conclusions, at least if they were derived from models that are articulated in a way they like' (p. 239). When asked about the importance of learning behaviour Lucas says that his methodology could easily incorporate it, and that indeed 'Nothing operational is at stake here.' (p. 39) Sargent points out that NCE models can include lots of what one would normally think of as Keynesian phenomena: 'Some models include roles for queues and unmatched agents. There are versions of models in which agents get thrown out of work and don't get matched right away.' (p. 67) He appears open-minded on the question of the optimality of *laissez faire*: 'it's not automatic that equilibria are optimal. If they're not, we try to analyze institutions and government interventions that will correct the non-optimality.' (p. 68) He even argues that the virtues of the NCE methodology have nothing to do with its empirical content: 'I claim that rational expectations is terribly fruitful, even if it never provides a single reliable answer. The reason is that it changes the way you think about policy.' (p. 75) Both he and Lucas claim that the main disadvantage of the disequilibrium approach is not that it leads to wrong answers but that to do it properly is technically too demanding.

Can it be that the most significant movement in macroeconomics since the Keynesian revolution has no substantive content? I don't think so. There is a substantive claim running through the writings of Lucas and Sargent. In general terms the claim is that Keynesian economics gives too pessimistic a picture of the self-regulating capacity of the economics system of free markets. More specifically, NCE claims that the main flaws in the Keynesian research program are twofold. First, the reason why aggregate-demand disturbances can cause employment fluctuations is not because nominal wages and/or prices are slow to adjust, and hence workers are sometimes forced off their notional supply curves. Instead, NCE offers the alternative paradigm of the Lucas–Phelps island, according to which less than perfect information about prices and/or the state of aggregate demand induces people to make choices that they later regret. The second error is the failure of Keynesian economics to incorporate rational expectations. According to NCE an empirically more fruitful theory is to be found by correcting these errors. Furthermore, such corrections destroy the Keynesian case for active stabilization policy.

These claims are so obviously characteristic of NCE that they hardly need to be documented. In case there is any doubt, one need look no further than the joint paper of Lucas and Sargent (1978), which was concerned with assessing the 'wreckage' of Keynesian macro models and with describing the NCE research program. Their main conclusion was 'that the difficulties [of Keynesian models] are *fatal*: that modern macroeconomic models are of *no* value in guiding policy and that this condition will not be remedied by modifications along any line which is currently being pursued' (p. 296). The main argument underlying this conclusion is based on the 'casual treatment of expectations' (p. 301) in Keynesian models. And in reconstructing what went wrong, they emphasize Keynes's 'unexamined postulate that money wages are sticky' (p. 307).

What perhaps makes these claims hard for Klamer to recognize is that they are not positive claims asserting that some proposition is true but negative claims that Keynesian economics is wrong. Without reference to Keynesian economics the claims would be meaningless, for by themselves the assumptions of clearing markets and rational expectations are just as empirically empty as the NCE methodology. But when phrased as they are above they are meaningful, for they assert that those potentially refutable propositions of Keynesian economics that depend upon nominal stickiness or non-rational expectations are false.

The style and substance of NCE complement each other. As Lucas has pointed out elsewhere (1980a), the Keynesian case for stabilization policy depends to a large extent upon the view that business-cycle fluctuations are disequilibrium movements around an equilibrium, and anything that reduces their amplitude is a good thing, not because it would enhance welfare in a way that we could demonstrate by the usual methods of microeconomists, but because of a presumption that anything that speeds up the process of disequilibrium adjustment is socially desirable. The NCE methodology deems such arguments inadmissible.

Furthermore, this methodology makes it comparatively easy for writers like Barro (1976) to make the case for the anti-Keynesian policy-ineffectiveness proposition that Lucas and Sargent are reluctant to endorse. The proposition might not follow directly from the methodology; but it does follow from the models that seem to embody that methodology in the simplest and most natural way; in short, from models that are 'paradigmatic' of the methodology.

Thus, while the methology has no substantive content as a matter of logic, it has a great deal of substantive content as a matter of practice. It forces the proponent of active stabilization policy to explain the precise nature of the impediments to transacting and communication that prevent private arrangements from exhausting all gains from trade, without forcing the defender of *laissez-faire* to address with any rigor the reciprocal Keynesian question of how exactly the economic system manages to overcome all the obvious coordination problems that stand in the way of attaining the state of equilibrium that he is postulating.

Any attempt to answer either question is bound to look feeble. Impediments to communication in a model simple enough for an economist to understand will typically also be simple enough that the economist can think of institutional changes that would overcome them. Similarly, any detailed attempt to explain how each agent acquires the information required of him in an NCE model must typically begin by assuming that the agents begin life endowed with an incredible amount of common knowledge. The NCE methodology has a substantive prejudice because it allows us to avoid the second question but forces us to submit to the first.

4.3 NCE AND MONETARISM

In my opinion the role of NCE in the development of macroeconomics can be seen most accurately by regarding it as phase II of what Friedman (1970a) called the monetarist counter-revolution. Both the substance and the style of NCE support the main message of that counter-revolution; that the Keynesian revolution was wrong on the central issue of self-regulation and that we should return to a pre-Keynesian style of analysis. Furthermore, the main substantive contributions of Lucas and Sargent have been extensions and refinements of central themes of monetarism. This is evident in the important role of money-supply disturbances and policy rules in their most prominent writings. More specifically, Lucas's pivotal article (1972) was written with the express purpose of making more precise some of Friedman's central ideas on the role of money. And the main point of the famous 'Lucas critique,' as elaborated by Lucas and Sargent (1978), was to corroborate one of Friedman's main points against activist stabilization policy; namely that we know less about the structure of the economy than Keynesians claim.

The contribution of NCE to the counter-revolution has been to add theoretical arguments and new techniques to the empirical generalizations upon which monetarism was based. This contribution can be seen more clearly in the light of Johnson's (1971) analysis. Johnson predicted at that time that monetarism would peter out, partly because it lacked a political 'cause' as important as unemployment was for the Keynesian revolution, and partly because it failed to provide an intellectually satisfying explanation of 'the supply-response of the economy to monetary impulses' (p. 12). I shall deal below with the first reason, but as for the second the achievement of Lucas's 1972 *JET* article was precisely to supply the ingredients for the missing explanation. In one stroke Lucas produced a theory that addresses why money should have the important short-run real effects that Friedman had been claiming, what determines their magnitude, how the explanation is consistent with Friedman's natural-rate doctrine, how it implies the optimality of a Friedmanesque constant money-supply growth rule, and how the argument can be based elegantly and precisely upon the fundamental principles of equilibrium and rationality.

Furthermore, Lucas and Sargent have supplied another ingredient which Johnson argued was necessary for the success of any counter-revolution: a framework of sufficient technical complexity and pure intellectual appeal to capture the imagination of large numbers of talented young economists. In Kuhn's terms, NCE has provided a rich framework in which to do 'normal science.' The challenges of redoing macroeconometrics to avoid the 'Lucas critique,' of integrating the analysis of uncertainty faced by individual decision-makers with the randomness of the economic time series used to test theories, of seeing how much of the dynamic, stochastic behavior of time-series data can be rationalized on the two principles of rationality and equilibrium, and of building bridges between macro and micro theories, have inspired technically oriented young economists in a way that monetarism never did.

This is not to say that NCE and monetarism agree on all issues. There are some important substantive differences. For example, Sargent and Wallace (1981) argue strongly against a simple Friedmanesque policy rule. And recent business-cycle theories like that of Kydland and Prescott (1982), which are clearly in the mainstream of NCE, assign no role at all to money. But these differences do not alter the point that the main substantive claim of NCE, namely that the Keynesian revolution was wrong on the central issue of self-regulation, is also the main point of the monetarist counter-revolution, and that to date the main substantive contributions of NCE have been extensions and refinements of key ideas in that counter-revolution.

Two of the most obvious differences between NCE and monetarism actually help to illustrate the contribution of NCE to the counter-revolution. The first is the one Tobin pointed out in his interview; namely that Friedman used a theoretical framework remarkably like the neoclassical synthesis that Lucas and Sargent are attacking. The *JPE* articles (1970b, 1971) that Friedman wrote in response to his critics' demands to see the theory underlying his empirical generalizations were based upon the same IS-LM framework as Keynesian theory.

While this difference is obviously real and important, it can be seen as a manifestation of the distinctive contribution of NCE to the monetarist counter-revolution, a contribution that embodies a factor that Lucas frequently emphasizes when discussing the development of economics – technical progress. Friedman's resort to Keynesian ideas to find theoretical support for his empirically based arguments was obviously damaging to the cause of the counter-revolution. For, if Friedman himself used Keynesian ideas, how could he claim that these ideas were essentially wrong? The technological breakthrough of NCE was to find a coherent and distinctly un-Keynesian set of theoretical arguments to buttress the counter-revolution, something which Friedman had been unable to do. This breakthrough supported Friedman's anti-Keynesian ideas with a set of arguments that appeal to more theoretically oriented economists, whether or not they appeal to Friedman.

The second obvious difference between NCE and monetarism is a methodological one. The monetarist Brunner makes it clear in his interview that he disagrees not only with the flexible-price assumption of many NCE models, but also with the NCE insistence upon deriving everything from first principles:

> This methodological position is quite untenable and conflicts with the reality of our cognitive progress over history. Science rarely progresses by working 'down from first principles'; it progresses and expands the other way. We begin with empirical regularities and go backward to more and more complicated hypotheses and theories. Adherence to the Cartesian principle would condemn science to stagnation. There are, moreover, as Karl Popper properly emphasized, no first principles (p. 195)

Likewise, the NCE methodology is obviously inconsistent with Friedman's 'as if' methodology which emphasized the importance of reduced-form predictions and denied the need to understand the structural details of individual decision-making and market interactions which the NCE methodology insists are crucial.

Johnson's analysis is again helpful for putting this methodological difference in perspective. As Johnson emphasized, Friedman's positivistic methodology was a major impediment to satisfying his critics' demands for a theoretical account of the transmission mechanism, because that methodology seemed to deny the need for any such explanation. Thus the development of a new methodology was almost a prerequisite for NCE to make its technical contribution to the counter-revolution. Just as Friedman needed a methodology that stressed the importance of factual content to support his empirical arguments, so Lucas and Sargent needed one that stressed the importance of first principles to support their theoretical arguments.

This new methodology was needed not only for the intrinsic reason of legitimizing the technical contributions of NCE, but also for the more extrinsic reason of aiding in the enlistment of young, technically oriented economists. It is hard to imagine that NCE would have been as successful as it was in its recruitment of such people if it had argued, as did Friedman, that what distinguished its analysis from that of its rivals was nothing more than an empirical judgment concerning the magnitude of a few key parameters in a simple and commonly agreed-upon theoretical framework.

One might wonder why, if Lucas and Sargent are part of a movement initiated by Friedman, they should place such emphasis on their un-Friedmanesque methodology. Before addressing the question I note that, strictly speaking, their emphasis does not constitute evidence for or against my view of their role in the development of macroeconomics, a role defined not by their intentions and states of mind but by their impact upon professional developments. Nevertheless it is possible to conjecture four different explanations for this emphasis that are consistent with, and thus further clarify, the view of NCE as part of the counter-revolution.

First, there is the obvious explanation that when asked to describe one's work any economist will naturally stress his own value-added. In the case of NCE that value-added is largely a nonsubstantive technical one. Although there is a strong substantive core claim in NCE, it is a core claim that was already embodied in monetarism.

Second, Friedman's main argument against activist stabilization policy was that our knowledge of economic reality is much less precise than Keynesians were claiming. A large part of his success resulted from his ability to debunk the more pretentious Keynesian claims to scientific knowledge. The scientific humility and open-mindedness displayed by Sargent and Lucas when they make no substantive claims can be interpreted as just what Friedman's critique called for.

Third, in emphasizing their methodology Lucas and Sargent are following Friedman in claiming the middle ground in their debates. Just as Friedman tried to saddle his opponents with the extreme position of a horizontal LM curve, and claim for himself the more reasonable position of anything else, so Lucas and Sargent are trying to saddle their opponents with the assumption of irrationality, while themselves taking the more reasonable-sounding position of being willing to entertain any proposition as long as it is formulated precisely and in terms of the innocuous-sounding principles that are almost part of the linguistic heritage of economics.

Fourth, in basing their claims on these time-honored principles Lucas and Sargent are coping with a problem that Johnson argued was faced by any counter-revolution, that of 'establishing some sort of continuity with the orthodoxy of the past' (Johnson, 1971: 10). Friedman coped with this problem by claiming a link to the 'oral tradition of Chicago' (a claim that Patinkin (1969) showed to be completely unfounded) as well as to generations of quantity theorists elsewhere. Lucas and Sargent (1978) do so by claiming that the Keynesian revolution was an

aberration that diverted attention from traditional 'equilibrium' explanations of the business cycle, and by adopting the label 'classical.'

4.4 WHY HAS NCE SUCCEEDED?

Klamer's claim that the success of NCE cannot be attributed to any
convincing theoretical or empirical arguments has merit, but his claim to
be able to deduce this from interviews with its exponents and detractors
is not credible; complex scientific theories cannot be assessed in this
format, and for two reasons. First, as Klamer recognizes, of all the
methods that economists use to persuade each other, the least
scientifically respectable are likely to come to the fore in informal
conversation. Second, the fact that economists use all sorts of rhetorical
devices to persuade does not imply that these devices are the decisive
elements in determining which arguments are ultimately successful.

Nevertheless, it is hard to argue with Klamer's conclusion. Nowhere
in the writings of NCE can one find decisive rejections of the core of
Keynesian economics. Sargent (1976) claimed only that his model
performs no worse than Keynesian models. Barro's (1977a) much
discussed work is well known to be roughly consistent with some very
Keynesian interpretations. Lucas (1973), McCallum (1976) and others
have found some support for NCE, but surely it would be an atrocious
theory for which talented people could not find any support. As for the
charge that Keynesian policy advice has failed, Keynesians like Tobin
deny that their advice was heeded, and in any event guilt by association
with bad policies hardly constitutes scientific grounds for rejecting a
theory.

Indeed there are still some empirical facts which on the whole seem
easier to account for with a simple Keynesian approach than with any
well-known NCE model: viz., the apparent lag in wages and prices
behind the business cycle (Gordon, 1982), the cyclical behavior of quits
and layoffs, the non-neutrality of perceived change in the money supply
(Boschen and Grossman, 1982), and the apparently 'involuntary'
character of a lot of unemployment. Likewise, persistent, large-scale
unemployment of the sort that occurred during the Great Depression
cannot be explained on the basis of existing NCE models without
invoking an implausible shift in people's preferences for leisure. Even
less dramatic cyclical fluctuations in employment seem to require such
preference shifts, given the absence of any pronounced procyclical
pattern to real wages; one can invoke information problems to account
for a negative correlation between the innovations in real wages and
employment over periods of a few weeks, but without a shift in

preferences existing NCE models imply that the lower-frequency movements in these variables should be positively correlated. Furthermore, most cross-section and panel-data studies indicate a real-wage elasticity of labor supply significantly less than unity, which, without shifts in preferences, or misinformation, would require the log of real wages to fluctuate with a standard deviation significantly greater than that of employment, a prediction which is clearly violated by the US data (Geary and Kennan, 1982).

The most recent empirical manifestation of NCE is Hansen and Singleton's (1982) strategy for uncovering the structural parameters of individuals' preferences. The work based on this strategy has not yet offered much support for NCE. As Rotemberg (1984) has argued, it tends to produce wildly different parameter estimates depending upon the econometrician's choice of instruments. In any event, as Hansen and Singleton emphasize, the strategy is not designed to test hypotheses concerning the overall working of the economy. Indeed its main attraction is that it offers a technique for consistently estimating individual choice functions without having to specify a model of the entire economy. Thus the consumption/asset demand functions estimated by this technique could just as easily be part of a Keynesian model as of an NCE model. The attempt by Mankiw, Rotemberg and Summers (1985) to use the strategy to estimate the labor-supply function jointly with the consumption function comes closer to discriminating between Keynesian and NCE models, because Keynesian theory denies that measured fluctuations in employment are movements along a supply curve. But their empirical results clearly reject the underlying choice theory.

This is not to say that the estimates reject NCE. There is obviously a way to explain any data set on the basis of equilibrium and rationality. But the use so far of the Hansen–Singleton strategy suggests that the attempt to do so with aggregate time series will require the researcher to postulate functional forms with many more free parameters than have been used so far, and hence to use up many more degrees of freedom. As more degrees of freedom are used up, the strategy becomes more one of describing the data than testing any fundamental economic propositions.

The lack of any decisive empirical evidence in favor of NCE seems to support Klamer's view of macroeconomics as an 'art of persuasion,' but it leaves us without an explanation for the spectacular success of NCE. The view of NCE as phase II of the monetarist counter-revolution suggests some reasons. Some of these reasons support Klamer's view, for they have little to do with the intrinsic scientific merits of NCE. But I shall argue that there are also strong scientific reasons for

NCE's success. Thus the case is less clear-cut than Klamer suggests.

Most of the nonobjective or extrinsic reasons for NCE's success suggested by viewing it as part of the monetarist counter-revolution have already been indicated. They are that NCE has provided a rich supply of 'normal science' puzzles for young economists to work on, that it has provided a methodology that appeals more to technically oriented young economists, that it has succeeded in building a bridge to an orthodoxy of the past, and that Lucas and Sargent have been effective debaters. To this list we can add the various extrinsic reasons that Johnson adduced for the success of monetarism, because the success of monetarism has obviously helped to make the profession more receptive to the similar message of NCE.

Another extrinsic reason is that NCE has acquired the politically important cause that Johnson argued was missing from monetarism; namely that of reducing the role of government in economic affairs. This cause is obviously aided by and in turn supports the central substantive message of NCE. The cause was likewise associated with monetarism, but it was not politically as important when Johnson was writing as it subsequently became with the 'neoconservative' movement in the mid to late 1970s.

However, this same point of view suggests an important intrinsic reason for NCE's success. Specifically, NCE has made important theoretical progress in areas where Keynesian economics was weak. The lack of a theoretically satisfactory account of the link between money and output was as much a defect of Keynesianism as of monetarism. It was this lack in Keynesian economics that inspired the work in the late 1960s and early 1970s on the micro foundations of macro theory. Thus it is hardly surprising to find that the work of someone who was as successful as Lucas in cracking a central theoretical problem in the existing approach should rise to prominence.[4] The fact that a profession dominated by Keynesian ideas was so willing to accept the anti-Keynesian conclusions of someone who had made progress in resolving a commonly acknowledged problem is hard to rationalize with Klamer's view of economists holding strongly entrenched prior positions, unwilling or unable to listen to the opposing point of view. Although some of this 'acceptance' was a result not of people changing their minds but of their being displaced by a new generation with different views, nevertheless much of it was also the result of the 'conversion' of theorists who had been searching for a micro foundation for Keynesian economics, including Barro and Grossman, authors of a widely cited series of articles on the disequilibrium foundations of macro theory, both of whom subsequently rejected the approach because of the difficulty of reconciling it with the principle of rationality.[5]

Even if Klamer's case is not wholly convincing, the above account supports his claim that the rise of NCE cannot be explained from the positivistic methodological viewpoint that economists like to preach. Empirical arguments played some role in that rise but not the decisive one that positive economics would dictate. Indeed, NCE fails on many accounts to predict as well as Keynesian theory does. Instead, the rise of NCE is attributable primarily to extrinsic factors that positive economics deems irrelevant and to theoretical arguments that it deems at best secondary. In short, insofar as intrinsic reasons mattered at all, the arguments of NCE have become accepted not because they predict well but because they have been judged to be 'theoretically coherent.' How a scientific community judges theoretical coherence is obviously a complicated question that the methodology of positive economics does not even begin to address.

4.5 THE FUTURE OF NCE

The preceding account suggests four reasons for thinking that the success of NCE will prove to be transitory. First, I doubt that theoretical coherence is enough of an intrinsic reason to keep the movement going despite its empirical failures. In particular, its failure to give an empirically plausible account of unemployment prevents it from thoroughly discrediting the Keynesian revolution, the main justification of which was that it did provide such an account. Also its failure to account empirically for the real effects of monetary policy will eventually undermine the support that it has received indirectly from the success of monetarism.

Second, it is not clear that the profession will continue to judge NCE theoretically coherent. Philosophers are raising important fundamental problems with the concept of rationality (e.g., Elster, 1979). Such problems become apparent in NCE when we ask what happens when an agent observes an event he had thought was impossible. The NCE methodology seems to deny the very possibility of such events.[6] To avoid paradoxes it seems that the methodology therefore requires people to consider anything possible, a requirement that would be difficult, if not impossible, to satisfy with any tractable model that gives a detailed account of the rational formation of expectations.

Furthermore, as NCE models are further developed to cope with anomalies they will inevitably become more complicated, and will thus lose much of the simplicity and elegance that give them their coherence. One does not have to perturb a model by much to make agents' decision rules appear intractable, and thereby to enhance the relative coherence of simple adaptive rules of behavior.

Third, even if the NCE methodology survives, it is not obvious that the substantive message of NCE will survive with it. The fact that the search for a micro foundation for Keynesian economics led first to un-Keynesian results may turn out to be merely a manifestation of the substantive bias to the NCE methodology, a bias that will not survive technical progress. The lack of micro foundation to Keynesian theory does not imply that the Keynesian conclusion regarding self-regulation is inconsistent with rationality and equilibrium, just that the transaction costs and coordination problems implicit in it were not clearly specified. Recent work that has focused on these costs and problems has begun to produce more Keynesian results (e.g., Shapiro and Stiglitz, 1984; also, Chapter 10 below).

Fourth, it is far from clear that 'big government' is as politically important as the Keynesian cause of unemployment. The persistence of double-digit unemployment in the major western industrialized countries that have not followed Reagan's Keynesian fiscal policies in the 1980s is adding to Keynesianism's political as well as scientific support.

Whatever the future holds for its core propositions NCE has clearly made a permanent mark on the history of our subject. Future historians will find Klamer's conversations invaluable in documenting and analyzing this fascinating counter-revolutionary movement.

NOTES

1. As Laidler (1981) has pointed out, some of the papers of the Phelps volume (e.g. those by Mortenson, Alchian, and Lucas and Rapping) were based on the assumption of market clearing that became one of the touchstones of the NCE movement. But the full extent of the anti-Keynesian bias of this kind of micro foundation was not yet apparent to the writers of those papers.
2. Robert Lucas, Thomas Sargent, Robert Townsend, James Tobin, Franco Modigliani, Robert Solow, Alan Blinder, John Taylor, Karl Brunner, David Gordon, and Leonard Rapping.
3. This point of view has also been taken by Tobin (1981) who builds, as I shall, upon Johnson's (1971) insights, but who pays little attention to the method-ological differences between NCE and old-style monetarism.
4. As Tobin (1981) has pointed out, however, NCE has been no more successful than old-style monetarism in explaining an important part of that link; namely the connection between money and aggregate demand. Lucas's contribution dealt mainly with the connection between aggregate demand and real output.
5. See, for example, Barro (1979) and Grossman (1979); these articles do not necessarily express the current (1985) position of the two authors, but they leave little doubt that in 1979 neither author saw much point in pursuing the

non-market-clearing approach of their famous joint 1971 *AER* article any further.

6. As Cooley, LeRoy and Raymon (1984) explain, this vitiates the concept of a 'régime change,' a concept which is necessary for econometric identification according to NCE methodology.

5 · THE KEYNESIAN RECOVERY

5.1 INTRODUCTION

It is an honor to be giving the Harold Innis Memorial Lecture for 1986. I am especially happy to be giving it in 1986 because this is the fiftieth anniversary of Keynes's *General Theory of Employment, Interest and Money*, and I would like to take this occasion to speak on the subject of what influence Keynes's central message in the *General Theory* has had on contemporary macroeconomics, and what influence it is likely to have in coming years.

If I had been asked to address this subject five or ten years ago I would have made the lecture very short. Although the Keynesian IS-LM apparatus was still the main organizing device of all intermediate macro textbooks, and of most policy-oriented economists, Keynesian theoretical ideas had virtually disappeared from the leading journals, having been displaced by such un-Keynesian ideas as perfect wage flexibility, perfect foresight, the absence of involuntary unemployment, the Pareto-optimality of business-cycle fluctuations, and so forth. Keynesian policy advice had become downright disreputable in some academic circles, and was clearly on the defensive everywhere.

As for the status of Keynesian ideas in society at large, Keynes once expressed the wish that some day 'economists could get themselves thought of as humble, competent people, on a level with dentists' (1972: 332). By 1979 Keynesian economists had become thought of the way I

The 1986 Harold Innis Memorial Lecture, presented at the Canadian Economics Association Meetings in Winnipeg, 29 May 1986. Robert Clower, David Laidler, Michael Parkin, and Douglas Purvis provided useful comments on the original lecture.

Reprinted from *Canadian Journal of Economics* (1986), **19**, November, 626–41. © Canadian Economics Association.

used to think of my dentist when I was ten years old, with a mouth full of cavities, and he could see no reason for using Novacaine – not humble or competent, but a menace to society who was all the more dangerous because of his belief that he knew better than others what was good for them, and because he now had his hands on some of the crucial policy instruments.

Since 1979 the public status of Keynesian ideas has fallen even further. The madmen in authority are now distilling their frenzy from other defunct economists. But I see signs of some recovery in the status of those ideas within the discipline of economics, signs that at least they are not yet completely dead. What I would like to argue is that there is an important aspect of Keynes's central message that was never incorporated into the mainstream of macroeconomic theory, that the failure to incorporate this aspect is largely responsible for the decline of Keynesian theoretical ideas, but that some recent theoretical developments offer hope that that failure may finally be rectified.

5.2 THE CENTRAL MESSAGE

The first part of my argument is to identify the central message of the *General Theory*. What were the main substantive claims that Keynes was making in the book? On this question I have little new to say beyond what is in Patinkin's (1976) authoritative account. However, the *General Theory* is sufficiently obscure in parts, and its central message is sufficiently different from what one finds in textbooks accounts, that the question is worth dwelling on.

First, the *General Theory*, as its title indicates, is a book on theory, not policy. As Patinkin has pointed out, although the *General Theory* was strongly motivated by the important policy issues of the day, and although it left no doubt about Keynes's position on those issues, nevertheless it devoted no more than a few paragraphs of its twenty-four chapters to discussion of monetary and fiscal policy *per se*. Instead, the book was intended to build a rigorous theory that would support the policy views that Keynes and others had already reached on more pragmatic or intuitive grounds.

Indeed the *General Theory* was devoted to what would now be called the micro foundations of macro theory. Keynes claimed that the fault of orthodox economics 'is to be found not in its superstructure, which has been erected with great care for logical consistency, but with a lack of clarity and generality in its premises' (p. xxi). As he explained in chapter 2, the fundamental postulates of classical economics that he sought to challenge were nothing less than those underlying the basic microeconomic concepts of demand and supply, as applied to the labor market. He was arguing that these concepts could not be used in the usual way to determine the level of employment. Instead he proposed an alternative micro foundation – his theory of effective demand.

So the central message of the *General Theory* has to do with how markets function. That central message has three parts to it. The first is that there is something wrong with a free-market system, because 'it seems capable of remaining in a chronic condition of sub-normal activity for a considerable period without any marked tendency either towards recovery or towards complete collapse' (p. 249). The system is not, to use a phrase that Keynes liked, self-adjusting. Instead, government intervention is needed to eliminate involuntary unemployment.

Keynes tried to support this claim with the idea of quantity adjustment as an equilibrating process. Following a disturbance to aggregate demand the ensuing quantity adjustments will not continue forever until a position of full employment or complete collapse is reached, but will generally lead to an equilibrium at less than full employment. This is the simple idea of the multiplier, the idea underlying Keynes's theory of effective demand, the familiar Keynesian cross diagram, the fixed-price equilibrium analysis of Barro and Grossman (1976) and Malinvaud (1977), and the IS half of IS-LM. As Patinkin has argued, this idea of quantity equilibration was the central analytical innovation of the *General Theory*.

So far we are on pretty familiar ground. This first component of Keynes's central message is the stuff of all the textbooks. But the second component is one that you will not find in many textbooks. It is that unemployment is not attributable to sticky wages, and that a policy of wage flexibility, far from alleviating the problem, would be likely to exacerbate it.

To anyone who has not read the *General Theory* I am sure this must sound 180 degrees from the truth. Nevertheless, it was a fundamental objective of the *General Theory* to show

> that a decline in employment, although necessarily associated with labour's *receiving* a wage equal to a larger quantity of wage goods, is not necessarily due to labour's *demanding* a larger quantity of wage goods; and a willingness on the part of labour to accept lower money-wages is not necessarily a remedy for unemployment. (p. 18)

It is true that Keynes assumed a fixed money wage for the first eighteen chapters of the book, but this, as he explained, was just 'to facilitate the exposition' (p. 27). In chapter 19, entitled 'Changes in Money Wages,' he relaxed the assumption and argued that it made no difference to the conclusions of the previous eighteen chapters.

To confuse matters more, Keynes even gave many reasons for believing that money wages are in fact sticky. Nevertheless, he made it perfectly clear in chapter 19 that this stickiness was, on the whole, a good thing. Some of the reasons he gave for this judgment had to do with broad questions of social justice, economic expedience, and the value of maintaining a stable price level. But he also argued that wage cuts in the face of unemployment would probably reduce aggregate demand even further, because of the effects of a lower wage on the distribution of income between workers and other factors, which would reduce the aggregate propensity to consume; because of the effects on bankruptcy, business confidence, and the propensity to consume of a higher real burden of debt resulting from a lower price level; and because the expectation of further deflation would depress aggregate demand.

The reason why it was central to Keynes's argument that sticky wages were not to blame for unemployment is that, as Patinkin, Leijonhufvud (1968) and others have stressed, that was the classical diagnosis of unemployment that he was trying to refute: 'the classical theory has been accustomed to rest the supposedly self-adjusting character of the economic system on an assumed fluidity of money-wages; and, when there is rigidity, to lay on this rigidity the blame of unemployment.' (p. 257) In the famous passage where he ridiculed the classical economists as being like Euclidean geometers in a non-Euclidean world who rebuke their lines for not keeping straight, he was referring to their 'conclusion, perfectly logical on their assumption, that apparent unemployment (apart from the admitted exceptions) must be due at bottom to a refusal by the unemployed to accept a reward which corresponds to their marginal productivity.' (p. 16)

The third component of Keynes's central message is more familiar. It is that the component of aggregate demand at the source of unemployment problems is investment, and that the main reason why investment demand cannot be counted on to stay at a level consistent with full employment is 'the extreme precariousness of the basis of knowledge on which our estimates of prospective yield have to be made' (p. 149). This pervasive uncertainty was the factor that Keynes identified in his reply (1937) to his critics as one of his two main points of departure from classical analysis (the other being his theory of effective demand). Because of it investment must rely not on rational calculation but upon the 'animal spirits' of entrepreneurs, which are subject to 'waves of optimistic and pessimistic sentiment' (p. 154). The development of organized security markets exacerbates the instability of investment because 'certain classes of investment are governed by the average expectation of those who deal on the Stock Exchange, rather than by the genuine expectations of the professional entrepreneur,' (p. 151) and those expectations are formed by forecasting the forecasts of others rather than being rooted in the fundamentals.

In short, Keynes's central message was a challenge to the classical conception of how the economic system functions. Now it may be inaccurate to speak of Keynes as attacking Walrasian theory; nevertheless, as a matter of pure economics, the conception underlying classical theory is that of Walrasian general equilibrium analysis. It pictures the system as one giant auction market, conducted by an auctioneer that establishes equilibrium prices and costlessly executes all trading plans.

The particular feature of the Walrasian conception that Keynes was challenging is the assumption that all social interactions are mediated by prices. In Walrasian theory the only social constraint on individual decisions is the single lifetime budget constraint. One person's action can impinge on another's only to the extent that it affects the prices in that constraint. It cannot have any additional effects by changing the probability that others can sell as much as they plan, or by making it more difficult for others to find trading partners, or by contributing to a shortage of liquidity. In Clower's (1965) terminology, all agents are free to base their trading plans on notional demands and supplies.

Classical theory portrays price adjustment as the system's main deviation-counteracting feedback mechanism. When an economy is disturbed by a change in tastes or technology that is first apparent only to a subset of agents, excess demands and supplies act as a signal that a changed allocation is called for. This signal is passed on to other agents in the form of a change in price. Sellers do not have to be informed by a rise in inventories, a shortening of order lists, or an increasing difficulty of locating buyers. They just have to watch the price.

Keynes was denying that prices are the main equilibrating variables. What signals a fall in demand is mainly an unexpected fall in sales. What makes demand fall is not a change in prices but a change in the level of output. What equilibrates the market for labor is not a change in wages but a change in employment. To the extent that price signals are sent, at least in the labor market, they are likely to be deviation-amplifying rather than deviation-counteracting.

The absence of non-price signals in Walrasian theory is what makes a Walrasian equilibrium a state of ideal coordination – that is what the first welfare theorem tells us. By implication it is the presence of non-price signals in Keynesian theory that makes a Keynesian equilibrium a state of coordination failure, one where a lack of coordination between savers and investors can prevent the buyers and sellers of labor from exploiting all mutually advantageous gains from trade.

5.3 THE FATE OF KEYNES'S CENTRAL MESSAGE

The IS-LM apparatus that Hicks extracted from the *General Theory* has had an enormous effect on the development of macroeconomics. It is what distinguishes the economics of the past fifty years from what went before. It is what allowed Keynes and his followers to formulate a theory of unemployment in familiar and tractable static equilibrium terms rather than the cumbersome, indeed sometimes impenetrable, disequilibrium dynamic terms of earlier writers. It is what finally permitted a systematic analysis of the interaction of real and monetary phenomena in determining the level of employment.

But although macroeconomics has almost immortalized the basic analytical model of the *General Theory*, it has been far less kind to the central message of the *General Theory*. The first component of that message, that there is something wrong with the way markets function, something calling for government intervention, was embraced by a generation of Keynesian economists; but for the past twenty years it has been roundly denied, not just in the political process but by the major schools of thought that have grown up within the discipline of macroeconomics: monetarism, New Classical Economics, and most recently, real business-cycle theory.

The second component, that unemployment is not attributable to wage stickiness, has ironically become a rallying cry for anti-Keynesian economics. And from Modigliani (1944) to Taylor (1979) the modern Keynesian position has been the classical one that Keynes was attacking: that sticky wages are to blame.

It is bad enough that the followers of Keynes and the classics have switched sides on this crucial aspect of Keynes's central message. In addition, hardly anyone in any camp today seems to agree with Keynes that wage adjustment is a destabilizing, deviation-amplifying mechanism. In the face of demand shocks Keynesians argue that employment fluctuates because wages do not. Real business-cycle theorists argue that employment does not fluctuate because wages do. New classics agree with Keynesians for unanticipated shocks and with real business-cycle theorists for anticipated shocks (although they prefer to base wage/price stickiness on deeper informational problems). All of them agree that wage and price flexibility is all it takes to maintain full employment.

As for the third component of Keynes's message, the idea that investment is by far the most volatile component of aggregate demand and thus is largely responsible for employment fluctuations, is certainly part of the mainstream Keynesian position. But the idea that pervasive uncertainty renders rational calculation impossible is certainly not.

Mainstream macroeconomics has become increasingly dependent upon the paradigm of rational, calculating agents that Keynes put down as being itself one of those pretty, polite techniques for coping with uncertainty. Modern investment theories of either the Eisner–Strotz variety, or the Tobin-q variety are firmly grounded on the assumption of expected profit maximization. The post-Keynesians that have embraced this third component of Keynes's message are generally regarded by mainstream Keynesians as beyond the fringe.

Now part of the responsibility for the fate of Keynes's central message undoubtedly lies in the message itself. History was unkind to it partly because it wasn't that compatible with history. There are good reasons for thinking that the economic system has better homeostatic properties than Keynes was claiming. Part of it is probably also attributable to a changing *Zeitgeist*. Anti-Keynesian economics is part of the more general neoconservative movement that gained force in the 1970s.

But to my mind the main reason for the decline of Keynes's ideas is the one that Robert Clower (1986) recently proposed. Neither Keynes nor any of his followers ever succeeded in presenting a clear conception of how markets function that would serve as an alternative to the Walrasian auction, and that would bear out his message that wage and price adjustment are not the system's main homeostatic mechanisms.

Keynes did come close. His theory of effective demand did portray an equilibrium in which quantities rather than prices were the equilibrating variables. But that equilibrium was one of less than full employment only under the assumption of a fixed wage. As Clower demonstrated in 1965, the Keynesian idea of effective demand can be derived from the very Walrasian framework that Keynes was challenging, just by assuming that traders were aware of the consequences of trading at disequilibrium prices. Once the auctioneer succeeded at getting prices right, the notional demands of classical economics would prevail and there would be no coordination failure.

Furthermore, the argument in the crucial chapter 19 went well beyond the neat comparative statics of IS-LM. In presenting this argument Keynes had to fall back on to the murky and unpersuasive disequilibrium dynamic arguments of his predecessors. Since everyone agreed that wages were not very flexible anyway, and since the IS-LM apparatus was such a fruitful one as long as you imposed a fixed wage, small wonder that Keynes's followers were content to assume a fixed wage, and to ignore the message of chapter 19. As Paul Samuelson (1983: 216) recently put it,

> The fiction that Keynes assumed rigid wages was found to be a useful fiction. That was so even if one could be persuaded by his purported

demonstration that wage cutting might induce such perverse dynamic effects as to be incapable of helping the unemployment problem.

In short, Keynes had an important message, and he proposed an ingenious and fruitful model. But the model does not support the message. IS-LM without wage stickiness does not yield Keynesian implications. That is why Friedman (1970b, 1971) was able to use it as the theoretical framework of his attack on Keynesianism, and why such writers as Ben McCallum and Michael Parkin have been able to combine it with the Lucas aggregate supply schedule to produce new classical models.

The reason why this failure led to a decline in Keynesian ideas was threefold. First, by resting their case on sticky wages Keynesians diverted attention from what Keynes believed to be the important fundamental coordination problem – the problem of coordinating the intentions of savers with the expectations of investors.[1]

Second, the failure to provide a coherent conception of how trade is organized left too many questions unanswered. The fact is that you can use IS-LM, together with some *ad hoc* assumptions about wage behavior and expectations, to present a mathematically rigorous argument that approximates that of Keynes's chapter 19. James Tobin (1975) did it with an expectations-augmented Phillips curve and adaptive expectations. Bradford DeLong and Lawrence Summers (1986b) did it with Taylor-style overlapping wage contracts and rational expectations. But even these modern arguments leave unanswered such basic questions as who sets prices, and under what motivation, and why transaction quantities are determined the way they are, and why the unemployed do not underbid those who have signed the sticky contracts, and so on.

It was the presence of unanswered questions like these that motivated the search for a micro foundation for macro theory in the 1960s and 1970s, the search that led initially to the informational foundations of Phelps *et al.* (1970). At first many writers conjectured that the conception of the Phelps island would provide the missing micro foundation for Keynesian economics. And it did indeed help to explain why the initial reaction to an unanticipated fall in nominal demand should come in the form of a change in quantity rather than in price. But once Lucas added rational expectations to that conception in his seminal 1972 *JET* paper, all trace of Keynesian implications vanished.

The third, and in my opinion the most crucial, reason why Keynes's failure to propose a coherent alternative to the Walrasian auction led to the decline of Keynesian ideas is that the hypothesis that mass unemployment is due to wage stickiness is simply not tenable. As

Keynes was aware, the big downturn in the early 1930s in the United States coincided with a massive wage deflation. And the downturn did not come to an end until, partly under the influence of the NIRA, wages stopped falling some time in 1933. As Keynes was even more keenly aware, the huge wage deflation of the early 1920s in the UK had not prevented the big rise in unemployment at the time.

Furthermore, in a model like that of Malinvaud or Taylor, the only reason why a worker can remain involuntarily unemployed is his failure to offer his services for less than the going wage. Why doesn't he? One might invoke the exclusion powers of trade unions, but surely that is no explanation of the Great Depression, which occurred when the labor force had hardly begun to be unionized. One might also argue that the unemployed workers are caught by surprise – as they reduce their asking wages the price level keeps falling, reducing their marginal value product, and thereby frustrating their attempts to regain employment. But this is the argument of Friedman and Lucas. The men riding the rails are voluntarily speculating on real-wage movements and are making forecast errors on the price level. Is this what Keynesian economics is all about?

5.4 MACROECONOMICS AT THE CROSSROADS

Despite the weakness in the empirical basis of Keynesian economics, the empirical basis of New Classical Economics strikes me as even weaker. Nonetheless, New Classical Economics managed with amazing speed to displace Keynesian economics as the main source of new ideas in macro. This success was due not so much to any convincing empirical arguments as to the great theoretical appeal New Classical Economics had to technically oriented young economists. A character in the movie 'Sweet Liberty' asserted that to attract young people a movie had to do three things: defy authority, destroy property, and take people's clothes off. New Classical Economics defied the Keynesian orthodoxy. It rendered obsolete a lot of Keynesian human capital. And it permitted young people the thrill of exhibiting their raw technical skills, uninhibited by the literary conventions that clothe their elders' flabby equipment.

Fortunately economics is not entirely dominated by these considerations. The facts also matter. As the memory of Woodstock fades, reality sets in. New Classical Economics did not succeed in providing a convincing explanation for why monetary policy should have more than fleeting real effects, or for why wages and prices should be so slow to respond to demand shocks. It failed to explain the time-series properties of real wages and employment, at least without invoking implausible shifts in preferences for leisure. It has yielded no insights into the apparently involuntary nature of unemployment in periods like the Great Depression. The Lucas aggregate supply schedule that lies at the heart of New Classical Economics is now admitted by economists of all persuasions to be an empirical failure.[2]

Because of these empirical failures I see macroeconomic theory at an important crossroads today. Many of the exciting new theoretical developments are coming from real business-cycle theory, which goes beyond the classics, new or old, to argue that money is neutral even in the shortest of runs, and that the business cycle is the Pareto-optimal outcome of a perfectly competitive economy with instantaneous price flexibility and a complete set of Arrow–Debreu markets.[3] But there are also some exciting new developments that may finally offer a micro foundation to support the central message of the *General Theory*.

Which of these two paths will be the main attractor of graduate students in the years to come is impossible to predict. Personally, I sense an increasing receptiveness of young people to Keynesian ideas, which I attribute to the severity of the 1981–2 recession and the continuation of high unemployment since then throughout most of the industrial world. Just as inflation brings out monetary cranks, so unemployment brings out those who maintain that capitalism is fundamentally flawed.[4] But that effect may well be transitory. Meanwhile, I would like to describe some of the new theoretical developments that might bring about a recovery in the status of Keynesian ideas.

The first set of developments I have in mind are those summarized by Peter Diamond (1984b), developments in the theory of search and transaction externalities. This work is closely related to the matching theories of Mortenson (1982a), and others, and it is something that I have been trying to develop in a recent series of papers, some of them together with my colleague Preston McAfee.[5]

When you ask a thoughtful Keynesian economist to explain his wage-adjustment equations, and to explain why the unemployed do not underbid the employed, he will tell you that the slowness of wages to fall is supposed to represent transaction costs and coordination problems. It takes time for people to find matches in the job market, job search is inhibited by the unwillingness of firms to recruit during recession, and so on. The main problem with these explanations is that they come from Keynesian economists but not from their models. The new literature on transaction externalities starts with a more or less explicit conception of the market organization that gives rise to transaction costs and shows how they impinge directly on individual decision-making.

The important transaction cost in these models is the cost of contacting potential trading partners. And the important feature of this cost is what I call a thin-market externality. The more active interest there is on one side of the market, the easier it is to find a partner. As in any communication network one person's efforts to undertake a transaction confers external benefits on other agents, whose marginal cost of transacting is thereby reduced.

This thin-market externality has some very Keynesian implications. To begin with it is a non-price market interaction that cannot be eliminated by price flexibility. It implies that consumers' trading plans will be affected by the level of employment (the key idea underlying effective demand) even if wages are fully flexible, because an increase in employment makes jobs easier to find, and this has a direct effect of relaxing the constraints faced by a household. Because of the non-price interaction the equilibria of these models are typically Pareto inefficient.

These models also typically yield a multiplier process. This is because the non-price interaction involves what Haltiwanger and Waldman (1985) call synergism, or what Cooper and John (1988) call strategic complementarity.[6] That is, an exogenous increase in activity by one set of agents induces other agents to want to increase their activity too, thus reinforcing the initial disturbance.

One of the most striking features of these models is their tendency to produce multiple equilibria. If everyone believes that markets will be inactive they will anticipate a high cost of transacting; this will discourage them from undertaking transactions, and the initial beliefs will be self-fulfilling. On the other hand, the expectation of a high level of activity can also be self-fulfilling. The low-level equilibria are reminiscent of the chronic states of subnormal activity that Keynes was trying to explain. In simple models they are Pareto-dominated by the high-level equilibria.

This approach also gives meaning to the elusive concept of involuntary unemployment. In the simplest of models the unemployed are all actively searching for trading partners. In a low-level equilibrium they will remain unemployed for longer than in a high-level equilibrium because with less recruiting jobs are harder to find, not because any change in the real wage has induced them to substitute leisure for work.

Finally, although the approach does not rely on the assumption of sticky money wages it is ideally suited for studying the effects of wage flexibility (as I have in Chapter 9). This is because a worker and firm that have made contact will typically be bargaining in a situation of bilateral monopoly. If there is a going market wage for the worker's services his reservation wage will be less than that because of the cost of finding someone else willing to pay the going wage; and the firm will be willing to pay more – otherwise it would not have incurred the cost of contacting in the first place. The indeterminacy of the outcome to this bilateral monopoly bargain lends an indeterminacy to the equilibrium wage contract in the market as a whole.[7]

This indeterminacy implies that the economist is at liberty to vary the nature of the wage contract without assuming any change in taste or technology. Both sticky and not-so-sticky wage contracts can be compatible with the assumption that both sides to the bargain are exhausting all mutually advantageous and privately attainable gains from trade. Such indeterminacy is an important feature for any Keynesian model to possess because although Keynes's central message does not rely on wage stickiness it does say something about the consequences of altering the degree of wage stickiness, and conceptual experiments that postulate an exogenous change in the degree of wage flexibility with no associated change in taste or technology are logically inadmissible without indeterminacy.

The other set of developments I have in mind is recent work on indeterminacy in rational-expectations models.[8] (This is a different kind of indeterminacy from the bilateral-monopoly indeterminacy of the previous paragraph.) Writers such as Robert Shiller (1978) and John Taylor (1977) have shown that in linear rational-expectations models there are always equilibria in which expectations are conditioned not just upon the fundamentals that directly influence supply and demand but also upon extrinsic random variables of no fundamental importance. The expectations are rational because if everyone else thinks the extrinsic variables will influence prices then they will, and it is therefore rational for you too to think they will. These equilibria are generally referred to as 'sunspot' equilibria, although I hasten to add that the implied reference to Jevons is misleading because to Jevons sunspots constituted an intrinsically important variable.

Early examples of rational sunspot equilibria seemed to require very special assumptions, like a backward-bending labor-supply curve, or else implied that the equilibrium path was dynamically unstable. However, neither of those implications is necessarily true. Blanchard and Watson (1982) have shown examples of speculative bubbles which, although they yield nonstationary price distributions, do get pricked. The bubble is expected on average to grow at the rate of interest, but with probability one it will eventually come to an end. The point is that this is not the same kind of egg-standing-on-end instability that ought to make us reject the equilibrium as being unobservable.

Furthermore, a recent paper by Michael Woodford (1988) has shown that nonexplosive, indeed stationary sunspot equilibria do not require any peculiar behavioral assumptions if there are heterogenous agents and credit-market imperfections.

I think Woodford's examples of sunspot equilibria have a great potential as a vehicle for expressing the third component of Keynes's central message. The sunspot variable in the examples can be interpreted as an indicator of the animal spirits of investors. When spirits are high the capitalists in his model expect a high level of output next period; that induces them to invest more today, which raises the equilibrium level of employment today.[9]

The indeterminacy of sunspot equilibria is bothersome to many economists. Because of the influence of the sunspots the evolution of the economy cannot be predicted from knowledge of tastes and technology alone. But Woodford makes a strong case that there is at least as much empirical content in sunspot theory as there is in modern real business-cycle theory, where everything is driven by essentially unobservable technology shocks.

The assumption of rational expectations in these models hardly seems consistent with Keynes's emphasis on the impossibility of rational forecasting in a world of uncertainty. Nevertheless, this line of research seems capable of generating precisely the sort of extrinsic volatility of investment that Keynes was talking about. And the fact that it can be shown to be consistent with rational expectations means that this aspect of Keynes's central message can now be brought back within the fringe of conventional macroeconomics.[10]

5.5 THE IMPORTANCE OF MICRO FOUNDATIONS

I would like to finish with some comments on the importance of micro foundations for Keynesian economics. Keynesian economists have generally taken a fairly cavalier attitude towards abstract work on micro foundations, sometimes passing it off as silly purism.[11] The main reason for their attitude is pretty obvious. Work on micro foundations for the past fifteen years or so has tended to undermine their policy position. Milton Friedman used to take a similar attitude to people that put his work down as lacking any theoretical basis, and I think for similar reasons.

There is perhaps some justification to this Keynesian attitude. To insist that every macro model be based upon explicit optimization problems rather than on ad hoc behavioral equations really is silly purism. There is a one-to-one correspondence between ad hoc behavioral equations and the ad hoc functional forms that have to be assigned to utility and production functions to give empirical content to so-called 'maximizing' models. The assumptions of equilibrium and rationality are nothing more than conventions – they are part of our common language. Sometimes conventions like that are useful, but models that violate these conventions are not automatically unscientific, or lacking in rigor.

Still, I think the Keynesian attitude towards micro foundations has been seriously mistaken. The simple truth is that Keynesian economics needs a micro foundation, not in order to gratify anyone's methodological urges but because Keynes's central message had to do with fundamental questions of how markets function. Doing Keynesian economics without a clear focus on how trade is organized and how different people's trading decisions interact is like doing welfare economics without reference to people's preferences.

Furthermore, the microeconomic conventions of equilibrium and rationality are far more conducive to Keynes's central message than Keynesians have thought. The fact that Lucas, Sargent and co. got non-Keynesian results from their micro foundations is attributable to their exclusive focus on competitive equilibria with no sunspots. These equilibria tend to have classical welfare properties. But the more general class of Nash equilibria does not. When social interactions are not all mediated by prices, you get Keynesian results. Nash equilibria are generically non-Pareto optimal.[12] And as soon as you have positively sloped reaction functions it is child's play to construct models with multiple, Pareto-ranked equilibria that exhibit multiplier phenomena. Transaction-externality models are just one example. Furthermore, almost any rational-expectations model you can construct with money and capital is going to have sunspot equilibria.

There is a certain irony to this that I cannot resist pointing out. Eight years ago Lucas and Sargent were writing stridently about the death of Keynesian economics. There was no doubt that the central message of their writings was to deny the central message of the *General Theory*. But more recently their tone has changed. For example, in their interviews with Arjo Klamer (1984) both insisted that their central message was methodological, not substantive. Specifically, they asserted that the central message of New Classical Economics was nothing more than that to do economics right you had to be committed to the microeconomic principles of equilibrium and rationality.[13] If I am right, then this new classical methodology may turn out to be the mainspring of a Keynesian recovery.

NOTES

1. This argument has been elaborated by Leijonhufvud (1981a).
2. I have presented this argument in greater detail in Chapter 4 above.
3. Kydland and Prescott (1982), Long and Plosser (1983). The work has recently been summarized by Prescott (1986), who makes the case that

equilibrium real business-cycle models are not only attractive theoretically but are also capable of mimicking the time-series data remarkably well, including data on unemployment and real wages, once one adopts Rogerson's (1984) device of modeling unemployment as the random outcome of a contingent contract entered into by firms and workers. How persuasive one finds Prescott's claims must depend upon a subjective judgment of how remarkable is this ability to mimic, since the results that Prescott describes involve no confidence intervals or formal hypothesis tests, and on whether one judges Rogerson's device to be plausible or contrived.

4. Keynesian policy ideas have also received support from the fact that recovery from the 1981–2 recession has tended to be strongest in those countries with the most expansionary fiscal policies. The economic recovery has thus been itself a Keynesian recovery, and has helped to promote the 'Keynesian recovery' of the present lecture.

5. For example, Chapters 10 and 11 below.

6. More generally it involves what Schelling (1978, esp. pp. 89–110) calls the phenomenon of critical mass.

7. Recent work by Rubinstein (1982) and others has made a lot of progress in narrowing down the range of possible outcomes in bilateral monopoly, but only on the basis of very special institutional assumptions concerning the precise rules by which offers and counter-offers can be made.

8. Recent work by George Akerlof and Janet Yellen (for example, 1985b) is also promoting a recovery of the Keynesian idea of imperfect coordination. Although I believe this work to be important I have not stressed it in this lecture because it does not bear out the message that unemployment is attributable to something other than wage/price stickiness. Instead it shows that such stickiness need not involve any gross violation of the principle of rationality.

9. In Woodford's model the rise in employment is an un-Keynesian movement along a supply-of-labor schedule. If transaction externalities were added it could be modeled as a result of a reduced cost of job search due to firms' increased recruiting activity.

10. It should be noted, however, that the assumption of rational expectations is particularly strained in these models, because it requires everyone somehow to have agreed upon which among the vast set of possible equilibria will be the one realized. There is obviously a serious coordination problem to be dealt with here.

11. I have borrowed the phrase from Solow (1981), although he used it in a somewhat different context. I should also note that most of the important theoretical developments in Keynesian economics have been applications of the maximizing paradigm to give the behavioral equations of Keynesian models a micro foundation. Thus the micro foundations that Keynesian economists have neglected are not so much the choice-theoretic foundations of their behavioral equations as the conceptual foundations underlying their entire macro model.

12. The proposition is obvious upon reflection of how a Cournot equilibrium

fails to maximize joint profits. A formal proof is less obvious, but has been provided by Dubey and Rogawski (1982).

13. In Chapter 4 I asserted that this methodology had an anti-Keynesian bias, because the models employing it that come most readily to hand seem to yield anti-Keynesian results, but that this bias might not survive technical progress. I think the work I have surveyed in this lecture constitutes that kind of technical progress.

PART II

THE MACROECONOMICS OF PRICE ADJUSTMENT

6 · STABILITY AND THE QUANTITY THEORY

6.1 INTRODUCTION

The neoclassical long-run quantity theory consists of two basic propositions. The first is the familiar quantity theorem – that in equilibrium the level of money prices will be directly proportional to the quantity of money. The second proposition, without which the quantity theorem would have little empirical significance, is that this equilibrium is stable.

Patinkin (1956) showed that the neoclassicals had no satisfactory explanation of the stability proposition. He suggested that such an explanation could be provided by considering the real balance effect on excess demands. If there were no distribution effects, and if appropriate restrictions were placed on the substitutability of commodities,[1] it could then be shown that a Walrasian tâtonnement would converge on a vector of money prices proportional to the stock of money. Archibald and Lipsey (1958) provided a method for extending this analysis to the case of distribution effects.[2] If we disturb a long-run equilibrium by, say, doubling the quantity of money, the temporary equilibrium established by a tâtonnement might contradict the quantity theorem unless each transactor's money balances are exactly doubled. However, these distribution effects are transitory. Money balances will change hands from one equilibrium to the next, until in the limit each transactor holds exactly twice his original money holdings and the money price of each commodity exactly doubles.

This paper is a revised version of one chapter of my doctoral dissertation, which was written with financial support from the Canada Council. I am indebted to Robert Clower, John Ledyard, Axel Leijonhufvud, and Joseph Ostroy for helpful comments and discussions.

Reprinted from *Journal of Political Economy* (1974), **82**, January/February, 133–51. © 1974 The University of Chicago.

As amended by Archibald and Lipsey, Patinkin's analysis does provide an explanation of the stability proposition. It is in fact the only such explanation in the literature. However, the analysis has the well-known drawback of Walras' original formulation of the tâtonnement process – that no transactions occur until market clearing prices have been established. To state the issue in familiar language, our understanding of the quantity theory is still impaired by a dichotomy. There are two basic forces that act to propel the economy from one long-run equilibrium to the next. First, there is the force of competitive bidding that makes prices adjust to their market clearing values. Second, there is the force of ongoing transactions that makes each transactor's money holding tend to its stationary level. While it is commonly acknowledged that the quantity theory is meant to apply to a world where these forces act simultaneously, the most complete explanation available of the quantity theory requires that we consider them separately – while the one is operating, the other must be suspended.[3]

Clower (1965) and Leijonhufvud (1968) have demonstrated that the basis of Keynes's attack on orthodox monetary theory was the contention that this dichotomy was invalid. They show how false trading gives rise to the multiplier process that can make the economy move away from its full-employment equilibrium, even with flexible wages and prices. If the quantity theory is to be maintained in the face of the Keynesian challenge, or if we are to have a monetary theory that can in fact reconcile Keynesian economics with the quantity theory, we need some method for presenting the stability proposition that does not rely on the dichotomy of price adjustment and transactions.The purpose of this chapter is to present such a method.

In order to do away with this dichotomy we must re-examine the micro foundations of the quantity theory. This is because, first, there is nothing in accepted general equilibrium theory to tell us how transactions occur even in equilibirum,[4] much less when there are nonzero excess demands. Because the time path of prices is affected by the false trading (see Edgeworth, 1881: 22–30; Kaldor, 1934), it becomes important to determine what transactions take place. Second, a meaningful monetary theory must specify a money commodity that changes hands with each transaction; this is not done by accepted general equilibrium theory (Clower, 1967). Third, the excess-demand functions of general equilibrium theory are usually derived under the implicit assumption that all planned trades will in fact be made, an assumption which appears to be inconsistent with the existence of false trading (Clower, 1965: 117).

To deal with these issues we shall describe a highly simplified exchange system organized by a group of shopkeepers. One of the consequences of this approach is that we are able to handle these problems, which arise in Patinkin's Walrasian approach, with a model that is formally very similar to Patinkin's. Indeed the long-run equilibria of the two models are identical. This allows us to demonstrate the stability proposition using many of the tools developed for the Walrasian system.

6.2 THE EXCHANGE ENVIRONMENT

In order to keep track of actual transactions, our description of the shopkeeper system will be very explicit about how these transactions occur. There are in the economy B transactors and $C + 1$ commodities. For reasons that will soon be apparent, the $(C + 1)$st commodity is called 'money.' Each transactor b begins each period with the endowment $W_c^b \geq 0$ of commodity c; $c = 1, \ldots, C$, and an endowment $M_b \geq 0$ of money. The first C commodities are nondurable goods that disappear after each period.[5] These endowments reappear at the beginning of each period in unchanging quantities. There are C shops in the economy. In shop c the only exchanges that may be made are trades of money and commodity c for each other. Each shop is presided over by a separate shopkeeper whose job it is to set the price for his commodity and to facilitate the exchange of that commodity from seller to buyer by acting as middleman.

Trading proceeds once a period in each shop. During the 'morning,' shopkeeper c posts a money price, p_c, that will prevail for all exchanges on that day. Later in the day each transactor goes to all the shops where he wishes to do business, placing an order to buy or sell a specific quantity of each commodity. We denote by X_c^b the bth transactor's order for commodity c.

In order to make money a well-defined medium of exchange we suppose that the shopkeepers require all purchase orders to be accompanied by the total money payment. This requires that:[6]

$$\sum_{c \in P(b)} p_c X_c^b \leq M_b \qquad \text{for all } b \tag{1}$$

where

$$P(b) = \{c: X_c^b \geq 0\}$$

For a sell order the transactor must deposit with the shopkeeper the entire quantity offered for sale. This requires that

$$X_c^b \geq -W_c^b \qquad \text{for all } b \text{ and } c \tag{2}$$

These conditions ensure that the transactor can only offer to trade commodities that are available at the beginning of the period. This rules out forward transactions and eliminates the possibility of bankruptcy.[7]

The sum of all orders for commodity c,

$$X_c = \sum_{b=1}^{B} X_c^b$$

is called the 'excess demand' for commodity c.

Once all orders are placed, the shopkeepers have two tasks. First they convert orders into transactions. If commodity c has zero excess demand, we assume all orders for commodity c are executed.[8] If excess demand is not zero, the shopkeeper has some rule to determine what transactions occur. The quantity of commodity c the shopkeeper for that commodity allows transactor b to exchange is T_c^b, which is positive (negative) for a purchase (sale). The shopkeeper's transaction rules make T_c^b a function of all orders for commodity c and the vector of money holdings.[9] That is: $T_c^b = T_c^b(X_c^1, \ldots, X_c^B; M)$ for all b and c; where $M = (M_1, \ldots, M_B)$. We assume that for all b and c, T_c^b is a continuous function of all arguments, satisfying a Lipschitz condition on every compact set, and

$$T_c^b = X_c^b \quad \text{if } X_c = 0$$

$$|T_c^b| \leq |X_c^b|$$

and

$$T_c^b \cdot X_c^b \geq 0$$

The first of these conditions has already been explained. The others say that no orders will be overexecuted and no purchase (sale) order will be converted into a sale (purchase). If follows from the second condition that if no order is placed, no transaction will occur.

In the 'afternoon' the shopkeepers allow these transactions to occur and return the deposits corresponding to unexecuted orders. Thus the transactors' money balances for the beginning of the next period are given by the difference equations

$$\Delta M_b = - \sum_{c=1}^{c} p_c T_c^b \quad \text{for all } b^{[10]} \tag{3}$$

The shopkeeper's second task is to determine next period's price. We assume he follows the usual adjustment rule of raising (lowering) his price when there is a positive (negative) excess demand. That is,

$$\Delta p_c = H_c \quad \text{for all } c \tag{4}$$

where

$$H_c \gtreqless 0 \quad \text{as} \quad X_c \gtreqless 0$$

These tasks of the shopkeepers are not meant to be literal accounts of all exchange and bargaining activities in a monetary economy. Instead they are intended to personify the 'forces of competition.' In this respect the shopkeepers are much like the Walrasian auctioneer. When X_c is positive there will be some buyers who, in the absence of the shopkeeper, would be unable to find a supplier of commodity c. In a Walrasian tâtonnement all trading would be suspended, some frustrated buyers would suggest that trading resume with a higher p_c, and orders would again be submitted on the basis of the new price. The auctioneer is supposed to embody these forces acting on prices. In the environment outlined above, the bargaining cannot be suspended in the middle of a period. Excess demands become apparent to the transactors only after trade has taken place; only then can frustrated buyers and sellers make known their willingness to trade at different prices. We assume that the shopkeepers have been provided with some incentive to reflect these competitive forces in their pricing decisions.

6.3 EXCESS-DEMAND FUNCTIONS

Within this shopkeeper system we can derive excess-demand functions similar to Patinkin's. However, the possibility of false trading means these functions cannot be derived in the usual way because the typical transactor's transactions depend not only upon his orders but also upon how the shopkeepers convert orders into transactions. Although shopkeepers have deterministic transaction rules, the relationship between a transactor's orders and transactions will appear to him as being stochastic because he does not have all the information that is available to the shopkeepers.

One implication of this false trading is that the transactor's current sales income can have a direct effect on his demand orders, which cannot occur in the general equilibrium theory of Patinkin with no false trading.[11] With no false trading, a change in one transactor's demands can only affect another transactor's demands if it somehow results in a price change. With false trading, a reduction in some transactor's demand for one commodity can cause sellers of that commodity to reduce their demands for other commodities, even at unchanged prices, because their current sales income will have fallen. This intermarket connection that arises from false trading has been interpreted by Clower

(1965) and others (Barro and Grossman, 1971; Leijonhufvud, 1968) as the theoretical essence of the Keynesian consumption function.

Another implication of false trading is that the typical transactor will be especially concerned with the state of his money balances. Money provides him with a form of insurance against the possibility that sell orders might not all be executed in the future, which would force a reduction in purchase orders if sufficient money balances were not held. Even if some commodities other than money were durable, money would still be especially important to the transactor because of the constraint (1) that assigns the role of medium of exchange to only the one commodity, money. Because money is the only medium of exchange it is also the only commodity that can provide that particular form of insurance. Even if current sales income were to have no direct effect on excess demands, this special role of money would provide the same sort of intermarket connection as explained above. An exogenous decrease in demand for one commodity will reduce the money holdings of sellers of that commodity, providing them with an incentive to reduce their demands for other commodities even with no change in prices.[12]

To be perfectly explicit about all this we would characterize the transactor's decision problem as the maximization of the expected value of an intertemporal utility function, where actual transactions depended upon orders placed but with random error terms to account for the shopkeepers' activities. Money balances would not enter this utility function directly but would be involved in the constraint (1), which would have to hold in every time period. Money would become the 'state variable' of the decision problem. To include the direct effect of current sales income we could assume that the transactor revised his estimates of the probability distribution of the error term every time a new observation was generated by the shopkeepers. If a reduction in demand for a commodity he was selling caused a decrease in his sales without an initial change in his sell order, he would form more pessimistic expectations about how the shopkeeper for that commodity was rationing him. This would cause him to reduce his demands elsewhere because of a reduction in his future sales prospects.[13]

Rather than describe the intertemporal decision problem explicitly we proceed in the following way. We make the simplifying assumption that the transactor has no idea how the future relationship between orders and transactions will be affected by variables about which he has any information, including the current decisions of the shopkeepers. In this case the subjective probability distribution of error terms is an unchanging one, and there is no longer any direct effect of current sales income. To incorporate the direct effect of money balances, we characterize the decision process as a single-period choice, where the choice variables are this period's orders and the money balances the transactor would have at the end of the period if all orders were executed. The bth transactor's objective function is $U^b(X^b; M_b + m_b, p)$, where $X^b = (X_1^b, \ldots, X_C^b)$, $p = (p_1, \ldots, p_C)$, and the intended change of M_b over the period is

$$m_b = - \sum_{c=1}^{C} p_c X_c^b \tag{5}$$

Prices enter into this objective function because the usefulness of money depends upon its future purchasing power. We make the usual homogeneity assumption with respect to all nominal variables, namely, that $U^b(X^b; M_b + m_b, p) = U^b(X^b; \lambda M_b + \lambda m_b, \lambda p)$ for all $\lambda > 0$ (Samuelson, 1947: 119). This is equivalent to saying that real instead of just nominal balances are considered important. The most convenient rationalization is to assume that all future price expectations are unit elastic with respect to current prices (Hicks, 1946: 205). Therefore if p, m_b, and M_b were all to double, all future price expectations would double, and the future purchasing power of the transactor's end-of-period money balances would be unaffected.

The transactor's decision problem is to choose X^b and m_b so as to maximize U^b subject to (1), (2), and (5). The solution to this decision problem implicitly defines the transactor's net demand functions:

$$X^b = X^b(p, M_b) = (X_1^b(p, M_b), \ldots, X_C^b(p, M_b))$$

$$m_b = m_b(p, M_b) = - \sum_{c=1}^{C} p_c X_c^b(p, M_b)$$

We assume X^b and m_b possess continuous first-order partial derivatives. The net demands may be summed to form the excess-demand function

$$X_c(p, M) = \sum_{b=1}^{B} X_c^b(p, M_b)$$

This is the same formal model of the transactor's decision process as Archibald and Lipsey's (1958) except for the constraint (1). This constraint makes the model very similar to Clower's (1967).[14] Including the constraint allows us to avoid the anomalous results found by Clower (1967) and Hahn (1965) in Patinkin's general equilibrium theory – that the economic system could proceed as usual even without the medium of exchange because there is no peculiar characteristic of money that would require any transactor to hold positive quantities of it in equilibrium. This anomalous result is avoided with the constraint (1) because there is now a compelling reason to hold money – a transactor needs to have some at the end of this period in order to submit purchase orders at the beginning of the next period. Although we have derived this demand for money partly from putting money into the utility function, this is not subject to the usual criticism that it begs the question of why transactors hold money: they hold it in order to place purchase orders.

6.4 THE DYNAMICAL SYSTEM

We may complete the description of price adjustment given in (4) by assuming that there exist continuously differentiable functions $H_c(p, M)$, for all c, such that $H_c = H_c(p, M)$. If we approximate the time paths generated by (3) and (4) by their continuous time analogs, we get the following system:[15]

$$\dot{p}_c = H_c(p, M); \qquad c = 1, \ldots, C$$

$$\dot{M}_b = - \sum_{c=1}^{C} p_c T_c^b [X_c^1(p, M_1), \ldots, X_c^B(p, M_B); M];$$

$$b = 1, \ldots, B$$

We refer to this system as Q. An equilibrium to Q is a vector $(p, M) > 0$[16] such that the right-hand side of Q equals zero. We assume that at least one such equilibrium exists. In equilibrium excess demands are all zero and each transactor's money holding is stationary. This is the long-run equilibrium analyzed by Archibald and Lipsey (1958).

The two stages of the Patinkin, Archibald–Lipsey process are merged into one by Q. The tâtonnement stage could be represented by holding M constant and allowing prices to adjust. If this were stable it would establish a temporary equilibrium p with $X_c(p, M) = 0$ for all c. The second stage could be represented by assuming the tâtonnement to take place instantaneously, so we are always in a temporary equilibrium. The adjustment of money balances would then be given by $\dot{M}_b = m_b(p, M_b)$ because there would be no rationing in the temporary equilibrium.

The system Q satisfies the following two properties:

1. Walras' law:

$$\sum_{c=1}^{c} p_c X_c(p, M) + \sum_{b=1}^{B} m_b(p, M_b) = 0;$$

2. Homogeneity of net demands: For any $\lambda > 0$,

$$X_c^b(p, M_b) = X_c^b(\lambda p, \lambda M_b); \quad \text{and} \quad m_b(p, M_b) = \frac{1}{\lambda} m_b(\lambda p, \lambda M_b).$$

In proving the stability proposition we make the following two assumptions:

1. Gross substitutability:

$$\frac{\partial}{\partial p_k} X_c^b(p, M_b) > 0 \text{ and } \frac{\partial}{\partial p_k} m_b(p, M_b) > 0$$

for all k, b, c $(c \neq k)$;

2. Real balance effect:

$$\frac{\partial}{\partial M_b} X_c^b(p, M_b) > 0 \qquad \text{for all } b, c.$$

The system Q together with gross substitutability and real balance effect is referred to as Q^*. There is a very striking resemblance between Q and the Walrasian system. Some of the results which have been developed in the Walrasian framework carry over directly to Q, and we make use of this strong analogy in proving the quantity theorem and the stability proposition.

Before proving the quantity theorem we state a result very similar to a lemma proved by Arrow, Block, and Hurwicz (1959: 88).

ABH lemma: Given gross substitutability and the real balance effect, the relations $0 < (p', M') \leq (p'', M'')$; $p_c' = p_c''$ for $c \in R \subset \{1, \ldots, C\}$ $M_b' = M_b''$ for $b \in S \subset \{1, \ldots, B\}$; imply that (a) $X_c(p', M') < X_c(p'', M'')$ for all $c \in R$; and (b) $m_b(p', M_b') < m_b(p'', M_b'')$ for all $b \in S$ if and only if $p' \neq p''$.

We may now prove a strong version of the quantity theorem.[17]

Quantity theorem: Given any value $\mathbf{M} > 0$ of the money supply, there is exactly one equilibrium to Q^* for which

$$\sum_{b=1}^B M_b = \mathbf{M}$$

Given two values of the money supply, $\mathbf{M}$ and $\mathbf{M}'$, if (p, M) and (p', M') are the corresponding equilibria, then $(p', M') = (\beta p, \beta M)$ where $\beta = (\mathbf{M}'/\mathbf{M})$.

Proof: To prove uniqueness for a given $\mathbf{M}$, suppose (p, M) is an equilibrium to Q^* such that

$$\sum_{b=1}^B M_b = \mathbf{M}$$

Take any other vector, $(\bar{p}, \bar{M})$ such that $(\bar{p}, \bar{M}) \neq (\bar{p}, \bar{M})$, and such that

$$\sum_{b=1}^{B} \bar{M}_b = \mathbf{M}$$

We show that $(\bar{p}, \bar{M})$ cannot be an equilibrium. Define $\lambda = \min \{\bar{p}_1/p_1, \ldots, \bar{p}_C/p_C, \bar{M}_1/M_1, \ldots, \bar{M}_B/M_B\}$. Since

$$\sum_{b=1}^{B} \bar{M}_b = \sum_{b-1}^{B} M_b$$

it cannot be that $(\bar{p}, \bar{M}) = (\lambda p, \lambda M)$, for this would imply that $(p, M) = (\bar{p}, \bar{M})$. Therefore, $(\lambda p, \lambda M) \leqslant (\bar{p}, \bar{M})$. There are two cases to consider:

1. If there is some c such that $\lambda = \bar{p}_c/p_c$, then by part (a) of the ABH lemma and by homogeneity, $0 = X_c(p, M) = X_c(\lambda p, \lambda M) < X_c(\bar{p}, \bar{M})$. Therefore $(\bar{p}, \bar{M})$ is not an equilibrium.
2. If there is no such c, then $\lambda p \neq \bar{p}$, and there is some b such that $\lambda = \bar{M}_b/M_b$. Therefore, by part (b) of the ABH lemma and by homogeneity, $0 = \lambda m_b(p, M_b) = m_b(\lambda p, \lambda M_b) < m_b(\bar{p}, \bar{M}_b)$. Therefore, $(\bar{p}, \bar{M})$ is not an equilibrium.

The rest of the proof follows directly from the homogeneity of net demands. If (p, M) is an equilibrium to Q^* such that

$$\sum_{b=1}^{B} M_b = \mathbf{M}$$

and if $\beta = (\mathbf{M'}/\mathbf{M})$, then by homogeneity $X_c(\beta p, \beta M) = X_c(p, M) = 0$, for all c, and $m_b(\beta p, \beta M_b) = \beta m_b(p, M_b) = 0$ for all b. Therefore $(\beta p, \beta M)$ is an equilibrium to Q^* and

$$\sum_{b=1}^{B} \beta M_b = \mathbf{M'}$$

It follows from the previous paragraph that $(\beta p, \beta M)$ is the only such equilibrium for $\mathbf{M'}$.

This is the quantity theorem in its fullest sense. If, starting from a longrun equilibrium, the stock of money is doubled in the economy, then, regardless of how this money is initially distributed, the economy will not come to rest again until all prices have exactly doubled and every transactor's money holdings have exactly doubled.[18] All that is missing from the quantity theory as stated in the introduction to this chapter is a proof that the economy would indeed come to rest if it were disturbed in this or in any other way.

6.5 THE STABILITY PROPOSITION

We interpret the stability proposition to mean that Q is asymptotically stable. That is, for any initial position $(p^0, M^0) > 0$, every solution $(p(t; p^0, M^0), M(t; p^0, M^0))$ to Q starting at (p^0, M^0) converges to an equilibrium as $t \to \infty$. We assume that for any initial position a unique solution exists to Q, which is continuous with respect to the initial position and which is bounded.[19] We can demonstrate that $\mathbf{Q}^*$ is asymptotically stable under three different sets of restrictions, as in the following three theorems.

For the first two theorems we shall use the result, due to Uzawa (1961: 619), that Q^* is quasi-stable[20] if there exists a continuous function, $V(p, M)$, called a 'modified Lyapunov function,' defined on R_+^{B+C},[21] such that for every $(p^0, M^0) > 0$ the function $v(t) = V[p(t; p^0, M^0), M(t; p^0, M^0)]$ is a strictly decreasing function with respect to t unless $p(t; p^0, M^0), M(t; p^0, M^0)$ is an equilibrium to Q^*.

First, suppose the shopkeepers can maintain stocks of the commodities and do not ration the transactors. All excess demands are absorbed by the shopkeepers' inventories. In this case we can use the modified Lyapunov function: $V_1(p, M) = \max J(p, M) - \min J(p, M)$, where $J(p, M) = \{p_1/\bar{p}_1, \ldots, p_C/\bar{p}_C, M_1/\bar{M}_1, \ldots, M_B/\bar{M}_B\}$, and $(\bar{p}, \bar{M})$ is an equilibrium to Q. An intuitive sketch of this stability proof is helpful. If $\min J(p, M) = p_c/\bar{p}_c$, then p_c is so low that $X_c > 0$ and therefore $\dot{p}_c > 0$. If $M_b/\bar{M}_b = \min J(P, M)$, then M_b is so low that $m_b > 0$. Because there is no rationing, the bth transactor's attempt to increase his money holding will be successful, and $\dot{M}_b > 0$. Similarly, the maximum of the ratios will be decreasing.

Theorem 1: If $T_c^b \equiv X_c^b$, Q^* is asymptotically stable.
Proof: In this case $\dot{M}_b(t) = m_b[p(t), M_b(t)]$ for all b.[22] We define:

$$\bar{v}_1(t) = \max J[p(t), M(t)]$$

$$\mathbf{v}_1(t) = \min J[p(t), M(t)]$$

$$v_1(t) = \bar{v}_1(t) - \mathbf{v}_1(t)$$

$$\omega_1(t) = \lim_{d \to 0} \sup [v_1(t + d) - v_1(t)]/d$$

$$\bar{\omega}_1(t) = \lim_{d \to 0} \sup [\bar{v}_1(t + d) - \bar{v}_1(t)]/d$$

$$\mathbf{w}_1(t) = \lim_{d \to 0} \inf [\mathbf{v}_1(t + d) - \mathbf{v}_1(t)]/d$$

$V_1(p, M)$ is continuous on R_+^{B+C}. Take any t such that $(p(t), M(t))$ is not an equilibrium. To prove $v_1(t)$ is strictly decreasing we show that $\omega_1(t) < 0$. It can be shown that

(i) $\omega_1(t) \leqslant \bar{\omega}_1(t) - \mathbf{w}_1(t)$

First consider $\mathbf{w}_1(t)$. It can be shown (Arrow et al., 1959: 96–7) that (a) there is some c such that $\mathbf{v}_1(t) = p_c(t)/\bar{p}_c$ and $\mathbf{w}_1(t) = \dot{p}_c(t)/\bar{p}_c$, or (b) there is some b such that $\mathbf{v}_1(t) = M_b(t)/\bar{M}_b$ and $\mathbf{w}_1(t) = \dot{M}_b(t)/\bar{M}_b$. If (a) then, defining $\lambda = \mathbf{v}_1(t)$, $(p(t), M(t)) \geqslant (\lambda\bar{p}, \lambda\bar{M})$ and $p_c(t) = \lambda\bar{p}_c$. Therefore, by homogeneity and the ABH lemma, $X_c[p(t), M(t)] > X_c(\lambda\bar{p}, \lambda\bar{M}) = 0$; therefore $\mathbf{w}_1(t) > 0$. If (b) and $p(t) \neq \lambda\bar{p}$, then $m_b[p(t), M_b(t)] > m_b(\lambda\bar{p}, \lambda\bar{M}_b) = 0$; therefore $\mathbf{w}_1(t) > 0$. If (b) and $p(t) = \lambda\bar{p}$, then $m_b[p(t), M_b(t)] = m_b(\lambda\bar{p}, \lambda\bar{M}) = 0$, and $\mathbf{w}_1(t) = 0$. It follows that

(ii) $\mathbf{w}_1(t) \geqslant 0$ with equality only if $\mathbf{v}_1(t)\bar{p} = p(t)$

By an analogous argument,

(iii) $\bar{\omega}_1(t) \leqslant 0$ with equality only if $\bar{v}_1(t)\bar{p} = p(t)$

The equality cannot hold in both (ii) and (iii) because this would imply $\mathbf{v}_1(t) = \bar{v}_1(t)$, in which case $(p(t), M(t))$ would be an equilibrium. Therefore, combining (i), (ii), and (iii), $\omega_1(t) < 0$, and hence Q^* is quasistable. It can also be shown (Uzawa, 1961: 624) that $\bar{v}_1(t) - \mathbf{v}_1(t) \to 0$ as $t \to \infty$, so that $(p(t), M(t)) \to (a\bar{p}, a\bar{M})$ for some $a > 0$. Therefore Q^* is asymptotically stable.

Next, suppose that at least some rationing does take place out of equilibrium. We can demonstrate the stability proposition again, provided the transaction rules satisfy a restriction that we shall now describe. It is clear from the proof of theorem 1 that Q^* will also be stable if for all b, $T_c^b = X_c^b$ for $X_c^b \geqslant 0$ whenever $M_b(t)/\bar{M}_b \geqslant M_k(t)/\bar{M}_k$ for all k, and $T_c^b = X_c^b$ for all $X_c^b \leqslant 0$ whenever $M_b(t)/\bar{M}_b \leqslant M_k(t)/\bar{M}_k$ for all k. This restriction is referred to as 'competitive rationing.' Given competitive rationing then, referring to our intuitive sketch of theorem 1, if $M_b/\bar{M}_b = \min J(p, M)$, then transactor b will not be rationed on sell orders and $\dot{M}_b \geqslant m_b > 0$. Similarly if $M_b/\bar{M}_b = \max J(p, M)$, then $\dot{M}_b \leqslant m_b < 0$.

We call this restriction competitive for two reasons. First, it says that the shopkeepers must assign the most favorable queueing position to those who have the greatest incentive to be first in line, in the sense that a transactor with low money balances will want to sell more than the same transactor with high money balances. Second, we generally think of the forces of competition underlying the price adjustments as being the bids and offers made by those who have been unsuccessful in trading at the previous prices. Their competitive bidding should have the effect not only of changing prices but also of allowing those who have been rationed most in the past to be rationed least in the present, because unless there are barriers to entry, the unsuccessful seller has only to underbid his competititors in order to sell his goods.[23] If the transactor with the 'lowest' money balances is also the one whose sell orders have been most heavily rationed, the competitive rationing restriction can be interpreted as reflecting his successful competitive bidding. Thus we have the second version of the stability proposition:

Theorem 2: Given competitive rationing, Q^* is asymptotically stable.

For the final version, suppose the shopkeepers hold no inventories at all, in which case

$$\sum_{b=1}^{B} T_c^b = 0$$

for all c. With no inventories we cannot be sure that there exists a set of transaction rules satisfying competitive rationing. Even the transactor who is first in line might have to be rationed if, say, his net demand is negative and exceeds in absolute value the sum of all positive demands for that commodity. Therefore the stability proposition cannot be demonstrated using the same method as in theorems 1 and 2. However, it can be demonstrated for the case of no distribution effects; that is, $X_c(p, M) = X_c(p, M')$ for all p, M, and M' such that

$$\sum_{b=1}^{B} M_b = \sum_{b=1}^{B} M_b'$$

Theorem 3: Given no distribution effects, if

$$\sum_{b=1}^{B} T_c^b = 0$$

for all c then Q^* is asymptotically stable.

Proof: Take any $(p^0, M^0) > 0$. Define

$$\mathbf{M} \equiv \sum_{b=1}^{B} M_b^0$$

Let $(\bar{p}, \bar{M})$ be the unique equilibrium such that

$$\sum_{b=1}^{B} \bar{M}_b = \mathbf{M}$$

Because

$$\sum_{b=1}^{B} T_c^b = 0$$

for all c, we have

$$\frac{d}{dt} \sum_{b=1}^{B} M_b = - \sum_{b=1}^{B} \sum_{c=1}^{C} p_c T_c^b = 0$$

Therefore for all $t \geqslant 0$

$$\sum_{b=1}^{B} M_b(t) = \mathbf{M}$$

and, because of no distribution effects, $X_c[p(t), M(t)] = X_c[p(t), M]$ for all c. Suppose $(p(t), \bar{M})$ is not an equilibrium. Then by the ABH lemma, if $p_c(t)/\bar{p}_c = \min \{p_k(t)/\bar{p}_k\}$ then $X_c[p(t), M(t)] = X_c[p(t), \bar{M}] > X_c(\bar{p}, \bar{M}) = 0$, and $\dot{p}_c(t) > 0$. Similarly, if $p_c(t)/\bar{p}_c = \max \{p_k(t)/\bar{p}_k\}$ then $\dot{p}_c(t) < 0$. It follows (Uzawa, 1961: 624) that (i) $p(t) \to \bar{p}$ as $t \to \infty$. Because of (i) and the continuity of X_c it follows that for all c, $X_c[p(t), M(t)] = X_c[p(t), \bar{M}] \to X_c(\bar{p}, \bar{M}) = 0$ as $t \to \infty$. Therefore, because T_c^b and X_c^b are continuous, and becaue $T_c^b = X_c^b$ whenever $X_c = 0$, for all b, $\dot{M}_b(t) \to m_b[p(t), M_b(t)]$ as $t \to \infty$. It follows from (i) and the continuity of m_b that for all b, $m_b[p(t), M_b(t)] \to m_b[\bar{p}, M_b(t)]$ as $t \to \infty$. Therefore the motion of M_b for any b is given by the nonautonomous system: $\dot{M}_b(t) = m_b[\bar{p}, M_b(t)] + h_b(t)$, where $h_b(t) \to 0$ as $t \to \infty$. The corresponding autonomous system, $\dot{M}_b = m_b[\bar{p}, M_b(t)]$, is asymptotically stable because, from the real balance effect, $(d/dt)(M_b - \bar{M}_b)^2 = 2(M_b - \bar{M}_b)m_b(\bar{p}, M_b) < 0$. Therefore (Coddington and Levinson, 1955: 327) the nonautonomous system is also stable and, (ii) $M_b(t) \to \bar{M}_b$ for all b as $t \to \infty$. The conclusion follows from (i) and (ii).

6.6 RELATIONSHIP TO THE NONTÂTONNEMENT LITERATURE

Mathematical economists who have studied the dynamics of nonrecontracting exchange models have not had to impose gross substitutability on the excess-demand functions in order to prove the convergence of prices and commodity holdings.[24] This has given rise to the conjecture that the recontracting itself was a source of instability – that by permitting false trades an unstable exchange model could be made stable.[25] The question naturally arises why we had to impose gross substitutability in the present model.

There are two fundamental differences between the present model and those of the 'nontâtonnement' literature. Both of these rule out the stability proofs that have been used in that literature. First, prices enter the utility functions in the present model but not in the nontâtonnement literature. Second, the nontâtonnement literature has been concerned exclusively with pure stock models, whereas we are dealing here with a stock-flow model.

Uzawa's (1962) method of proof was to use the negative of the sum of all transactors' utilities as a modified Lyapunov function. This function will be decreasing over time in his model if every transactor refuses to make any trade that results in a decrease in utility. However, once prices enter the utility function a transactor's refusal to accept a utility-decreasing trade will no longer guarantee that his utility will be increasing over time, for the price changes can make it decrease. There appears to be no way of avoiding this in a model of monetary exchange where money is only held with a view to its future purchasing power. Also, in a stock-flow model where the flow commodities disappear after the trading period, the transactor's utility might be decreasing if he is unable to engage in the same trades as in the previous period, even if he refuses to engage in utility-decreasing trades.

Hahn and Negishi's (1962) proof depends upon an assumption that the value of this period's endowments for any transactor, evaluated at last period's prices, is the same as last period's endowment evaluated at last period's prices. In a pure stock model this assumption is natural because this period's endowments are all the result of last period's trades, none of which can change the value of the transactor's commodity holdings. However, this assumption cannot be carried over to a stock-flow model where production and consumption also change the endowments. Arrow and Hahn (1971) and Fisher (1972) have transposed Hahn and Negishi's analysis to a model of monetary exchange, but they too have a pure stock analysis without prices in the utility function.

6.7 SUMMARY AND CONCLUSION

We have presented a method by which the stability proposition of the quantity theory can be verified without the artificial separation of exchange and price adjustment. The basic features of the formal model were that sales income was not an argument of the excess-demand functions, that all commodities were gross substitutes, and that the real balance effect was operative on all transactors' net demands. It was shown that the long-run equilibrium of the quantity theory was asymptotically stable if there was no rationing, if there was a form of 'competitive rationing,' or if there were no distribution effects.

Of course it does not follow from the acceptance of this stability proposition that one must then accept the policy recommendations of the quantity theorists, even if the proposition were to be proved in a much more realistic model than the one used here. The main reason for this is that the stability proposition refers only to the behavior of an unchanging system as time goes to infinity. We still have no well-articulated theory to tell us what to expect in the short run, the period of interest to policymakers. What is needed, as Leijonhufvud (1968) has argued so convincingly, is a short-run theory that can explain the dynamics of an economy in which the coordination of economic activities is not costless. Only after this has been accomplished can we begin to understand the importance of Keynesian economics and its relation to the quantity theory. All this study shows is that the quantity theory can still be valid in the long run even in such a world of costly coordination.[26]

One of the lessons of Keynesian economics is that the short-run behavior of an economy is very much affected by the intermarket connections, other than price changes, that make one transactor's decisions dependent upon other transactors' expenditures. In particular, this is the essence of the multiplier process. Our problem is that the only short-run theory capable of describing such connections in a multimarket context is the textbook Keynesian theory which postulates that one set of prices (money wages) is completely inflexible. On the other hand, the only theory that allows all prices to adjust is the Walrasian theory of Patinkin which does not allow for any of the intermarket connections because it cannot handle false trading (Leijonhufvud, 1973). The difficulty that has stood in the way of allowing for false trading in a model like Patinkin's is that the microfoundations have not been strong enough to handle the problems mentioned above. Because the 'shopkeeper' approach used in this study attempts to deal with these problems it provides one way of allowing for the intermarket connections without postulating any absolute price rigidities. Thus it appears capable of handling some of the short-run questions that have traditionally been the exclusive domain of Keynesian economics.

In fact, it can be shown (Howitt, 1973) by using this approach that a monetary economy can behave in a Keynesian fashion in the short run even though it has a stable neoclassical long-run equilibrium. In particular, there can be a Keynesian multiplier process at work in the short run that amplifies the effects of an exogenous change in aggregate demand. Many practical macroeconomists have viewed Keynesian economics as important in the short run when prices have not fully adjusted to their equilibrium levels, and the quantity theory as important in the longer run when the economy approaches its long-run equilibrium.[27] The present approach appears to provide a way of incorporating this view in a formal theory.

NOTES

1. See Patinkin (1956, pp. 342–44). Arrow and Hurwicz (1958) showed that a sufficient condition is for all goods to be gross substitutes.
2. Archibald and Lipsey's analysis was the subject of the symposium by Baumol *et al.* (1960). Their model was extended by the exchange between Hahn (1962) and Clower (1963) to include a richer description of intertemporal choice.
3. Grossman's (1971) interesting analysis of price dynamics in a Patinkinesque model with false trading fails to do away with the dichotomy because prices do not change until quantities have all adjusted to a 'fix-price' equilibrium; the effect is to retain the dichotomy by reversing the relative speeds of price adjustment and transactions. The same is true of Frevert (1970).
4. This point is made very forcibly by Ostroy (1973).
5. Even if money were not the only durable commodity it would still have the distinguishing feature of being the unique medium of exchange (see below). However, the nondurable nature of nonmoney commodities means that they will not be demanded for speculative purposes.
6. This condition is similar to Clower's (1967) 'dichotomized budget constraint.'
7. The possible complications of bankruptcy have been stressed by Hahn (1965).
8. This rules out the sort of phenomenon that Phelps (1970) described with job vacancies and involuntarily unemployed workers at the same time.
9. The reason for including money balances will become apparent in Section 6.5; in short, it allows us to include the competitive-rationing restrictions (see below).
10. The Δ represents a first difference. Time subscripts are omitted here.
11. This point is made very forcibly by Clower (1965: 111–12).
12. I have shown elsewhere (1973) how this intermarket connection can produce, in a model like the present one, the sort of Keynesian short-run behavior usually associated with current income having an important effect on excess demands in the form of the consumption function.
13. This way of accounting for the direct effect of sales income differs from Clower's (1965) 'dual decision hypothesis' used by Barro and Grossman (1971) and Grossman (1971). The difference is that for these writers sales income during the current period is known before demand orders are placed. This is equivalent to making expected income always equal to current income, implying a much closer relationship between income and consumption than implied by modern consumption theories. This point has been made by Leijonhufvud (1973). The present analysis would allow for a 'looser' dependence of consumption on income.
14. Clower's excess demand functions have been analyzed by Lloyd (1971) and Clower (1971).
15. The 'dots' refer to time derivatives.
16. We use the following notation throughout: for any n-dimensional vectors, $x = (x_1, \ldots, x_n)$ and $x' = (x'_1, \ldots, x'_n)$; $x > x'$ means $x_i > x'_i$ for all i, $x \geqq x'$ means $x_i \geqq x'_i$ for all i, and $x \geq x'$ means $x \geqq x'$ and $x \neq x'$.

17. This proof is similar to the proof of the analogous uniqueness theorem of Arrow *et al.* (1959: 89–90).
18. We have been unable to find in the literature a proof that the long-run quantity theory equilibrium of stocks and prices is unique. Patinkin (1965: 45) *assumed* the uniqueness of equilibrium in order to derive the quantity theorem. The same is true of Archibald and Lipsey (1958). Arrow *et al.* (1959: 89–90) proved the uniqueness of prices for given stock holdings. Hadar (1965) proved the uniqueness of stock holdings for given prices.
19. I have elsewhere (1973) shown that the system Q^* satisfies all three assumptions under the premises of theorems 1–3 below.
20. The system Q^* is defined to be quasi-stable if for any initial position $(p^0, M^0) > 0$ any solution to Q^* is bounded and every limit point of the solution is an equilibrium.
21. For any integer n, R_+^n is the set of all n-dimensional vectors x such that $x > 0$.
22. The arguments (p^0, M^0) are omitted whenever no ambiguity results.
23. This phenomenon would be more easily formalized in a model where each transactor is allowed to set his own bid or asked price, which in turn would determine his share of the rationing. This is the approach of Bushaw and Clower (1957: pp. 176–90) and Fisher (1972).
24. The two most important works in this area are those of Hahn and Negishi (1962) and Uzawa (1962). The literature is summarized by Negishi (1962).
25. This conjecture is referred to (although not necessarily maintained) by Negishi (1962: 658–9) and Arrow and Hahn (1971: 328).
26. That is, costly in the sense that the activities of production, consumption, and exchange cannot be suspended during the search for equilibrium prices.
27. Of course this is not the view of the monetarists, who view the quantity theory as important in the short run also.

7 · THE LIMITS TO STABILITY OF A FULL-EMPLOYMENT EQUILIBRIUM

7.1 INTRODUCTION

This chapter addresses the question of the stability of a full-employment equilibrium. In particular it examines the notion, recently proposed by Leijonhufvud (1973) that a full-employment equilibrium is locally stable but globally unstable. Leijonhufvud called this neighborhood of stability "the corridor," and suggested several reasons for believing in its likely existence. The notion has yet to find concrete embodiment in any precisely articulated economic model, and Grossman (1974) has suggested good reasons for doubting that it will. The present chapter is intended to clarify some of the issues involved and to demonstrate some simple formal models in which such a corridor exists. Section 7.2 contains a general discussion of the notion of the corridor. Section 7.3 investigates the appropriate concept of stability. Sections 7.4 and 7.5 contain the examples, and Section 7.6 contains a summary and suggestions for future research.

7.2 THE CORRIDOR

The basic notion of the corridor is that although the economic system usually exhibits desirable stability properties there are limits to the size of shock that it is capable of handling. Formally, the system is locally stable but globally unstable. Such a notion has an intuitive appeal if the economic system is compared to other sorts of control systems, such as

Helpful comments and criticisms of Åke Blomqvist, Joel Fried, Herschel Grossman, David Laidler, Michael Parkin, Tony Santomero, and an anonymous referee, are gratefully acknowledged. The research underlying this paper was aided by a grant from the Canada Council.

Reprinted from *Scandinavian Journal of Economics* (1978), **80**, September, 265–82.

an automatic pilot device on an airplane, or the human body, most of which can continue to function normally in the presence of small enough perturbations, but which break down if enough of a shock is applied, as when the plane is thrown into a tailspin or the human body becomes mortally ill. Generally speaking there are probably good reasons why such systems are not designed to withstand shocks of unlimited magnitude. At some point the gains from increasing the system's ability to function under even more severe, and perhaps unlikely, conditions become outweighed by the added costs of complexity, strength of materials, and general informational requirements.

The notion also has a place in the history of economic thought. It is at least implicit in a long line of literature dealing with financial factors in economic stability, a recent case in point being the work of Hyman Minsky (1964, 1968, 1969). One notable contributor to this literature was Irving Fisher (1931, 1933). The following passage of Fisher's (1933: 339) expresses vividly the notion of a corridor:

> There may be equilibrium which, though stable, is so delicately poised that, after departure from it beyond certain limits, instability ensues, just as, at first, a stick may bend under strain, ready all the time to bend back, until a certain point is reached, when it breaks. This simile probably applies when a debtor goes "broke" or when the breaking of many debtors constitutes a "crash" after which there is no coming back to the original equilibrium. To take another simile, such a disaster is somewhat like the "capsizing" of a ship which, under ordinary conditions, is always near stable equilibrium but which, after being tipped beyond a certain angle, has no longer this tendency to return to equilibrium, but, instead, a tendency to depart further from it.

The particular nature of corridor effects that Leijonhufvud has argued exist in the economic system can be pictured in terms of the following conceptual experiment. Suppose that we displace a position of full-employment equilibrium by some deflationary shock. This will call into play two broad classes of forces. On the one hand the general excess supply that will exist in markets will cause prices to fall. On the other hand, the build-up of inventories, the involuntary unemployment, and the decline in income expectations will cause a secondary decline in aggregate demand through the multiplier process. These two forces are respectively the deviation-counteracting and the deviation-amplifying feedback effects. The price effects tend to make real output rise back to its full-employment value, but the multiplier effects tend to make it fall by even more than the initial shortfall. The overall movement of real output following the displacement will depend upon the relative strengths of these two opposing tendencies. Leijonhufvud has argued that if the original displacement is small enough the deviation-counteracting price effects will dominate, but that for large enough displacements the deviation-amplifying multiplier effects will dominate.

7.3 THE CONCEPT OF STABILITY

This account of the corridor naturally brings to mind the question of what we mean by saying that a system does or does not function "normally"; or that a system can or cannot "handle" a shock. Much of the difficulty of Leijonhufvud's argument arises from its vagueness on this point. Obviously, some concept of stability is involved here, but for many purposes the concept most familiar to economists, that of asymptotic stability, is not appropriate. For the particular purpose of Keynesian macroeconomics, some concept of short-run stability is called for. Leijonhufvud's argument regarding price effects versus multiplier effects makes sense only when related to such a short-run concept. Although the multiplier effects tend to make real output go in the wrong direction they do not rule out an eventual return to equilibrium. Our task in the present section is to clarify this concept of short-run stability.

Let us begin with some purely formal analysis. Suppose we have a system of differential equations:

$$\dot{x}(t) = f(x(t); \alpha); \ t \geq t_0; \ x(t_0) = x_0 \tag{1}$$

where x is a vector of dynamical variables, α a vector of parameters, and x_0 the predetermined initial value. Suppose the system solves uniquely for the time path:

$$x = x(t; x_0, \alpha); \ t \geq t_0 \tag{2}$$

We are interested in measuring the performance of the system over time. Suppose that the degree of performance at any point of time can be measured by an indicator function, $V(x)$. The time path of this indicator is:

$$v(t; x_0, \alpha) \equiv V(x(t; x_0, \alpha)); \quad t \geq t_0 \tag{3}$$

We are interested in systems in which the best possible state of the system is an equilibrium, and, in the case of multiple equilibria, in which all equilibria are equally good. If x^* represents any equilibrium to (1), then the number $V^* \equiv V(x^*)$ is the best possible value of the indicator; and for all x that are not equilibria, $V(x) \neq V^*$.

Any concept of stability is merely a single dichotomous measure of how well the system (1) performs in the presence of exogenous displacements. Ideally the performance of the system should be judged in terms of the entire time path of the indicator function for different values of x_0 and α, as in the example of the intertemporally additive social welfare functionals of optimal growth theory. The usefulness of a concept of stability lies in its simplicity. The stability of a system (or of a motion) can often be determined without detailed knowledge of the nature of the system or of the exact nature of the appropriate welfare functional. Thus no one concept of stability is ideal for all purposes, but may be more or less useful than another for particular purposes.

Of the many concepts of stability that have been explored in economics and other disciplines, four are particularly worth examining here:[1]

1. A motion (2) exhibits *asymptotic stability* if $\lim_{t \to \infty} v(t; x_0, \alpha) = V^*$.
2. It exhibits *finite-time stability* if, for some prespecified values of b and T, $|v(t; x_0, \alpha) - V^*| \leq b$ for all $t \geq T$.
3. It exhibits *practical stability* if, for some prespecified value of c, $|v(t; x_0, \alpha) - V^*| \leq c$ for all $t \geq t_0$.
4. It exhibits *direct stability* if for all $t > t_0$, $|v(t; x_0; \alpha) - V^*| < |v(t_0; x_0, \alpha) - V^*|$.

The concept of asymptotic stability needs no further comment. Finite-time stability occurs if it does not take the system "too long" to return "close" to equilibrium from its initial position. Practical stability occurs if at all times the motion remains within an "acceptable" region. Direct stability occurs if the motion is never again as bad as its initial position.

Whatever concept of stability is used, we say that a corridor effect occurs if, following some displacement from equilibrium, the resulting motion is stable if the displacement is small enough but unstable if the displacement is large enough; that is, if there is some pair of initial positions and vector of parameter values, (x_0, α) and (x_0', α'), and some number $\bar{\lambda} > 0$, where x_0 is an equilibrium with respect to α, such that all motions $x(t; \lambda x_0' + (1 - \lambda)x_0, \lambda \alpha' + (1 - \lambda)\alpha)$ are stable if $0 \leq \lambda \leq \bar{\lambda}$ but not for some values of $\lambda \geq \bar{\lambda}$.

For the concept of asymptotic stability, corridor effects seem unlikely to occur; although there are well known examples of systems that are locally asymptotically stable and globally asymptotically unstable,[2] they are rare. For the practical and finite-time concepts trivial corridor effects will occur in the sense that every well-behaved system (if it is locally asymptotically stable) will be locally stable, but large enough displacements will *automatically* result in unstable motions if an initial position is displaced outside of the acceptable region (in the case of practical stability) or far enough outside that the return time is greater than T (in the case of finite-time stability).

Note that, except for asymptotic stability, all these concepts depend upon the exact nature of the indicator function. According to concepts 2–4, a motion may be stable for one indicator function but not for another, whereas it can easily be established that as long as the motion is bounded, asymptotic stability occurs for one continuous indicator function if and only if it occurs for any other. This dependency upon the value judgment underlying the indicator function appears to be an unavoidable property of any short-run stability concept. Nevertheless it is a legitimate and potentially interesting problem in positive economics to investigate the short-run stability properties of macroeconomic models for particular indicator functions such as the rate of unemployment or the level of aggregate real income.

The concept suggested by Leijonhufvud's discussion is that of direct stability.[3] If the multiplier effects dominate immediately following a displacement then the indicator function (real income) will deviate even further from its equilibrium (full-employment) value. This is also the concept used in the examples below. The main advantage of this concept is that, while it depends like the other short-run concepts upon the particular indicator function used, it does not depend like the others upon the exact definition of "too long," "close," or "acceptable." Also, if a motion is directly stable then it will necessarily be practically stable as long as it begins within the acceptable region: thus the concept conveys as much information as the practical concept without requiring as much detailed, knowledge of what is "acceptable." However, it is a highly restrictive stability concept. Only the "perfect" system, in which the indicator function behaves like a Lyapounov function (see LaSalle and Lefschetz, 1961) will have motions that are all directly stable.

This discussion suggests that a general theory of corridor effects may require the employment of a variety of short-run stability concepts, as none seems to be clearly preferable to all others. The examples below using the direct concept must therefore be regarded as nothing more than a first step towards such a theory. Nevertheless, while each of the concepts discussed above seems generally unappealing as an absolute measure of performance, it should be remembered that corridor effects involve only relative measures; that is, the performance of motions following small displacements is being compared with the performance following large displacements. Thus the proposition that a large displacement of real income from its full-employment value may be followed by an even larger departure may not be important in itself, but it does tell us something about how the system handles shocks if we also know that small displacements result in a direct return.

7.4 LONG-TERM INCOME EXPECTATIONS AS A SOURCE OF CORRIDOR EFFECTS

It should be clear that any corridor effect involving direct stability is going to require a nonlinearity in either the system or the indicator function. Otherwise the directness of return cannot be affected by the size of the displacement. Leijonhufvud's argument suggests that an important source of such nonlinearities might lie in a qualitative change in the aggregate demand relationship associated with large displacements. The purpose of the present section is to present a formal demonstration that this type of nonlinearity will indeed produce corridor effects for deflationary displacements.

Consider an aggregate model with four distinct commodities: money, output, bonds, and labor services. There are the usual market participants – households, firms, and the government. There is also a market authority that always adjusts the rate of interest, r, to equilibrate the bond market, which we may take as meaning that the demand and supply of money are always equal.[4] But the market authority only adjusts the wage rate, W, and the price level, P, gradually in response to excess demands for labor services and output. Thus if a situation of full-employment equilibrium is displaced, false trading will occur during the return to equilibrium. This will give rise to income and spillover effects that bring into play Clower's (1965) dual-decision process whereby notional demands and supplies are replaced by their effective counterparts. Suppose that the resulting multiplier process works itself out to a final fix-price equilibrium before W and P have begun to adjust.[5] To keep matters simple suppose also that if a full-employment equilibrium is displaced to create excess supply in the labor and output markets then both W and P fall at the same proportional rate, keeping the real wage rate constant.[6]

The representative household formulates its effective demands for goods and money by solving an intertemporal decision problem:

$$\max \int_0^\infty e^{-\varrho t} u(c(t)) dt$$

subject to: $A(0) = A$; $A(t) \geqslant 0$ for all $t \geqslant 0$

$$\dot{A}(t) = r(A(t) - m(t)) - c(t) - f(m(t), y^c(t)) \qquad (4)$$

where $c(t)$ is the planned time path of consumption, u is a utility function with positive but diminishing marginal utility, ϱ is the (positive) rate of time preference, $m(t)$ is the planned time path of real balances, $y^c(t)$ is expected income at date t, $A(t)$ is the planned time path of wealth, both human and non-human, and $f(m(t), y^c(t))$ is the cost of transacting at date t. This model is similar in construction to Sidrauski's (1967) except that the expected rate of inflation is assumed here to be zero, and the desirability of money holdings arises from the associated saving in transaction costs, rather than from having real balances enter directly into the household's utility function. Assume that $f_m < 0$, $f_y > 0$, $f_{mm} > 0$, $f_{my} < 0$. An example of this transaction-cost function is provided by the well-known Baumol–Tobin model, in which $f(m, y) = by/m$, where b is a fixed cost per transaction.

The variable t in (4) denotes planning time, not actual time. At each point in actual time the household plans to follow the time paths: $\{c^*(t), m^*(t)\}_{t=0}^{t=\infty}$ that solve (4), where the current actual date is taken as the origin of the scale of planning time. The initial choices $(c^*(0), m^*(0))$ in this plan are the household's current-period choices of consumption and moneyholding, and they clearly depend upon the current actual value of wealth A, the current rate of interest r, and the time path $\{y^c(t)\}_{t=0}^{t=\infty}$ which the household currently expects will be followed by income. Let y denote the current actual value of income, let y^c denote the current value of a parameter influencing the household's expectations, and let T denote the (fixed) length of the household's short-term horizon. Suppose that the expected time path of income takes the simple form:

$$y^c(t) = y \quad \text{for } 0 \leqslant t \leqslant T; \qquad y^c(t) = y^c \quad \text{for } T < t \qquad (5)$$

In other words, the household expects income to remain at its current level until T, at which time it expects income to jump to the level y^c and to remain there forever. It follows that the household's current-period choices can be expressed as functions of the four variables: A, r, y, and y^c. In particular, the current period choice of consumption can be written:

$$c^*(0) = \hat{c}(A, r, y, y^c) \qquad (6)$$

The current value of wealth is the present value of future expected disposable income.[7] Assume that the government always balances its budget, so that the level of government spending, g, always equals the flow of tax collections, which is expected to remain constant forever. Then, from (5):

$$A \equiv (y + e^{-rT}(y^c - y))/r - g/r \qquad (7)$$

From (6) and (7) we may express the current-period choice of consumption as:

$$c(\underset{(?)}{y}, \underset{(?)}{y^c}, \underset{(-)}{g}, \underset{(?)}{r}) \qquad (8)$$

where the indicated sign can be determined from the preceding assumptions. The ambiguity of the effects of y and y^c arise because increases in income may, in principle, increase the size of transaction costs by enough to make the household worse off.

The current-period choice of money holdings can be determined more simply. An optimality condition that must be satisfied by the solution to (4) is (see Intriligator, 1971: 351):

$$-f_m(m^*(t), y^c(t)) = r \qquad \text{for all } t \geqslant 0 \tag{9}$$

Solving (9) for $t = 0$, and recalling from (5) that $y^c(0) = y$, we can express $m^*(0)$, the current-period choice of money holdings, as a function of y and r only:

$$m(y, r) \tag{10}$$
$$\text{(+) (−)}$$

As actual time elapses there will generally be unanticipated changes in the variables y, y^c, g, and r, which will induce the household to revise its plans. At each point in time the household will be implementing its current choices, which may differ from the choices that it had earlier planned for this date. Thus the household's effective demands are always given by (8) and (10).

For simplicity suppose that the household supplies a totally inelastic quantity of labor, N, each period.

The representative firm forms its effective demands for inputs by solving an intertemporal cost-minimization problem.[8] Suppose that the firms expect to be sales-constrained now and in the future, and that the sum of all firms' expected sales at any date equals the sum of all households' expected incomes. Then the firm's decision problem is:

$$\min \int_0^\infty e^{-rt}(wL(y^c(t), K(t)) + C(\dot{K}(t)))dt$$

$$\text{subject to: } K(0) = \bar{K}; \; K(t) \geqslant 0 \text{ for all } t \geqslant 0 \tag{11}$$

where $L(y, K)$ is the firm's effective demand for labor, defined by the equation: $F(K, L) = y$; $\bar{K}$ denotes the historically given stock of capital; and F is a smooth, concave production function with positive marginal products and in which capital and labor are both normal inputs. The function $C(\dot{K})$ represents the cost of investment (including the cost of purchasing and installing the capital goods), which is assumed to be positive and increasing at an increasing rate. The (assumed constant) real wage rate is w.

At each point in time the firm plans to follow the time path $\{K^*(t)\}_{t=0}^{t=\infty}$. Its planned time path of investment is just the time derivative of this path: $\{I^*(t)\}_{t=0}^{t=\infty} \equiv \{\dot{K}^*(t)\}_{t=0}^{t=\infty}$. Likewise it is planning a time path of employment $\{L^*(t)\}_{t=0}^{t=\infty} \equiv \{L(y^c(t), K^*(t))\}_{t=0}^{t=\infty}$. As with the household's plans, only the current-period choices $(I^*(0), L^*(0))$ ever get implemented. It follows from (5) and (11) that the current-period choice of investment can be expressed as a function of y, y^c, r, w, and $\bar{K}$. However, w is assumed to remain constant and we follow standard practice in ignoring the influence of $\bar{K}$ in the short-run determination of investment demand. Thus we may express the firm's effective demand for investment as the current period choice:

$$I(y, y^e, r) \tag{12}$$
$$\text{\small (+) (+) (−)}$$

Since the firm takes as given the initial values $y^e(0) = y$ and $K^*(0) = \bar{K}$, its effective demand for labor is the current-period choice $L^*(0)$, which equals

$$L(y, \bar{K}) \tag{13}$$
$$\text{\small (+) (−)}$$

The firm's notional supply of output is given by the short-run profit-maximizing condition:

$$L_y(y, \bar{K}) = 1/w \tag{14}$$

Suppose that the above individual demand and supply functions can be taken to represent the corresponding market functions. Then the structural form of the macro model (i.e., the set of fix-price equilibrium conditions) is:

$$d(y, y^e, g, r) + g - y = 0 \tag{15}$$
$$\text{\small (?) (?)   (−) (?)}$$

$$Pm(y, r) - M = 0 \tag{16}$$
$$\text{\small (+) (−)}$$

where $d(y, y^e, g, r) \equiv c(y, y^e, g, r) + I(y, y^e, r)$, M is the nominal stock of money, and all variables are now taken to be aggregates rather than per capita magnitudes.

In addition to the restrictions already implied by earlier assumptions, assume, following standard practice, that:

$$\partial d/\partial r < 0, \qquad 0 < \partial d/\partial y < 1, \qquad 0 < \partial d/\partial y^e < 1 \tag{17}$$

The last two of these restrictions assert that the marginal propensities to spend out of current income and out of long-term expected income are both less than unity. A stronger restriction that is standard, and that plays an important role in the theory of corridor effects, is that the sum of those marginal propensities to spend be less than unity:

$$\partial d/\partial y + \partial d/\partial y^e < 1 \tag{18}$$

Such a restriction would assert that the marginal propensity to spend out of permanent income is less than unity.

This structural form produces the reduced-form equation:

$$y = y(P, y^e; g, M) \tag{19}$$

with partial derivatives:

$$\partial y/\partial P = (M/P)(\partial d/\partial r)/\Delta < 0 \tag{20}$$

$$\partial y/\partial y^e = -P(\partial d/\partial y^e)(\partial m/\partial r)/\Delta > 0 \tag{21}$$

where the Jacobian of the structural form is

$$\Delta = P((\partial d/\partial y - 1)(\partial m/\partial r) - (\partial d/\partial r)(\partial m/\partial y)) > 0 \tag{22}$$

Suppose that the real wage, which is assumed to be fixed, takes on its full-employment market-clearing value, $w^* = F_L(\bar{K}, N)$, and let $y^* = F(\bar{K}, N)$ be the full-employment level of output, which in turn equals the notional supply of output. Then we may assume that the rate of change of the price level is proportional to the gap between the effective demand for and notional supply of output,[9] which, in the fix-price equilibrium, equals $y(P, y^e; g, M) - y^*$.[10] Suppose furthermore that long-term income expectations are formed adaptively. Then the rate of change of y^e will be proportional to the gap between actual and expected output, $y(P, y^e, g, M) - y^e$. In other words, the behavior over time of the economy will be governed by the differential equations:

$$\begin{cases} \dot{P} = \alpha(y(P, y^e; g, M) - y^*) \\ \dot{y}^e = \beta(y(P, y^e; g, M) - y^e) \end{cases} \quad t \geq t_0 \tag{23}$$

with initial conditions:

$$P(t_0) = P_0; y^e(t_0) = y_0^e \tag{24}$$

where α and β are positive adjustment coefficients. There is a unique equilibrium, (P^*, y^*), to this dynamical system. This equilibrium is a position in which full-employment output has been attained and long-term expectations are fully adjusted; that is, actual output equals long-term expected output equals full-employment output.

The local behavior of this system can be represented by the linear approximations:

$$\begin{bmatrix} \dot{P} \\ \dot{y}^e \end{bmatrix} = \begin{bmatrix} \alpha\dfrac{\partial y^*}{\partial P} & \alpha\dfrac{\partial y^*}{\partial y^e} \\ \beta\dfrac{\partial y^*}{\partial P} & \beta\left(\dfrac{\partial y^*}{\partial y^e} - 1\right) \end{bmatrix} \begin{bmatrix} P - P^* \\ y^e - y^* \end{bmatrix} \tag{25}$$

where the starred derivatives are all evaluated at the equilibrium (P^*, y^*). Assume that the system is locally asymptotically stable, which, in addition to (20) and (21) requires that:[11]

$$\alpha\partial y^*/\partial P + \beta(\partial y^*/\partial y^e - 1) < 0 \tag{26}$$

Suppose that the equilibrium is displaced by some deflationary shock that does not directly affect long-term expectations – say a fall in g or M.[12] This will immediately disturb both of the differential equations. On the one hand, real output will now be below full employment, so that prices will start falling. On the other hand, real output will be below long-term expected output, so that long-term expectations will also start falling. These two forces represent respectively the deviation-counteracting and deviation-amplifying feedback effects.

Suppose that the indicator function is the value of real output (19). Then immediately following such a displacement the rate of change of the indicator function will be:

$$\dot{y} = (\alpha\partial y/\partial P)(y - y^*) + (\beta\partial y/\partial y^c)(y - y^*) \qquad (27)$$
$$\underset{(+)}{} \qquad\qquad \underset{(-)}{}$$

where the partial derivatives are evaluated at the new (displaced) initial position. Whether or not the resulting motion is directly stable will depend upon the relative strengths of the two terms in (27), which represent the two opposing feedback effects. A corridor effect will occur if the first dominates in the neighborhood of equilibrium but the relative strength of the second term increases sharply with the size of the displacement.

An example of such a corridor effect can be generated by postulating a nonlinearity in the aggregate demand function, such that the marginal propensity to spend out of expected income, $\partial d/\partial y^c$, varies inversely with aggregate wealth, A, defined in (7).[13] Consider the extreme, limiting case in which $\partial d/\partial y^c$ equals zero at the equilibrium of the system but rises sharply when wealth falls. (Of course, if corridor effects occur in this case they will also occur whenever these exists a less extreme but 'sharp enough' nonlinearity.) In this limiting case it follows from (20)–(22) that in the neighborhood of equilibrium the second term in (27) vanishes but not the first; but if the displacement is large enough the second term may dominate the first because the fall in y produces a fall in A as defined in (7), which produces a rise in $\partial d/\partial y^c$. In other words, a small displacement will be followed by a direct return because of the relative weakness of the deviation-amplifying expectation effect in the neighborhood of equilibrium, but a large displacement may be followed by an indirect return because of the relative strength of the same effect far away from equilibrium. Hence the existence of a corridor effect.

The nature of this particular source of corridor effects, while strongly suggested by Leijonhufvud's discussion (see especially the discussion of 'dysfunctional revisions of permanent income expectations,' (1973), p. 43), does not involve the role of inventories that was stressed by Leijonhufvud. It also illustrates two crucial features of corridor effects which were not adequately dealt with by Leijonhufvud or Grossman. First, it involves a short-run stability concept in a crucial way that was apparently not recognized by Leijonhufvud; according to the more conventional concept of asymptotic stability, all of the motions of this system are stable. Second, it requires the existence of a crucial nonlinearity. Grossman is correct that both price effects and multiplier effects increase in strength with the size of the displacement; but whereas Grossman infers from this (1974: 361) that 'there would appear to be no analytical support for Leijonhufvud's concept of "the corridor",' we have shown on the contrary that corridor effects require merely that the *relative* strength of the price effects diminishes as the size of the displacement increases.

Thus simple macro models are capable of exhibiting corridor effects if the marginal propensity to spend out of expected income is small in the neighborhood of full-employment equilibrium but rises sharply when aggregate demand is substantially reduced. However, this particular source of corridor effects does not always work for all kinds of displacements. For example, consider what would happen if the equilibrium were displaced by a spontaneous wave of pessimism; i.e., a downward displacement of y^c.[14] Once more the return to equilibrium will be direct for a small displacement. In general the rate of change of y immediately following the displacement will be:

$$\dot{y} = \alpha(\partial y/\partial P)(y - y^*) + \beta(\partial y/\partial y^c)(y - y^c) \tag{28}$$

If we impose the restriction (18) that the marginal propensity to spend out of permanent income is less than unity, then it follows from (18), (21), and (22) that a one unit decline in long-term expectations will always cause real output to fall by less than one unit, that is:

$$\partial y/\partial y^c - 1 < 0 \tag{29}$$

This implies that immediately following the decline of long-term expectations from y^* to y^c we have:

$$y - y^c = \int_{y^*}^{y^c} [\partial y(P, \theta; g, M)/\partial y^c - 1]d\theta > 0 \tag{30}$$

Therefore the expression in (28) is positive, and we should expect a direct return to equilibrium for all sizes of displacements.

Of course, a corridor effect following a reduction in y^c could occur if, once wealth fell sufficiently, the marginal propensity to spend out of permanent income could become greater than unity, in which case (29) might no longer hold. This is not as implausible as it might seem, because (a) it does not violate the conditions for asymptotic stability of the system, and (b) it does not imply that the marginal propensity to consume out of permanent income exceeds unity, because y^c affects investment as well as consumption spending.

7.5 BANKRUPTCY AS A SOURCE OF CORRIDOR EFFECTS

Another potential source of corridor effects stressed by Leijonhufvud is the disruption of normal credit arrangements following a large displacement. From a historical point of view this source seems particularly worth pursuing, as so many severe economic downturns in modern history have been associated with financial crises of various sorts (see Friedman and Schwartz, 1963; Clapham, 1944). This section presents an example of a corridor effect arising from the effect on the incidence of bankruptcy following a deflationary disturbance.

The potentially destabilizing effect of bankruptcy is a factor stressed in Fisher's (1931, 1933) debt-deflation theory of depressions. The fundamental idea of this theory can be stated quite simply. Following a deflationary disturbance, the subsequent decline in prices tends to bring the level of output back towards its full-employment value, through the usual direct and indirect effects of changes in the real quantity of money. However, deflation also increases the real value of existing debt, which may offset the effects on the level of output by increasing the incidence of bankruptcy and thereby reducing the level of aggregate demand. In terms of our earlier example, if the effects on bankruptcy are strong enough the price effects may themselves be deviation-amplifying.[15]

How this might produce corridor effects can be seen in terms of Figure 7.1. Consider a model like that of the previous section, but in which the adaptive expectations assumption is replaced by completely static expectations: $y^e = y$. Then the level of real output is a function of

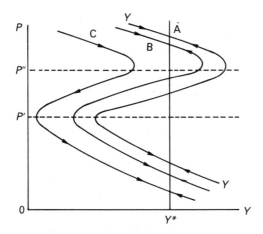

Figure 7.1 The corridor effect of bankruptcy.

P and the policy parameters only. The dynamic behavior of the economy is governed by the single differential equation:

$$\dot{P} = \alpha(y(P, g, M) - y^*) \tag{31}$$

The curve YY in Figure 7.1 represents the function $y(P; g, M)$. Thus the motion will follow the direction of the arrows over time. The slope of YY is $(\partial y/\partial P)^{-1}$, which according to the analysis of the previous section ought to be negative everywhere. However, as we shall see, when the effects of bankruptcy are taken into account the curve may take on a positive slope. Suppose that, as in Figure 7.1, there is a critical range for the price level (from P' to P'') over which the bankruptcy effects dominate the 'normal' price effects. Then YY will take on the 'backward-S' shape of Figure 7.1. A small deflationary shock that displaces the system from A to B will clearly be followed by a direct return to the new equilibrium, but a larger displacement that displaces the system to C will result in an indirect return, as the price level must fall into the range of dominant bankruptcy effects.

This example of instability is one of Thom's (1972) elementary catastrophes. Not only does it produce corridor effects with respect to direct stability, it may also produce them according to practical and finite-time stability. The motion from C may take too long to return to equilibrium and may stray outside the acceptable neighborhood of full employment, whereas these might not be true of any motion from a point like B that never enters the backward-bending part of the curve.

In order to bring these bankruptcy effects into our model, suppose first that the households behave exactly as in the previous section, giving rise to the consumption function $\bar{c}(y, g, r) \equiv c(y, y, g, r)$. Next, suppose that all firms are identical except for the amount of debt outstanding, and that all debt takes the form of perpetuities paying one dollar per period. Let B_f represent the outstanding stock of perpetuities issued by firm f. The real market value of this debt is B_f/rP. Define

$$V(y, r) \equiv \int_0^\infty y e^{-rt} dt - \min \int_0^\infty \{wL + C(I)\} e^{-rt} dt$$

the value of the firm. It is easily seen that if the firm is presently sales-constrained (i.e., $y < y^*$), then $\partial V/\partial y > 0$. The sign of $\partial V/\partial r$ is ambiguous. Next, suppose that all agents share the same expectations. If a firm is solvent its demand for investment goods will be the amount $\bar{I}(y, r) \equiv I(y, y, r)$. However, in the case of insolvency the firm goes into receivership and for the short run its demand for investment goods becomes zero. The reason why insolvency should affect the firm's demand for investment is that in the event of liquidation the creditors will have to pay legal and transaction costs of dismantling the firm's capital equipment. The present approach makes the simplifying assumptions that the probability of liquidation is seen to be zero when the firm is insolvent and the costs of liquidation are seen to be so high in the case of insolvency that it eliminates all investment demand. Thus the firm's demand for investment is

$$I_f(y, r, P) = \begin{cases} \bar{I}(y, r) \text{ if } B_f/rP \leq V(y, r) \\ 0 \qquad \text{otherwise} \end{cases} \tag{32}$$

and the aggregate demand for investment is

$$\bar{I}(y, r, P) = \bar{I}(y, r)F(rPV(y, r)) \tag{33}$$
$$\text{\small (+) (?) (+)}$$

where F is the cumulative distribution of B_f across firms. Thus $F(rPV(y, r))$ indicates the number of firms still solvent.[16]

The structural form of the macro model is:

$$\bar{d}(y, r, g, P) + g - y = 0 \tag{34}$$
$$\text{\small (+) (-) (-) (+)}$$

$$Pm(y, r) - M = 0 \tag{35}$$
$$\text{\small (+) (-)}$$

where

$$\bar{d}(y, r, g, P) \equiv \bar{c}(y, g, r) + \bar{I}(y, r, P) \tag{36}$$

and where all the signs in (34)–(35) except for $\partial\bar{d}/\partial y$ and $\partial\bar{d}/\partial r$ can be deduced from the preceding assumptions.

The (inverse of the) slope of YY in Figure 7.1 is

$$\partial y/\partial P = (M/P)(\partial d/\partial r)/\Delta - P(\partial\bar{I}/\partial P)(\partial m/\partial r)/\Delta \tag{37}$$

where once again $\Delta > 0$, as in (22). The two terms in (37) represent, respectively, the deviation-counteracting price effect discussed in the previous section (compare (20)), and the deviation-amplifying bankruptcy effect resulting from the influence of P on investment demand. Thus a backward-bending portion of YY in Figure 7.1 requires a sharp nonlinearity involving a rise in $\partial\bar{I}/\partial P$. The value of this partial derivative is

$$\partial\bar{I}/\partial P = \bar{I}(y, r)rV(y, r)f(rPV(y, r)) \tag{38}$$

where f is the frequency distribution of B_f. It follows from (38) that the nonlinearity in $\partial\bar{I}/\partial P$ requires a high peak in this frequency distribution; in other words, a high degree of clustering of firms around the same degree of indebtedness. In the extreme case where all firms are equally indebted, the backward-bending part of YY will be horizontal, representing an actual discontinuity in the aggregate demand relationship.

While there is no apparent reason for thinking that the degree of indebtedness of different firms is sufficiently clustered to produce this sort of corridor effect, a similar result may occur because of the phenomenon of debt layering stressed by Minsky. The above analysis simply requires that the distribution across firms of critical price levels at which each firm will become insolvent is sufficiently clustered. This may occur because of the domino effect of an initial bankruptcy in an economy with a highly interdependent system of financial claims. The analysis of such a possibility seems worth pursuing, particularly in the light of recent events that have generated widespread fears of such domino effects. Whether or not it occurs would appear to depend crucially upon the extent to which the initial bankruptcy is anticipated and the extent to which its repercussions upon the solvency of other economic agents are anticipated.

7.6 SUMMARY AND SOME SUGGESTIONS

In summary, this chapter has tried to clarify the notion of corridor effects, first by suggesting various concepts of short-run stability that could be employed, and second by demonstrating two concrete examples of economic models in which a corridor could exist according to the concept of direct stability. The first example was directly suggested by Leijonhufvud's analysis of deviation-amplifying multiplier effects versus deviation-counteracting price effects. The second example dealt with financial factors which are not stressed by Leijonhufvud but are central elements in the writings of Minsky. These examples as well as the others mentioned by Leijonhufvud show that the notion of the corridor does have an analytical foundation and suggests that corridor effects ought to be taken seriously in the analysis of economic systems, just as they are quite naturally in the analysis of systems in other sciences.[17]

Much more theoretical research needs to be undertaken before the empirical usefulness of the concept of the corridor can be assessed. The present examples contain suggestions for possible directions to that research. One suggestion is that the formalism of catastrophe theory might usefully be employed, as it has already in such diverse fields as biological theory and bifurcation theory (see Dold and Eckmann, 1976). The configuration in Figure 7.1 is a pattern that occurs frequently in the theory of catastrophes.

Both of the present examples involve asymmetrical corridors. A deflationary shock will lead to instability if the shock is large enough, but an inflationary shock will in all cases lead to a direct return regardless of the size of displacement. It would be interesting to investigate the possibility of corridor effects on the other side. Their existence is suggested by Cagan's (1956) observation that the speed of adjustment of expectations and the elasticity of money demand with respect to expected inflation both rise as the expected rate of inflation rises, implying a greater likelihood of unstable inflation, the higher is the expected rate of inflation.

It would also be interesting to extend the approach of this chapter to situations of ongoing inflation. The approach ought to be able to deal with such questions as the effect of eliminating inflation with a sudden drop in the rate of monetary growth, rather than a gradual one. The example in Section 7.5 suggests that a sudden enough drop might lead to instability through its financial repercussions. It also suggests that the higher the rate of inflation, the less stable the economy will be, given the convention of repaying debt in constant nominal sums. The higher the expected rate of inflation, the larger will be current nominal repayment obligations relative to the current price level, and hence the higher up in Figure 7.1 will lie the backward-bending portion of YY.

NOTES

1. For a treatment of similar stability concepts, see LaSalle and Lefschetz (1961), and Weiss and Infante (1967).
2. For example, the Van der Pol equation: $\ddot{x} - \varepsilon(x^2 - 1)\dot{x} + x = 0$, with $\varepsilon > 0$.
3. This is also the stability concept implicit in the analysis of Lorie (1977) and that of Ize (1977).
4. This assumes that we have appropriately defined the 'effective' demand for money. See Tucker (1971).
5. This assumption of an 'instantaneous multiplier' implies that, following a deflationary shock, much of what might otherwise be regarded as a deviation-amplifying feedback effect is instead treated as part of the initial displacement. However, the full working out of the multiplier process involves the downward revision of long-term income expectations, which, as we shall see, is enough in itself to cause an indirect return to equilibrium.
6. This simplifying assumption was also made by Patinkin (1965: 324–6). Relaxation of this assumption would require us to deal with extraneous complications of the sort analyzed by Barro and Grossman (1976: ch. 2). In any event, the observed difficulty of discerning a cyclical pattern to the behavior of real wages suggests that the approximation involved in our simplifying assumption is roughly compatible with historical experience.
7. The role of real balances in wealth is omitted for notational simplicity.
8. A discrete-time version of this problem is analyzed in depth by Brechling (1975: 63–5). The connection between such a cost-minimization problem and the theory of effective demand was analyzed by Grossman (1972b).
9. The contrary assumption by Varian (1977) and others that the relevant gap

is that between effective demand and *effective* supply implies extremely unaggressive behavior on the part of entrepreneurs who, when faced by a sales constraint, do not even bother to compete against one another.

10. The modern literature on inflation suggests that this equation should also include a term for the expected rate of price change. However, the equilibrium value of this variable is zero in the present context of a fixed money supply, so that ignoring this term can be rationalized by assuming that the expectation adapts too slowly to experience for it ever to depart significantly from zero.

11. If this condition is satisfied then the Routh–Hurwitz conditions for local stability are satisfied. See, for example, Gantmacher (1959). This condition also guarantees the *global* stability of the system; see Olech (1963).

12. In order for a fall in g to be deflationary we must assume the further restriction that $-1 < \partial c/\partial g$.

13. Empirical evidence of such a non-linearity has been produced by Clower and Johnson (1968).

14. This particular conceptual experiment illustrates the phenomenon mentioned by Leijonhufvud (p. 34) of 'prices that were at their G[eneral] E[quilibrium] values [but that] may tend ('automatically') to move *away* from those values...'. Following the displacement both W and P are at their ultimate equilibrium values but markets will not clear, and W and P will fall, because of the pessimistic expectations. Grossman's claim (1974: 362) that such a phenomenon would be impossible clearly ignores the possibility that some other variable (in this case y^e) might not be at its general equilibrium value, although the claim is valid if the term – 'GE values' is interpreted as the values that would temporarily clear the market given the values of all other such variables.

15. The possibility that price effects might themselves be deviation amplifying plays a large role in the literature following Keynes's *General Theory*, which was summarized by Patinkin (1948). The role of bankruptcy, while mentioned, does not appear to have played a large part in this debate (although see the second paragraph added to p. 263 of the revised version of Patinkin's article in Lutz and Mints (1951).) Nor was it conducted in terms of explicit concepts of short-run stability. In the terminology of the present chapter, Patinkin's stated conclusions can be summarized in the proposition that while a full-employment equilibrium does exist, it may be asymptotically unstable or finite-time unstable. Finally, Patinkin's summary contains no suggestion that local stability properties might differ systematically from global properties.

16. We are implicitly assuming that the household demand for output of the insolvent firms continues to be satisfied, and that the insolvency of some firms does not affect the prospective sales of the firms that remain solvent.

17. For another possible example of corridor effects, see Howitt (1979). In this example prices are set by dealers who maintain inventories which they allow to fluctuate to accommodate the demands and supplies of other traders.

With a large enough shock these inventories may get depleted, and normal market relationships may thereby be disrupted. This example is more closely related to Leijonhufvud's discussion than are any of the examples in the present chapter, because of its focus upon the crucial role of inventories as buffer stocks.

8 · ACTIVIST MONETARY POLICY UNDER RATIONAL EXPECTATIONS

8.1 INTRODUCTION

By an activist monetary policy I mean a policy whereby the monetary authority permits the money supply to react systematically to information concerning aggregate disturbances. The proposition commonly known as the Sargent–Wallace (hereafter SW) proposition[1] asserts that an activist monetary policy cannot succeed in offsetting aggregate disturbances when people's expectations are formed rationally, unless the monetary authority possesses information unavailable to private agents. It asserts that in the absence of such superior information systematic variations in the money supply will be anticipated and thus neutralized even in the short run.

The SW proposition has been criticized by previous writers. Taylor (1975) pointed out that it will take private agents time before they learn the exact nature of the monetary policy.[2] During this transition period the SW proposition is invalid. Poole (1976), Fischer (1977), and Phelps and Taylor (1977) have pointed out that even if private agents possess the same information as the monetary authority they may not be able to act upon it immediately because of contractual precommitments, in which case the SW proposition is invalid. It has also been widely acknowledged that if the arguments underlying the SW proposition

An earlier version of this paper was presented at the meetings of the American Economic Association, New York, December 1977. I am indebted to Russell Boyer, Stanley Fischer, Joel Fried, Herschel Grossman, Robbie Jones, David Laidler, Robert E. Lucas, Jr., Michael Parkin, Arthur Robson, and an anonymous referee for helpful comments and criticisms, and to the Social Sciences and Humanities Research Council of Canada for financial support.

Reprinted from *Journal of Political Economy* (1981), **89**, April, 249–69. © 1981 the University of Chicago.

were valid it would be difficult to explain the observed persistence of movements in output and employment.[3]

The present chapter focuses on another objection to the SW proposition: namely, that it fails to take into account (1) the costs of gathering and processing information, and (2) uncertainty concerning the structure of the economic system. People may choose not to collect and process the monetary authority's information concerning aggregate disturbances when it is costly to do so.[4] Indeed, everyday observation suggests that most people pay no attention to such information. In such circumstances people may still be forming their expectations rationally, in the sense that they are making efficient use of (costly) information, yet they are not in a position to anticipate and neutralize the effects of an activist monetary policy. In order for the SW proposition to be true the monetary authority's information must not only be available to private agents, it must also be economically usable by private agents.

This qualification to the SW proposition has been noted by Barro (1976), who argued nevertheless that the monetary authority could do just as well by disseminating its information as it could by varying the money supply. However, this chapter attempts to show that such a disseminating policy may be inferior to an activist policy when there is uncertainty concerning the values of parameters in the economic system because (1) people may not have enough incentive to process information, and (2) even if people do process the information there is no guarantee that this will produce the same outcome as would a properly designed monetary policy. A demonstration of this argument can be made precise only in terms of a formal model, but it can be sketched in the following terms.

First, even if the information concerning aggregate disturbances is provided to people they must still incur the cost of processing it if they are to use it. But they may not find it economical to incur that cost if they think that not many other people will be using the information, even when its social value exceeds the processing cost. Consider, for example, an agent who is deciding what price to charge for the single good that he sells. Suppose he is told that the demand for money has doubled. If he thinks that all other agents are using this information he can calculate that his best course of action will be to cut his price in half, along with everyone else. The information may be quite valuable to him and to society because failure to conform in reducing his price would leave him charging a suboptimal relative price. But if he thinks that no other agent is using the information his best course of action will depend on the effects of that change in the demand for money on the demand for his product. If this effect is difficult to estimate accurately then the information may have little value to him. A convention like universal indexing that leads people to believe that everyone else will be using the information as well may be necessary for the private value of such information to be as great as its social value. Everyday observation again suggests that such a convention rarely exists.

Second, in a world without complete Arrow–Debreu contingent-claim markets there is no guarantee that even an otherwise frictionless competitive equilibrium will be efficient with respect to the information possessed by private agents. It is possible that the monetary authority is in a position to make better use of aggregate information than are private agents, even if the above-mentioned indexing convention could be established. In the example of the previous paragraph, Brainard's (1967) analysis suggests that if the values of the parameters of the economic system are not known with certainty then the optimal reaction of the monetary authority is to allow the money supply to increase, but by less than 100 percent. But if the information is disseminated, prices may indeed fall by half, which would be equivalent to a 100 percent increase in the money supply. As in the theory of the second best, full information results in the best equilibrium, but when information is incomplete then more information does not necessarily result in a better equilibrium.[5]

The remainder of the chapter attempts to make these arguments more precise by developing a simple model of a monetary economy in which prices are costly to adjust. Section 8.2 describes the basic features of the model; Section 8.3 analyzes the private decision whether or not to use information; Section 8.4 characterizes the optimal policy of the monetary authority showing how an activist policy may be justified by the first of the above arguments; Section 8.5 considers a variant of the model in which the second of the above arguments may be used to justify an activist policy; and Section 8.6 contains some concluding remarks.

8.2 THE BASIC MODEL

Preliminaries

This section describes a simple hypothetical economy possessing the features described above. In this economy there are two tradable objects: money and a good. There are also two classes of economic actors: a monetary authority, whose job is to determine how much money will exist and to distribute the money, and a set of private agents (referred to simply as 'agents'), who produce and consume the good. In the interest of simplicity we suppose that each agent possesses identical tastes, technology, and initial endowments. (Thus we are making no distinction between firms and households.) In order to establish a basis for exchange among these identical agents we assume that each of them has an absolute aversion to consuming units of the good that he himself has produced. Thus he is induced to sell all of these units and to purchase for consumption units of the good that are produced by others.

To keep the demand and supply functions simple we suppose that each agent evaluates his demands according to a Stone–Geary utility function and produces subject to a quadratic cost function. That is, each agent's utility during a period depends upon $\hat{q}$, the amount of the good consumed during the period, $\hat{m}$, the real value of money balances held at the end of the period, and q, the amount of the good produced during the period, according to the particular function

$$U = K\hat{q}^a(\hat{m} + x)^{1-a} - (k/2)q^2 \qquad (1)$$

where k is a positive, nonstochastic parameter equal to the slope of the agent's marginal cost schedule, a and x are independent stochastic parameters with $0 < a < 1$, and K is a stochastic parameter defined as $K \equiv a^{-a}(1 - a)^{-(1-a)}$. For reasons that will become apparent later we shall refer to the parameter x as 'the level of aggregate demand.'

In order for purely monetary changes potentially to have real effects even in the short run we must not assume that there exists a central Walrasian auctioneer who is able each period to compute a single market-clearing price at which all trades are to occur. The actual transaction prices must be determined before the agents have collected enough information for them to be able to compute this Walrasian equilibrium price. We accomplish this by assuming that each agent is responsible for setting his own selling price. He must set the price before learning exactly how much he will be able to sell, and all trades must occur at these posted prices whether or not markets are clearing in the usual sense.[6] Assume also that the quantities transacted at these prices always equal the quantities demanded. In other words, when markets are not clearing the sellers bear all the resulting quantity rationing.[7]

At the time of the price-setting decision each agent's expected utility will depend negatively on the variance of his error in forecasting demand, because he must produce subject to increasing marginal cost. Thus he will have an incentive before setting his price to gather and process information concerning the demand function facing him so as to reduce the variance of this forecast error. The decision on what information to use at this stage will be the main focus of the following analysis.

When determining the value of M, the nominal per capita stock of money, the monetary authority is assumed to be unaware of the exact state of aggregate demand. Suppose, however, that he is able to acquire partial information by observing a variable, s, that is correlated with aggregate demand. In particular, assume that

$$x = cs \tag{2}$$

where c is a stochastic parameter. We shall refer to s as the 'indicator' of monetary policy. The monetary authority is assumed to obey the following rule:[8]

$$M = \bar{M}(1 - gs) \tag{3}$$

where $\bar{M}$ (> 0) is the average per capita stock of money and g is the 'policy reaction coefficient.' Thus the monetary authority follows a 'feedback' rule of reacting to observable information concerning the level of aggregate demand, and its two decision variables are $\bar{M}$ and g. The SW proposition asserts that the stochastic behavior of aggregate output in the economy will be independent of the monetary authority's choice of g.

The sequence of activities

During each period activities proceed according to the following sequence. First, there is a stage in which the monetary authority decides on his policy. That is, he chooses values for g and $\bar{M}$. When making this decision he is assumed to possess an accurate model of the economy, including exact knowledge of all deterministic variables, parameters, and functions, and the probability distributions of all stochastic variables. He does not, however, know the exact value that will be assumed during the period by any stochastic variable. As soon as he makes his decision all of his information is conveyed to each private agent, including the chosen values of g and $\bar{M}$. Thus there is no scope for the monetary authority to fool private agents, even in the short run, about the nature of his policy, or to make this policy decision using information that is not available to private agents.

Second, there is a stage in which private agents make their monitoring decision. That is, each one must choose whether to pay the cost of learning the exact value of s before setting his price, in which case he will be able to reduce the variance of his forecast error, or to wait until after his price has been set, when the value of s will be revealed to him at no cost. In the interest of simplicity we assume that the indicator is the only stochastic variable whose value is potentially observable before the price-setting decision is made.

Third, there is a stage in which the exact value of the indicator s is determined. Any agent who has decided to monitor observes s and pays the cost at this stage, as does the monetary authority (unless he has set g

= 0). Note that once again we are not giving the monetary authority any informational advantage. At this stage, before he chooses his price anyone can choose to be as well informed as the monetary authority.

The fourth stage is the one in which the values of all prices and of the money supply are decided. The money supply is determined automatically by equation (3), and the private agents choose their prices in such a way as to maximize expected utility. If they have decided to monitor the indicator (to learn the value of s), then private agents can forecast the exact value of M by using equation (3) and can use this knowledge in making their price decision. Otherwise they must make their decisions on the basis of expectations concerning M, which they form using (3) and their knowledge of the probability distribution of s. When setting his own price no agent is able to observe the others' prices. However, he is able to tell whether or not the others are monitoring the indicator, and this will be enough in most cases to allow him to predict exactly what the others' prices will be.

The fifth stage is the one in which all uncertainty is resolved. In this stage the monetary authority distributes money to the private agents in equal amounts, and the exact values of a, x, K, c, and s are revealed to everyone. Whatever values of the utility parameters a, x, and K are determined in this stage, they are shared by all agents in common. Thus, with this information each agent is able (1) to calculate exactly how much his sales will be for the period and (2) to compute his own demands for money and the good.

In the sixth and final stage the agents visit one another to execute their planned purchases, and each agent must produce to meet the demands placed upon him. Up until this stage each of the identical agents will have been led to make identical decisions. Thus every agent will be charging the same price. Assume that in such a situation the quantity demanded from each agent will be identical.[9]

To understand what happens in this sequence we must start at the end and work back. Consider an agent who, during the sixth stage, is going to be called upon to produce the quantity q. Suppose that all other agents have set the same price, P, and that he himself has set the price rP. Then during the fifth stage he will be aware of the value of q and of the exact values of all the parameters in his utility function (equation (1)). He will formulate his own demands, $\hat{q}$ and $\hat{m}$, so as to maximize this utility function subject to the budget constraint

$$\hat{m} + \hat{q} = m + rq \tag{4}$$

where $m = M/P$ denotes his initial holding of real balances.[10] Thus his demand for the good will be

$$\hat{q} = a(m + rq + x) \tag{5}$$

and by substituting from (4) and (5) into (1) we can see that the level of utility that he will obtain is determined by the indirect utility function

$$V(m, q, x, r) = m + rq + x - (k/2)q^2 \qquad (6)$$

During the fifth stage each agent will also be able to predict his sales, q, in the following way. First, suppose that every agent is charging the same price, P. Then every agent will sell the same quantity, q, and will formulate demands according to (5) with $r = 1$. But every agent will also realize that his sales, q, will be equal to the per capita demand, $\hat{q}$. Thus the values of q and $\hat{q}$ can be computed by substituting $q = \hat{q}$ into (5), with $r = 1$, to produce

$$q = b(m + x) \qquad (7)$$

with

$$b = \frac{a}{1 - a} > 0 \qquad (8)$$

Equation (7) indicates the amount that each agent would demand in stage 5, as well as the amount that he would expect to sell, under the assumption that $r = 1$. And indeed the equilibrium will be one in which $r = 1$. But to see how prices are chosen we must indicate how much each agent would expect to sell if $r \neq 1$. Let us suppose that this quantity is given by the expression

$$q(m, x, b, r) = \max\,[b(m + x) + n(1 - r), 0] \qquad (9)$$

where $n > 0$ is a measure of the 'conjectured competitiveness' in the economy. In other words, it measures the extent to which each agent supposes that he would lose sales by raising his price above the market price. The limiting case in which $n = +\infty$ is the one usually associated with the assumption of perfect competition.

We now have introduced a total of seven random variables: $b, c, s, x,$ $a, K,$ and M. Let us suppose that the probability distributions of the first three of these are mutually independent and that

$$E(b) = \beta > 0; \qquad E(c) = \gamma > 0; \qquad E(s) = 0$$
$$\text{var}\,(b) = \sigma_b^2 > 0; \text{ var}\,(c) = \sigma_c^2 > 0; \text{ var}\,(s) = \sigma_s^2 > 0. \qquad (10)$$

At the outset of the fourth stage each agent realizes that if he sets the price rP his utility will equal

$$\frac{\bar{M}}{P}\,(1 - gs) + cs + rq\left[\frac{\bar{M}}{P}\,(1 - gs),\, cs,\, b,\, r\right]$$
$$-\left(\frac{k}{2}\right)q\left[\frac{\bar{M}}{P}\,(1 - gs),\, cs,\, b,\, r\right]^2 \qquad (11)$$

(This is obtained by substituting from [2], [3], and [9] into [6].) He will know that the stochastic variables b, c, and s obey (10), and he may or may not know the exact value of s, depending on whether or not he has chosen to monitor s in the second stage. Suppose that in stage 2 he has made the same monitoring decision as every other agent. Then he will be able to calculate P, the price set by all other agents. He will also know the values of $\bar{M}$, g, and k. Thus he will choose a relative price so as to maximize the expected value of (11) conditional on the information set I, where $I = \{s\}$ if he has monitored and $I = \phi$ otherwise. The first-order condition of this maximization (assume that $q[m, x, b, r] > 0$ with probability 1) can be expressed as

$$E\{b[\bar{M}(1 - gs)/P + cs] + n(1 - r) \,|\, I\} = r\bar{q}_n \tag{12}$$

where

$$\bar{q}_n = n/(1 + nk) \tag{13}$$

Let the superscript i denote the information set, $i = 1$ denoting $I = \{s\}$ and $i = 2$ denoting $I = \phi$. Then the solution to (12) can be written as the relative-price function

$$r = r_n^i(P, \bar{M}. g, s), \qquad i = 1, 2 \tag{14}$$

In order to tell what price to set, each agent must also calculate P, the price that the other agents each will set. To do this he calculates the value of P that makes the value of r in (14) equal to unity. That is, he expects the price to be one such that every agent (including himself) is induced to conform. This will also be the actual price set by all agents in stage 4. It can be expressed as

$$P = P_n^i(\bar{M}, g, s), \qquad i = 1, 2 \tag{15}$$

and, from (12), it must satisfy the condition

$$E(q\,|\,I) \equiv E\{b[\bar{M}(1 - gs)/P + cs]\,|\,I\} = \bar{q}_n \tag{16}$$

In the limiting case of perfect competition, (16) states that the market price will be set so that the expected market demand (per capita) equals the competitive market supply (per capita), $\bar{q} \equiv \lim_{n \to \infty} \bar{q}_n = 1/k$. In other words, there is expected market clearing.[11]

Let $\bar{m}_n \equiv \bar{q}_n/\beta$. From (10), (15), and (16) the prices can be expressed as

$$P_n^1(\bar{M}, g, s) = \bar{M}(1 - gs)/(\bar{m}_n - \gamma s) \tag{17}$$

$$P_n^2(\bar{M}, g, s) = \bar{M}/\bar{m}_n. \tag{18}$$

Thus the quantity of output that will be produced per person in stage 6 can be expressed as a function of the information set, the reaction coefficient g, and the random variables b, c, and s by substituting from (2), (3), (17), and (18) in (7) to obtain

$$q_n^1 = b[\bar{m}_n + (c - \gamma)s] \tag{19}$$

$$q_n^2 = b[\bar{m}_n(1 - gs) + cs] \tag{20}$$

The essence of the SW proposition is contained in (19). If agents monitor s then the behavior of the quantity q is independent of the reaction coefficient g. On the other hand, (20) shows that q is affected by g if no monitoring occurs.

From (10), (19), and (20) the mean and variance of output per person, as seen at the beginning of stage 3 (i.e., before the exact value of s has been ascertained), can be expressed as

$$E(q_n^1) = E(q_n^1|s) = E(q_n^2) = \bar{q}_n \neq E(q_n^2|s) \tag{21}$$

$$\text{var } q_n^1 = \sigma_b^2 \bar{m}_n^2 + \sigma_s^2(\beta^2 + \sigma_b^2)\sigma_c^2 \tag{22}$$

$$\text{var } q_n^2 = \sigma_b^2 \bar{m}_n^2 + \sigma_s^2(\beta^2 + \sigma_b^2)[\sigma_c^2 + (\gamma - g\bar{m}_n)^2] \tag{23}$$

From (6) and (17)–(21) the utility that each agent expects at the end of stage 2 may be expressed as

$$V_n^i(g) = EV(M/P_n^i, q_n^i, x, 1) = \bar{m}_n + \bar{q}_n - (k/2)\bar{q}_n^2 - (k/2) \text{ var } q_n^i;$$
$$i = 1, 2 \tag{24}$$

It follows from (22)–(24) that the gain to society from everyone monitoring the indicator (i.e., $V_n^1[g] - V_n^2[g]$) arises solely from the consequent reduction in the variance of output. This reduction in variance yields a welfare gain because the marginal utility of more production is (by assumption) a constant but the marginal cost is increasing, so that total utility is a concave function of the level of output.

8.3 THE MONITORING DECISION

Equations (17)–(24) show how each agent's price, output, and expected utility will depend on the monitoring decision made in stage 2 and the reaction coefficient chosen in stage 1. This section analyzes the monitoring decision.

Let z_m (> 0) denote the cost, in utils, of monitoring the indicator. This cost will generally equal $z_c + z_p$ where z_c is the cost of collecting the information (i.e., of determining the exact value of s) and z_p is the cost of processing the information (i.e., of computing and posting the optimal price given the value of s). Each agent will choose to monitor if the gain to him in expected utility is at least as great as z_m.

The size of this gain will depend on whether or not the other agents are monitoring. Consider first the case in which none of the other agents is monitoring. In this case the agent will derive the expected utility $V_n^2(g)$, as determined by (24), if he too chooses not to monitor. But if he chooses to monitor, the market price will continue to be P_n^2, as in (18), and he can now profit from knowing the exact value of the indicator before setting his own price. Because he can infer, as before, the exact value of P before determining his relative price, that relative price will be the one that satisfies the first-order condition (12) with $I = \{s\}$ and $P = P_n^2(\bar{M}, g, s)$. That is,

$$r_n^1(P_n^2, \bar{M}, g, s) = 1 + s\beta(\gamma - g\bar{m}_n)/(\bar{q}_n + n) \tag{25}$$

Let $V_n^3(g)$ denote the expected utility of the agent who monitors when no one else is monitoring. This can be obtained by substituting from (25) into (6) and using $q = q_n^3 \equiv q_n^2 + n(1 - r)$ with q_n^2 given by (20). As a result of this calculation it can be seen that the gain in expected utility from deciding to monitor when others are not monitoring is

$$V_n^3(g) - V_n^2(g) = \phi(n)\sigma_s^2\beta^2(\gamma - g\bar{m}_n)^2 \tag{26}$$

where $\phi(n) = (1 + nk)^2/2n(2 + nk)$. (This result is also derived in the appendix at the end of this chapter.) Note that

$$\phi(n) > (k/2) \quad \text{and} \quad \phi(n) \to (k/2) \text{ as } n \to \infty \tag{27}$$

The nature of this gain is easy to see. The expected output of the agent is not affected by the decision to monitor but its variance is, and, as we have argued, a reduction in variance increases expected utility. Specifically, whenever the level of aggregate demand is high ($s > 0$) the monitoring agent will, according to (25), raise his price, thereby damping the increase in his sales (assuming that $g < \gamma\bar{m}_n^{-1}$). Likewise, when $s < 0$ the monitoring agent will bolster his sales by reducing r. Not only does this reduce variability but it also adds to the agent's expected revenue. In the limiting case of perfect competition, (25) implies that these changes in r will be imperceptible. In this case the agent is able to adjust the mean position of his random sales schedule whenever a nonzero value of s is observed so that the expected value of his sales *conditional upon s* is equal to $\bar{q}$,[12] and the entire gain to the agent from deciding to monitor arises from the resulting reduction in the variance of sales. In particular, (26) and (27) imply that the gain is equal to $(k/2)$ times this reduction in variance.[13]

Next, consider the case in which all of the other firms are monitoring. In this case the agent will derive the expected utility $V_n^1(g)$ as determined by (24) if he too chooses to monitor. But if he chooses not to monitor then the price will continue to be P_n^1 as in (17), and the agent will lose by not being able to foresee, before setting his own price, the variations in s and in P_n^1 that his competitors are taking into account. The nonmonitoring agent will choose a price $\hat{P}$ so as to maximize $EV[M/P_n^1, q_n^1 + n(1 - \hat{P}/P_n^1), x, \hat{P}/P_n^1]$. Let $V_n^4(g)$ denote the expected utility of the agent who does not monitor when others are monitoring. Then, as the appendix demonstrates, the gain in expected utility from deciding to monitor when others are monitoring is

$$V_n^1(g) - V_n^4(g) = \psi(n) \frac{\text{var } e_n}{1 + \text{var } e_n} \tag{28}$$

where $e_n = P_n^1(\bar{M};g,s)^{-1}[EP_n^1(\bar{M};g,s)^{-1}]^{-1}$ is the reciprocal of the market price, expressed as a ratio to its mean value, and where $\psi(n) = n + n^2 k/2$. Note that

$$\psi(n) \rightarrow \infty \text{ as } n \rightarrow \infty \tag{29}$$

If everyone is to monitor then the gain from deciding to monitor when everyone else is monitoring must be at least as great as the monitoring cost; that is,

$$V_n^1(g) - V_n^4(g) \geq z_m \tag{30}$$

Likewise, if no one is to monitor, it is necessary that

$$V_n^3(g) - V_n^2(g) \leq z_m \tag{31}$$

From (26) and (28) it follows that for large enough n at least one of these conditions must be satisfied. But it also follows that both of them may be satisfied. In other words, convention appears to play an important role in the monitoring decision. It may be that everyone will monitor if they all expect everyone else to, but no one will monitor if they all expect no one else to.[14] I shall assume that monitoring will occur if and only if (31) is violated – in other words, that the convention of monitoring will develop only when the convention of nonmonitoring is unsustainable.[15] Notice, however, that when the reaction coefficient assumes the value

$$\hat{g}_n = \gamma/\bar{m}_n \tag{32}$$

then the convention of monitoring could never be sustained as long as $z_m > 0$, because from (17), (26), and (28),

$$V_n^1(\hat{g}_n) - V_n^4(\hat{g}_n) = V_n^3(\hat{g}_n) - V_n^2(\hat{g}_n) = 0 \tag{33}$$

In order to simplify the analysis further, let us assume the limiting case of perfect competition. Then, from (2), (26), (27), (31), and (32) the necessary and sufficient condition for monitoring to occur is

$$(k/2)\lambda_c\sigma_x^2\beta^2(1 - g/\hat{g})^2 > z_m \tag{34}$$

where $\lambda_c = \gamma^2/(\gamma^2 + \sigma_c^2)$ is a measure of the accuracy of the indicator, being the square of the coefficient of correlation between x and the conditional forecast γs of x based on the indicator, $\sigma_x^2 = \text{var } x$ is the variance in aggregate demand, and $\hat{g} = \gamma\beta k$, the limiting value of (32).

According to (34), the likelihood of monitoring occurring is larger, (1) the larger is the slope, k, of the typical producer's marginal cost schedule, because the larger this slope the more the firm loses from variability in its demand that could be avoided by monitoring; (2) the more accurate is the indicator, because an inaccurate indicator conveys little useful information; (3) the more variable is the level of aggregate demand, because there is little gain in monitoring a variable that is relatively constant; (4) the larger is β, because there is little gain to monitoring a variable if its expected effect on demand is small; and (5) the further is the reaction coefficient from $\hat{g}$, because when $g = \hat{g}$ then, as can be inferred from comparing (22) with (23), the monetary authority is already accomplishing everything that private agents could accomplish by monitoring.

8.4 OPTIMAL MONETARY POLICY AND THE INCENTIVE TO MONITOR

Three implications of this analysis are worth noting here. First, the SW proposition is valid for all values of g satisfying (34). For in this case monitoring will occur, and, as noted before, the behavior of output is unaffected by the value of g. According to (22) and (24) each agent's expected utility will also be unaffected by the value of g.

Second, whatever can be accomplished by monitoring can be accomplished just as well by having the monetary authority set $g = \hat{g}$. According to (34) no monitoring would occur, but according to (19), (20), and (24) the behavior of output and expected utility would be the same as if monitoring was occurring.

Third, as was argued in the introduction above, private agents may not have much incentive to monitor s even when the social gains from everyone deciding to monitor are large. That is, the private value of monitoring, $V^3(g) - V^2(g)$, may be small when the social value, $V^1(g) - V^2(g)$, is large. In particular, it follows from (22)–(24) and (26) that

$$[V^3(g) - V^2(g)] = \lambda_b[V^1(g) - V^2(g)] \tag{35}$$

where $\lambda_b = \beta^2/(\beta^2 + \sigma_b^2)$ is a measure of the predictability of the effect upon effective demand of changes in x, being the square of the coefficient of correlation between the actual effect bx and the predicted effect βx. If the value of the coefficient b is known with certainty, then the private and social values coincide. In the limiting case of pure uncertainty (when $[\beta/\sigma_b]^2 \to 0$) the private value is infinitesimal in comparison with the social value.

The reason for this divergence of private from social value is seen most easily in the case of a perfectly reliable indicator ($\sigma_c^2 = 0$) and a neutral monetary policy ($g = 0$). If everyone monitors then the price level will adjust to fluctuations in x so that the sum $m + x$ is constant and equal to $\bar{m}$, with output equal to $q^1 = b\bar{m}$. Thus everyone monitoring together will completely eliminate the effects of x upon output. An isolated agent monitoring when no one else is cannot stop $m + x = \bar{m} + x$ from fluctuating. He can, and will, through imperceptible changes in r alter the mean position of his demand curve so as to offset the predicted effect βx, but there will still remain an unpredicted effect $(b - \beta)x$. Specifically, by substituting (25) into (9) we see that his output will be $q^3 = b\bar{m} + (b - \beta)x$. Thus the social gain to monitoring comes from eliminating the total effect bx of changes in aggregate demand, whereas the private gain comes from eliminating only the predicted effect βx. The ratio λ_b of private to social gain is just the ratio of variances of the predicted and total effects.

Consider three different monetary policies:

1. Policy N is the neutral policy, $g = 0$, which is assumed to result in no administrative cost.
2. Policy D is the disseminating policy suggested by Barro of setting $g = 0$ but also publicizing the value of s, which is assumed to result in the administrative cost z_d per person.
3. Policy A is the activist policy of setting $g = \hat{g}$, resulting in the administrative cost z_a.

Assume that the cost z_a is incurred whenever any nonzero value of g is chosen. Then policy A will dominate any other policy with $g \neq 0$, and we may restrict our attention to policies A, D, and N. Which policy is optimal will depend upon the relationships between the costs and benefits of monitoring and the administrative costs of the different policies. Let

$$V^s \equiv V^1(0) - V^2(0) = (k/2)\lambda_c \text{ var } (bx) \qquad (36)$$

denote the social gain to monitoring and $V^p \equiv V^3(0) - V^2(0) = \lambda_b V^s$ denote the private gain to monitoring, when $g = 0$. Then according to (34) monitoring will never occur under policy A and will not occur

Table 8.1 Cost per person of monetary policy.

	Policy		
Situation	N	D	A
I. $z_c + z_p < \lambda_b V^s$	$z_c + z_p$	$z_d + z_p$	z_a
II. $z_p < \lambda_b V^s \leq z_c + z_p$	V^s	$z_d + z_p$	z_a
III. $\lambda_b V^s \leq z_p$	V^s	$z_d + V^s$	z_a

Note: N = neutral policy, D = disseminating policy, A = activist policy.

under policy N if $\lambda_b V^s \leq z_c + z_p$. Policy D is assumed to save the private agents any collecting costs, but if they are to use their knowledge of the value of s they must still incur the processing cost. Thus monitoring will not occur under policy D if $\lambda_b V^s \leq z_p$. Table 8.1 depicts the cost per person of the different policies in the three situations indicated, where the cost is measured as $V^1(0)$ minus the expected utility resulting from the policy plus the monitoring and administrative costs. In each situation the optimal policy is the one with the least cost.

Note that if the indicator is unreliable enough (i.e., λ_c small enough) or if effective demand is stable enough (var [bx] small enough), *ceteris paribus*, then a neutral policy will be optimal because both of these factors make V^s small. Both of these factors also figure prominently in Milton Friedman's (1953, 1968) case against activist policy. For the same reason, a small slope to marginal cost (small k) favors a neutral policy. Note also that in situation III the disseminating policy is dominated by the neutral policy.

For our purposes the most important implication to note about Table 8.1 is that an activist policy will be uniquely optimal whenever $z_a < V^s \leq z_p/\lambda_b$; that is, if (1) the indicator is reliable enough, effective demand is unstable enough, or marginal cost rises fast enough that V^s exceeds the cost of administering an activist policy; and (2) the cost of processing the information contained in the indicator is large enough or the predictability of the effect of changes in the level of aggregate demand is small enough that $V^s \leq z_p/\lambda_b$. These conditions do not require the monetary authority to possess any cost advantage. If λ_b is very small, they may hold even if the cost of administering an activist policy is much larger than the private cost of monitoring. If the conditions hold then an activist policy is optimal because despite the large social gain to monitoring no one will do it even if the cost of collecting information is saved. For even under a disseminating policy the user of the information contained in the indicator must incur a processing cost, and, as we have seen, he will be led to underestimate the gains from using the information.

8.5 A VARIANT OF THE BASIC MODEL: MONETARY POLICY AND THE EFFICIENCY OF MONITORING[16]

One special feature of the basic model employed above is that the terms m and x enter into the aggregate demand function (5) with the same coefficient. This is why the optimal reaction coefficient $\hat{g}$ always makes the expected level of output (conditional on s) equal to its optimal value, $\bar{q}$ (see (20)). When m and x have different random coefficients then Brainard's (1967) analysis suggests that the optimal value of the reaction coefficient will generally be smaller than this. Such a case is easily constructed by replacing the utility function (1) with the variant

$$U = K(\hat{q} - x)^a \hat{m}^{1-a} - (k/2)q^2 + 2x \tag{37}$$

in which case the indirect utility function is still given by (6), but the effective demand function changes from (7) to

$$q = bm + x \tag{38}$$

As in (19) and (20), the value of output with or without monitoring can be expressed as

$$q_n^1 = b(\bar{m}_n - \gamma s/\beta) + cs \tag{39}$$

$$q_n^2 = b\bar{m}_n(1 - gs) + cs \tag{40}$$

Once again the expected value of output is

$$E(q_n^1) = E(q_n^1|s) = E(q_n^2) = \bar{q}_n \tag{41}$$

and the variance of output is

$$\text{var } q_n^1 = \sigma_b^2 \bar{m}_n^2 + \sigma_s^2[(\sigma_c^2 + \gamma^2\sigma_b^2)/\beta^2] \tag{42}$$

$$\text{var } q_n^2 = \sigma_b^2 \bar{m}_n^2 + \sigma_s^2[\sigma_c^2 + (\gamma - g\bar{m}_n\beta)^2 + (g\bar{m}_n)^2\sigma_b^2] \tag{43}$$

Let us again restrict our attention to the limiting case of perfect competition. As before, the optimal value g' of the reaction coefficient will be the one that minimizes $\text{var}(q^2)$. That is,

$$g' = \lambda_b\gamma/\bar{q} \tag{44}$$

If the activist policy $g = g'$ is pursued and no monitoring occurs, then

$$E(q^2|s) = \bar{q} + (1 - \lambda_b)\gamma s \tag{45}$$

As in Brainard's analysis, only the fraction λ_b of the predicted effect of a change in the indicator is offset by optimal monetary policy. In contrast to this, (41) implies that all of the predicted effect will be offset by the outcome of monitoring. Thus optimal monetary policy without monitoring can in this case accomplish more than monitoring. With private monitoring the real money supply will overreact to information about aggregate disturbances. Specifically, it follows that the social gain to monitoring when $g = g'$ is

$$V^1(g') - V^2(g') = (k/2)\lambda_c\sigma_x^2\sigma_b^2[1/(\beta^2 + \sigma_b^2) - 1/\beta^2] < 0 \tag{46}$$

Optimal monetary policy can be characterized in this variant model as we did in the basic model with results that are similar but with a complication, because even when $g = g'$ and the social gain to monitoring is negative, the private gain in this case is actually positive. Specifically (see the appendix at the end of this chapter),

$$V^3(g) - V^2(g) = (k/2)\lambda_c\sigma_x^2(1 - \lambda_b g/g')^2 \tag{47}$$

from which it follows that $V^3(g') - V^2(g') > 0$. Thus optimal monetary policy may require g to be somewhat larger than g' so that people will not be motivated to monitor.

For our purposes the important feature of optimal monetary policy is that the activist policy ($g = g'$) will be optimal whenever

$$(k/2)\lambda_c\sigma_x^2(1 - \lambda_b)^2 \leq z_p + z_c < (k/2)\lambda_c\sigma_x^2 \tag{48}$$

and

$$z_a \leq (k/2)\lambda_c\sigma_x^2\sigma_b^2[1/\beta^2 - 1/(\beta^2 + \sigma_b^2)] \tag{49}$$

If (48) is satisfied then monitoring will occur under a neutral or disseminating policy but not under an activist policy. If (49) also holds then the activist policy is optimal because its cost (relative to $V^2(g')$) is z_a, whereas, from (46) and the fact that $V^1(g)$ is independent of g, the cost of each of the other policies will exceed the right-hand side of (49) by the sum of monitoring and administrative costs. As in the previous section, the monetary authority needs no cost advantage for these conditions to be satisfied if $\lambda_b < 1$. For example, they may be satisfied even if $z_a > z_c + z_p$, because the first term in (48) is just λ_b times the right-hand side of (49).

Thus, an activist monetary policy can be justified because the monetary authority, by avoiding the overreaction to the indicator that would occur with monitoring, is able to accomplish more than could be accomplished by private monitoring. The overreaction of private agents monitoring s occurs because each individual sees himself as being able to offset the effect of s by changing his relative price, the coefficient of which, n, is known with certainty. Thus, he will try to offset completely the predicted effects of a change in s. As Brainard has shown, this is the optimal policy when the effect of the price setter's action can indeed be predicted with certainty. But the effect of every agent trying to alter his relative price is a change in the absolute price level, the effect of which cannot be predicted with certainty. As Brainard has also shown, the optimal reaction when the effect of policy is uncertain is to attempt to offset less than 100 percent of the predicted effect of the disturbance. The crucial assumption in this argument is that the degree of uncertainty attached to the effects of relative price changes is different from that attached to absolute price changes. Private agents take the former into account but not the latter. In the particular model used above the former uncertainty is less than the latter, but this is not essential to the argument. In the reverse case private agents would underreact to monitored aggregate disturbances, once again giving a rationale to an activist policy.

8.6 CONCLUSION

In summary, this chapter has argued that an activist monetary policy may be justified even when people's expectations are formed rationally if there are costs of gathering and processing information and if there is uncertainty concerning the exact values of parameters in the economic system. The justification that we have presented is twofold: first, that private agents may not be motivated to use information that can be used profitably by the monetary authority and, second, that even if they are motivated to use it they may not make as good use of it as could the monetary authority.

The formal argument has been presented with a simple model employing specific functional forms chosen for their tractability. Therefore, much work remains before the degree of generality of the results can be ascertained.

The first rationale that we provided for an activist policy should be distinguished from that of Fischer (1977) and Phelps and Taylor (1977). Their models are similar to ours in that prices are set in advance of trading rather than being determined by an independent auctioneer according to market-clearing conditions. However, their models allow activist monetary policies to improve welfare because they postulate a temporary rigidity in prices that prevents private agents from realizing all mutually advantageous and perceived gains from trade. This raises the question of whether the contractual arrangements implicit in such models would be competitively sustainable (see, e.g., Barro 1977b). Our argument has gone one step further and shown conditions under which these contracts are in fact sustainable. We have not postulated any rigidity or imperfection that allows the monetary authority to react more quickly or with more flexibility to variation in the indicator than private agents can. Instead we have shown that private agents may *choose* not to act on as much information as the monetary authority possesses, or even as much as the monetary authority makes freely available to them, even when it would be Pareto improving for them to do so. In other words, this argument also provides an explanation for the fact that private contracts are typically written in nominal terms without being indexed to the money supply or other aggregate variables.

This chapter has not addressed the question of whether or not the particular conditions derived above for the optimality of an activist policy actually exist in any real-world situation. The purpose has been mainly to argue that as a matter of principle the assumption of rational expectations does not imply the uselessness of an activist policy. It depends at least on the factors discussed above. Any balanced evaluation of alternative monetary policies should also take into account at least two other important considerations. First, as Hayek (1945) has argued, the most important problem to be resolved is probably not what policy to pursue but whom to entrust with the task. An activist policy will work only if the authority can be entrusted or persuaded to pursue the public interest instead of his own and to pursue it competently. Second, as Hayek has also argued, the centralization of decision making is most easily rationalized when the decisions require the use of general knowledge rather than local, specific knowledge. In the model of the present chapter every individual agent is essentially identical, so there is no clear distinction between these two kinds of knowledge. But more generally one would expect the aggregate disturbances to which monetary policy reacts to come under the heading of general knowledge, about which most individual agents can be expected to have little expertise. Thus a further argument in favor of an activist policy is that it allows society to centralize, and thus to bring to bear an efficient degree of expertise on, decisions concerning such general knowledge.

APPENDIX

This appendix sketches a formal derivation of the private value of monitoring. In general terms, suppose that a decision maker has an information set I and his problem is to choose the value of decision variable x so as to

$$\max_{\{x\}} E(\alpha_0 + \alpha_1 x + \alpha_2 x^2 | I) \qquad (A.1)$$

where the α_i's are random parameters. Then the expected value of receiving the information contained in the new information set I' is the expected difference in the optimized value of (A1) resulting from replacing I by I'; that is,

$$E\{[E(\alpha_1|I)]^2/4E(\alpha_2|I) - [E(\alpha_1|I')]^2/4E(\alpha_2|I')\} \qquad (A.2)$$

1. To derive (26) from (A2) note that in this case $\alpha_1 = (q_n^2 + n)(1 + nk)$, $\alpha_2 = -(n/2)(2 + nk)$, $I = \Phi$, and $I' = \{s\}$.
2. To derive (28), let x be the *average* relative price, $PE[P_n^1(\bar{M}, g, s)^{-1}]$, and note that in this case $\alpha_1 = e_n(q_n^1 + n)(1 + nk)$, $\alpha_2 = -e_n^2(n/2)$ $(2 + nk)$, $I = \Phi$, and $I' = \{s\}$.
3. To derive (48) proceed exactly as in deriving (26) and take the limit as $n \to \infty$.

NOTES

1. See Sargent and Wallace (1975). The proposition is derived in a more general context by Barro (1976).
2. A similar point was made by Benjamin Friedman (1979), who showed the similarity of rational expectations to error learning during the learning process.
3. See, however, Lucas (1975) and Sargent (1976).
4. This point has been stressed by Rutledge (1974), Frenkel (1975), Feige and Pearce (1976), Laidler (1978), Shiller (1978), and Friedman (1979).
5. This result is similar to those of Hirshleifer (1971) and Grossman and Stiglitz (1976), who argued that equilibrium allocations with more information may be Pareto inferior to those with less.
6. This setup may be contrasted with Lucas's (1972), in which the agents are randomly divided into subgroups, each with a miniature Walrasian auctioneer, and with no communication between groups during the market period. Both setups require agents to make trading commitments before being completely informed of other agents' dispositions to trade. Lucas's approach has the advantage that market-clearing models have been more thoroughly analyzed in the literature than price-setting models. Ours has the advantage of replacing the Walrasian auctioneer with a scheme that bears some resemblance to the way prices actually get determined in many real-world markets. Whether our results could be transposed to a suitably constructed 'market-clearing' model is an open question.
7. This rule also appears to be compatible with the way transaction quantities are determined in many real-world markets, especially those organized by specialist traders – wholesalers, retailers, etc. – who post prices and hold inventories which they allow to act as buffer stocks against fluctuations in demand. By absorbing the non-price rationing they provide a service to customers, for which they are rewarded by a spread between their buying and selling prices. In effect we are assuming that each agent is a combination consumer-producer-trader. (However, we are ignoring the potentially important role of inventories by assuming that the good is not storable).
8. A purely random, unpredictable component could be added to (3) but, as

Barro (1976) has also shown, the optimal policy, if feasible, would be to set its variance to zero.

9. Alternatively, we could suppose that they all face a stochastic demand function with independent, identical probability distributions, the randomness representing the indeterminacy in the distribution of sales among identical sellers charging identical prices. However, the addition of one more random factor would add nothing but notational complexity to the analysis.

10. It has been argued that even in markets where demanders choose quantities at predetermined prices the demand decisions must take into account the future relationships between trading partners, as well as the usual objectives, in which case the quantities chosen may be on neither the demand nor the supply curve as usually conceived (Barro, 1977b). This consideration is probably important in markets where exchange is conducted on a highly personal basis because of the costs of switching trading partners, as in labor markets, markets for personal credit, and so forth. However, there are also many markets where exchange is quite impersonal and buyers may, because they can remain anonymous to the sellers, choose their quantities without taking this consideration into account. When we assume that demanders choose their quantities according to the usual sort of utility maximization we are implicitly assuming this sort of impersonal arrangement.

11. An almost identical condition was assumed to hold by Fischer (1977: 195–7) and by Phelps and Taylor (1977: 166–70).

12. The limiting case of perfect competition is denoted by the absence of the subscript n on the variables $\bar{q}_n$, $\bar{m}_n$, V_n^1, $\hat{g}_n$, etc.

13. Notice that we are not allowing a monitoring agent to gain by selling his information. Allowing a market for information would complicate the analysis without affecting our main result. For in the case that we focus on below where an activist policy dominates all others, the private value of information is less than the cost of processing it. In this case no one would willingly pay the monitoring agent anything for his information.

14. In such cases the private value of the information contained in s is larger when everyone else has the information than when no one else has it. This result may appear somewhat counterintuitive, but it arises from the following considerations. In stage 4 the agent who knows s may gain because this allows him to vary his price in anticipation of variations in (a) the variable x which is correlated with s, and (b) his competitors' price, which may be predicted once s is known. When n is large, then b will be the dominant factor if others are observing s, because variations in his competitors' absolute selling price imply variations in his own relative selling price, and thus large variations in his sales, if he is unable to anticipate them. But if no one else is observing s then b no longer applies because he does not need to observe s in order to anticipate his competitors' price. More generally, the result arises because the main use of the information is to allow the agent to coordinate his activities (specifically the activity of setting his nominal selling price) with the activities of other agents. As an analogy, the value of

knowing that you should drive on the left in England would be much less if none of the other drivers knew it. This analogy also illustrates why multiple equilibria that must be selected by convention can arise under such circumstances.

15. Thus we may say that an equilibrium with respect to any $(g, \bar{M}, n)$ consists of a monitoring decision $i \in \{1, 2\}$ and a price function $P_n^i(\bar{M}, g, s)$ such that (a) for any s the optimal relative price $r_n^i(P, \bar{M}, g, s)$ equals unity when $P = P_n^i(\bar{M}, g, s)$, and (b) the monitoring decision is $i = 1$ only if $V_n^1(g) - V_n^4(g) \geq z_m$, and $i = 2$ if and only if $V_n^3(g) - V_n^2(g) \leq z_m$.

16. The rationalization for activist policy presented in this section is similar to the one presented by Fane (1977).

9 · WAGE FLEXIBILITY AND EMPLOYMENT

9.1 INTRODUCTION

One of the central messages of Keynes's *General Theory* was that wage flexibility cannot be counted on to cure unemployment. One part of Keynes's argument was that wages were not in fact very flexible. But he did not rest his case on the assumption of sticky wages. In his chapter 19 he argued that if wages were more flexible, matters would be even worse. Greater wage flexibility would be detrimental to social justice, would lead to greater labor unrest, and would destabilize the value of money. More to the point it would probably also make unemployment even worse because wage reductions would cause the level of aggregate demand to fall.

Keynes pointed to several channels through which a wage reduction might reduce aggregate demand. The one he seemed to rely on most was an expectation effect:

> If...the reduction leads to the expectation, or even to the serious possibility, of a further wage-reduction in prospect, . . . it will diminish the marginal efficiency of capital and will lead to the postponement both of investment and of consumption. (p. 263)

He pointed out that if wages were suddenly to fall so low that they were believed to have 'touched bottom' then the expectation of wage inflation would stimulate aggregate demand. But he argued that this was 'scarcely practical,' and that:

> it would be much better that wages should be rigidly fixed and deemed incapable of material changes, than that depressions should be accompanied by a gradual downward tendency of money-wages, a further

---

David Laidler provided helpful comments on an early draft.

Reprinted from *Eastern Economic Journal* (1986), **12**, July–September, 237–42.

moderate wage reduction being expected to signalize each increase of, say, 1 per cent in the amount of unemployment. (p. 265)

Another channel was the distribution effect of a wage reduction, between wage earners and 'other factors entering into marginal prime cost whose remuneration has not been reduced' (p. 262). This effect he argued would probably diminish the propensity to consume.

Still another channel was the increase in the real burden of nominal debts. This would transfer income 'from entrepreneurs to rentiers' (Keynes's archetypical debtors and creditors), which he believed was more likely to lower than to raise the propensity to consume. It would also depress entrepreneurial confidence, with adverse effects on investment. And if the reduction was large enough it would even lead many entrepreneurs to the point of insolvency, 'with severely adverse effects on investment' (p. 264).

There are two separate propositions involved in Keynes's argument, although he was not careful to distinguish between them. The first is that the impact effect of a given wage reduction is to reduce employment. The second is that an increase in the degree of flexibility of wages will make employment more variable – that depressions will be deepened or prolonged by the expectation that they will cause wage deflation. The distinction between these two propositions corresponds to the now familiar rational-expectations distinction between the effects of a one-time policy action and the effects of a policy regime.

Despite the enormous influence that Keynes has had (and continues to have) on the development of macroeconomics, his ideas concerning wage flexibility have never 'caught on.' Modern Keynesian economics has been built on the assumption of sticky wages (and possibly prices). Most Keynesian models would exhibit no involuntary unemployment without this assumption. Several authors have noted that the impact effect of wage reductions might be perverse, but that possibility has played no part in the development of mainstream Keynesian models. Likewise, the idea that the variability of output is positively related to the degree of flexibility of wages seems hardly to have been examined in recent years.[1] Instead, it is commonplace to assert that wage and employment variability are substitutes.

The purpose of this chapter is to re-examine Keynes's two propositions using a simple rational-expectations macro model. The assumption of rational expectations is useful for distinguishing clearly between Keynes's two propositions. It is also appropriate for analyzing the second proposition, since it deals not with a once-over unique historical event but with a recurrent systematic pattern of wage behaviour that people can reasonably be supposed to anticipate.

The model distinguishes between two sorts of wage flexibility: sensitivity to employment, and speed of adjustment. Sensitivity is represented by the effect of a given increase in employment on a target wage. The change in the money wage each period is a fraction of the gap that existed last period between the target wage and the actual wage. That fraction represents the speed of adjustment.

The model also includes two kinds of random shocks that affect employment: shocks to aggregate demand and wage shocks. Demand shocks are included for obvious reasons; wage shocks are included in order to make the experiment of a once-over reduction in wages logically admissible in a rational-expectations model.[2]

Keynes's second proposition also has a temporal dimension to it that his analysis does not address. Specifically, if we interpret the variability of employment as the variance of a rational forecast of employment, it matters how far ahead that forecast is made. In the following analysis I consider two forecast horizons: one period and infinity. Thus I consider the effects of varying wage flexibility on both the one-period-ahead conditional variance of employment and on the unconditional stationary variance of employment.

This re-examination confirms that Keynes's first proposition is correct under the conditions that he postulated – a large real-debt effect or a large real-wage effect. It also tends to confirm the short-run version of his second proposition. Specifically, the one-period-ahead variance of employment is an increasing function of the sensitivity of wages to employment; it is also an increasing function of the speed of adjustment of wages if either demand shocks account for a large enough fraction of the variability of output or Keynes's first proposition is invalid.

The main reason for the confirmation of Keynes's second proposition is the expectation effect that he stressed in his own analysis. Through this effect wage adjustment generates a multiplier process. An increase in aggregate demand causes a rise in employment, and hence a rise in this period's target wage. This will cause a rise in wages next period. The anticipation of this rise in wages induces a secondary rise in aggregate demand this period. The greater the sensitivity of wages to employment, or the greater the speed of adjustment, the greater is the anticipated rise in wages and hence the greater the multiplier effect.

The analysis is less clear cut concerning the long-run version of Keynes's second proposition, because raising the flexibility of wages can cause shocks to be dampened more quickly, which tends to reduce the stationary variance of employment. However, the model does imply that an increased sensitivity of wages will raise the stationary variance of employment in the case where Keynes's first proposition is correct. It also implies that an increase in wage flexibility by either interpretation will raise the stationary variance in the special case where the only channel through which wages affect employment is the expectation effect.

The results depend heavily on the assumption that the effect on wages of an increase in employment works with a one-period delay. Without this delay the multiplier process resulting from Keynes's expectation effect would not arise, because an increase in demand would have an immediate effect on wages, which would start to go away in the following period. Thus it would give rise to the expectation of deflation, not inflation, an expectation that would dampen the impact on employment rather than amplify it. The sensitivity of the main result of the chapter to this timing assumption illustrates the importance of the considerations stressed by Keynes. If wages were to 'touch bottom' in response to a fall in demand, the expectation of the subsequent rise would stabilize employment. The model presented below rules out such a response by assumption. This is consistent with Keynes's view that the case is 'scarcely practical,' but it is nonetheless an arbitrary timing assumption in the context of the formal model.

9.2 THE MODEL

The model employs the following notation:

n_t – log of employment
p_t – log of price level
w_t – log of money wage rate
e_{dt} – demand shock
e_{wt} – wage shock

The shocks are independent white-noise processes with variances σ_d^2 and σ_w^2 respectively. The variables are related by the following three equations:

$$n_t = e(E_t p_{t+1} - p_t) + dp_t + r(w_t - p_t) + \varepsilon_{dt} \tag{1}$$

$$w_t = a(fn_{t-1} + p_{t-1}) + (1 - a)w_{t-1} + \varepsilon_{wt} \tag{2}$$

$$p_t = mw_t \tag{3}$$

All constants are suppressed, and E_t denotes the rational expectation conditional on an information set I_t that includes all parameters and current dated variables.

Equation (1) can be derived as the reduced form of an IS-LM system in which the distribution of wealth between debtors and creditors, and the distribution of income between workers and others are included as arguments in the IS curve, and where Mundell's (1963) analysis of real and nominal interest rates is included.

The parameter e in (1) represents Keynes's expectation effect, and is positive. A rise in expected inflation increases demand and hence employment. The parameter d is the effect on employment of an increase in demand caused by a rise in the price level. If Keynes's real-debt effect is large enough d will be positive, but if the Keynes or Pigou effect is large enough it will be negative. The parameter r embodies the income-distribution effect of a change in real wages, and is positive.

Equation (2) represents the assumed outcome of the wage bargain. It states that wages adjust with a lag to a target wage. The target wage adjusts one-for-one to changes in the cost of living. The speed of adjustment is measured by the parameter a, which lies between zero and one. The sensitivity of wages to employment is measured by the parameter f, which is positive.

Equation (3) is a log-linear approximation to a simple markup of price over a weighted average of short-run and long-run cost, under an assumption of constant returns. Thus the parameter m lies between zero and one.

9.3 EMPLOYMENT AND WAGES

It is straightforward to verify that the unique solution to equations (1)–(3) is given by the two equations:[3]

$$w_t = \lambda w_{t-1} + (af/(1 - afme))\varepsilon_{d,t-1} + \varepsilon_{wt} \tag{4}$$

$$n_t = \phi w_t + (1/(1 - afme))\varepsilon_{dt} \tag{5}$$

where:

$$\lambda \equiv \{af[(d - e)m + r(1 - m)] + am + 1 - a\}/(1 - afme) \tag{6}$$

$$\phi \equiv [(d - ae(1 - m))m + r(1 - m)]/(1 - afme) \tag{7}$$

Therefore, the impact effect on employment of a demand shock is:

$$\partial n_t/\partial \varepsilon_{dt} = 1/(1 - afme) \tag{8}$$

Assume that

$$afme < 1 \tag{9}$$

Then (8) can be interpreted as a multiplier formula. When a demand shock causes a one unit direct effect on employment, this causes the target wage to rise by f, causing the rational expectation that wages next period will rise by af, and that prices will therefore rise by afm. This expectation has a secondary effect of making employment this period rise by $afme$ through the expectation effect, causing another increase in the target wage, and so forth. The limit of this process is (8). The greater is the sensitivity of wages f or the speed of adjustment a, the larger is this multiplier.

Next, note that the impact effect on employment of an exogenous change in wages is:

$$\partial n_t / \partial \varepsilon_{wt} = \phi \tag{10}$$

Keynes's first proposition is that ϕ is positive. It follows from (7) and (9) that this will be the case whenever the real-debt effect d and/or the real-wage effect r are positive and large enough relative to the expectation effect e and/or the speed of adjustment a.

The expectation effect e works against Keynes's first proposition because in this model an exogenous increase in wages always reduces the rate at which wages are expected to rise next period. Thus a negative ε_{wt} works like the case discussed by Keynes of wages being thought to have 'touched bottom.'

To analyze Keynes's second proposition, consider the one-period-ahead conditional variance:

$$\text{var}(n_t \mid I_{t-1}) = (1/(1 - afme))^2 \sigma_d^2 + \phi^2 \sigma_w^2 \tag{11}$$

Note that an increase in either the sensitivity f or the speed of adjustment a of wages will increase the part of this conditional variance attributable to demand shocks, $(1/(1 - afme)^2)\sigma_d^2$, by increasing the size of the expectation multiplier. By (7), an increase in sensitivity will also increase the part attributable to wage shocks, because the coefficient ϕ can be expressed as the product of a direct effect $- (d - ae(1 - m))m + r(1 - m)$ – and the expectation multiplier, and an increase in f increases the multiplier. An increase in the speed of adjustment a has an ambiguous effect on the conditional variance attributable to wage shocks because it reduces the direct effect but increases the multiplier. Note, however, that under 'classical' conditions, i.e. assuming that $\phi < 0$, this effect ($\partial \phi^2 / \phi a$) is unambiguously positive.

Thus the short-run version of Keynes's second proposition is borne out by the model, with one exception. Specifically, the proposition is invalid only if demand shocks account for a small enough proportion of the variability of output, flexibility is interpreted as speed of adjustment, and Keynes's first proposition ($\phi > 0$) is valid.

The model is less clear cut concerning the long-run version of Keynes's second proposition. This is because an increase in the speed of adjustment a, while it may increase the impact effect on employment of a demand or wage shock, may increase the speed with which that effect is dampened by the system. The more rapid dampening tends to offset the larger impact with an ambiguous overall effect on the unconditional stationary variance of employment. The effect of an increase in sensitivity f is similarly ambiguous.

More specifically, the dampening factor of the system is the eigenvalue λ given by (6); the dynamic response of employment to a wage or demand shock is:

$$\partial n_{t+i}/\partial \varepsilon_{wt} = \phi \lambda^i; \qquad i = 0,1, \ldots$$

$$\partial n_t/\partial \varepsilon_{dt} = 1/(1 - afme)$$

$$\partial n_{t+i}/\partial \varepsilon_{dt} = \lambda^{i-1} af\phi/(1 - afme) \qquad i = 1,2, \ldots$$

Assume that the system is stable:

$$\lambda^2 < 1$$

Then the unconditional variance of employment is:

$$\text{var}(n_t) = (1 + a^2 f^2 \phi^2/(1 - \lambda^2))(1/(1 - afme))^2 \sigma_d^2 + (\phi^2/(1 - \lambda^2))\sigma_w^2$$

$$(12)$$

which could be increasing or decreasing in a or f because λ^2 could be increasing or decreasing in a or f.

There is, however, one important case in which the unconditional variance (12) is increased by an increase in sensitivity f. That is the case in which Keynes's first proposition is valid; i.e. where $\phi > 0$. Under this assumption the dampening factor λ is positive because, from (6) and (7):

$$\lambda = af\phi + am + 1 - a \qquad (13)$$

Since $\phi > 0$ it follows from (7) that $\partial \phi/\partial f > 0$; it follows from this and (13) that $\partial \lambda/\partial f > 0$. Therefore (12) implies that var(n_t) is increasing in f.

The economic interpretation of this result is as follows. If wage increases raise employment ($\phi > 0$) then the employment effect of a wage shock will remain positive into the future because high employment this period will raise wages next period, which will feed back positively on employment next period. An increase in sensitivity f makes the future employment effect stronger by raising the effect on next period's wage. Likewise, the employment effect of a demand shock will remain positive, to an extent that varies positively with f, because the induced high wages next period will keep employment high. Thus in this case raising the sensitivity of wages to employment will not only raise the impact effect on employment of either shock, it will also reduce the speed with which that effect is dampened.

Finally, there is a special case in which the unconditional variance of employment is an increasing function of the degree of wage flexibility under either interpretation of flexibility. That is the case in which the real-debt effect just cancels the Pigou and Keynes effects, and the real-wage effect is absent; that is, $d = r = 0$. To show this, according to (12), it suffices to show that the expression $\phi^2/(1 - \lambda^2)$ is increasing in a and f. In this case the expression equals

$$(mae(1 - m))^2/[(1 - afme)^2 - (1 - afme - a(1 - m))^2]$$
$$= m^2ae^2(1 - m)/[2(1 - afme) - a(1 - m)]$$

which is strictly positive, and increasing in a and f as required.

NOTES

1. Before the *General Theory*, Keynes's first proposition was a central aspect of Fisher's (1933) theory of depressions. Fisher's analysis has recently been revived by Tobin (1980). Keynes's first proposition was also invoked by Patinkin (1951, 271–7), who emphasized the possibly perverse effects of wage/price reductions working through expectations and through increased bankruptcy induced by greater real debt. None of these authors, however, articulated Keynes's second proposition. In particular, the idea stressed by Patinkin, and analyzed more formally by Tobin (1975), that a full-employment equilibrium might be dynamically unstable does not imply that greater wage flexibility would increase the likelihood of dynamic instability. In fact, it would decrease that likelihood in Tobin's (1975) model.

   More recently DeLong and Summers (1986b) have presented an analysis of Keynes's second proposition. Their paper, which was cast in terms of Taylor's (1979) overlapping-wage model does not include the possibility of Keynes's first proposition, because it excludes the real-debt effect and the real-wage effect. It deals exclusively with the unconditional stationary variance of output and it employs numerical simulations rather than the theoretical demonstrations of the present chapter. Caskey and Fazzari (1985) develop a model with a real-debt effect. They carry out simulations to show results like those of DeLong and Summers. They also show analytically that (a) the immediate output loss following a monetary contraction and (b) the likelihood of asymptotic instability are both increased by greater wage flexibility.

2. Shocks to the price equation could be added with little effect on the main results.

3. The presence of the expected inflation term in (1) does not yield indeterminacy because the lagged adjustment of wages and the rigid link between wages and prices prevent expectations formed at t from having any effect on w_t or p_t, and hence preclude any bubble-paths, stable or otherwise. To verify that (4) and (5) do indeed constitute a unique solution it suffices to derive them from (1)–(3). To do this use (3) to eliminate p_t, p_{t-1} and $E_t p_{t+1}$ from (1) and (2). Use the modified (2) to derive: $E_{t-1}w_t = w_t - \varepsilon_{wt}$. Use this to eliminate $E_{t-1}w_t$ from the back-dated version of modified (1), and use the resulting equation to eliminate n_{t-1} from modified (2), thus yielding (4). Then use (4) to eliminate $E_t w_{t+1}$ from modified (1), yielding (5).

PART III

THE MACROECONOMICS OF TRANSACTION EXTERNALITIES

10 · TRANSACTION COSTS IN THE THEORY OF UNEMPLOYMENT

10.1 INTRODUCTION

This chapter addresses the problem of accounting theoretically for the persistence of large-scale unemployment. It briefly reviews some of the well-known shortcomings of the Keynesian account based upon sticky wages and prices and upon Clower's (1965) concept of effective demand, arguing that these shortcomings can be seen as a failure explicitly to integrate transaction costs into the theory of unemployment. The main constructive contribution of the paper is an example of a simple macro model, along the lines of Barro and Grossman (1971), in which transaction costs are made explicit. An essential part of this example is an externality of the sort suggested by Diamond (1982b). The example provides an account of persistent unemployment with many Keynesian features, yet without some of the Keynesian shortcomings, In particular it assumes perfect wage and price flexibility.

10.2 THE KEYNESIAN ACCOUNT

For future reference, the standard Keynesian account is sketched in terms of Figure 10.1, reproduced in essence from Barro and Grossman (1971: 86). Both the output and labor market are in excess supply at a real wage equal to its general equilibrium value, w^*. The supply of labor equals its notional demand n^*. But the effective demand, as given by the schedule ABn', is only n', because collectively the firms find themselves

This paper has benefited from the helpful comments and criticisms of Joel Fried, Tom Kompas, Richard Manning, John McMillan, Tom Rymes, Dan Usher, and John Vanderkamp; none of whom is responsible for any shortcomings.

Reprinted from *American Economic Review* (1985), **75** March, 88–100.

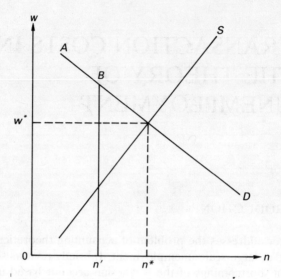

Figure 10.1 The standard Keynesian account of unemployment.

unable to sell any more output than can be produced by this amount. Thus the amount $n^* - n'$ of unemployment exists.

Over time the money wage and the price level will fall in response to excess supplies. This will generally raise the aggregate demand for goods, shifting the vertical portion of the effective demand for labor schedule to the right, and thus increasing employment. Less than full employment will persist if the process of deflation is slow, or if the effect of deflation on aggregate demand is small (or in the wrong direction). Involuntary unemployment will also persist, with w exceeding the supply price of labor, unless wages fall more rapidly than prices, driving real wages down to the point where effective demand equals notional supply.

This account has many virtues. It is consistent with the widely observed lags in wages and prices behind the business cycle, with the countercyclical pattern of layoffs, and with the absence of any pronounced cyclical pattern to real wages. The assumption of quantity rationing underlying Clower's distinction between notional and effective demands also makes the approach consistent with the apparently involuntary nature of large-scale unemployment, and with the observation that the typical business firm would usually prefer to increase its sales at the current price.

There are, however, some well-known shortcomings. As Barro (1977b) has pointed out, the account gives no clear explanation of why the mutually advantageous gains from trade implied by the fact that the supply price of labor at n' is less than its marginal product remain persistently unexploited. Defenders of the approach often take this failure as a logical consequence of wage-price stickiness. But Barro points out that such stickiness can be explained by theories that predict that all potential gains from trade will be exhausted. For example, implicit contracts might specify efficient quantities of goods and services to be traded, along with money payments that are set in fixed ratio to the corresponding quantities in order to satisfy an independent condition of optimal risk sharing.[1] Thus something in addition to price stickiness must be adduced in order to explain the market failure in Figure 10.1.

That additional something is usually presented by defenders of theories of nonclearing markets as being the limitations imposed by transaction costs upon people's ability to communicate offers to buy and sell (see, for example, Leijonhufvud, 1968; Okun, 1981; Laidler, 1982). The stickiness of prices in Keynesian economics results not from a full set of prearranged contractual agreements but from an institutional assumption that prices must be set and advertised by agents (often personified collectively by the 'auctioneer') before there is time for everyone to agree upon what quantities to trade. These costs are what prevent the exhaustion of all gains from trade. But the main problem with this line of defense is that the transaction costs are not integrated explicitly into the theory of unemployment. They do not appear in the decision problems faced by agents, except sometimes as part of an explanation of the demand for money.

The problem is manifested in a difficulty with the concept of effective demand. Specifically, why doesn't the firm in Figure 10.1 try to remove its sales constraint by undercutting its rivals' price? If it made the conjecture most compatible with the price-taking assumptions of the Barro–Grossman model, it would see itself as being able to supply anywhere up to the entire market demand at anything less than the going price. In this case there would be no reason why the demand for labor should not be determined by the notional schedule in Figure 10.1, because a rational firm would ignore any constraint that could be removed by a negligible price reduction.[2] The concept of effective demand for labor would be redundant and there would be no unemployment in Figure 10.1. This difficulty might be resolved by invoking any of a number of costs of price adjustment. But the costs are absent from the standard Keynesian account.[3]

The problem is also revealed by recalling that, even if we accept the effective demand schedule ABn' as defining the relevant demand for labor, unemployment can persist in Figure 10.1 only if the money wage rate falls slowly relative to the price level. According to the usual textbook interpretation of the tâtonnement process, this means that people remain unemployed only because they are slow to offer their services at less than the going wage. Similarly, the 'contract' interpretation of Fischer (1977) and others requires the assumption that unemployed workers do not attempt to underbid anyone working on an unexpired contract (see Fischer, 1977: 198, fn. 17). This is not a convincing description of 'involuntary' unemployment. As Leijonhufvud stressed in his well-known critique, Keynesian economics thus agrees with the pre-Keynesian diagnosis that people are unemployed only because they are asking too much. One might defend Keynesian economics from this critique by arguing that the slowness with which the unemployed offer their services at less than the going wage is a theoretical proxy for the time cost of communicating and forming new matches in the labor market. But again these costs are absent from the account.

10.3 TRANSACTION COSTS AND THIN MARKETS

The preceding discussion attributes many of the shortcomings of the Keynesian account to the absence of explicit transaction costs, broadly interpreted to include costs of communication. It is a commonplace that such costs are higher the thinner the market; that the per unit cost of transacting depends inversely upon the amount of activity in the market. This observation refers not to the well-known economies of scale from lumpy setup costs (for example, Baumol, 1952), but to an externality whereby one agent's trading costs are reduced by having agents on the other side of the market devote more resources to trading.

The observation usually refers to crossmarket comparisons, as between over-the-counter and regularly listed stock transactions, but it could equally well apply to intertemporal comparisons within any given market. For example, a decrease in the demand for labor makes it harder to find a job as well as reducing the wage, because potential employers advertise less and become less willing to arrange interviews, read job applications, return calls, and so forth.[4] From the potential employer's point of view, the labor market becomes less thin when the number of unemployed workers searching for jobs increases and the cost of finding suitable potential recruits thereby decreases. In markets for consumer durables, when demand falls many people stop reading advertisements, stop visiting sellers, and generally become more difficult for sellers to contact. The phenomenon is especially marked in the housing market, where a decrease in demand not only reduces the market price but also increases the expected waiting time required to sell at that price.

This externality works mainly through the cost of communication. The extra cost of dealing in a thin market is primarily that of identifying, contacting, and negotiating with a suitable trading partner. This suggests that the externality is particularly difficult to internalize. Such internalization would generally require some kind of collective agreement to coordinate the activities of potential traders on both sides of the market. But the agreements themselves would require communications whose costs are subject to the externality. Once two potential trading partners have contacted one another, it is generally too late for them to agree to an arrangement to share the costs of contacting in such a way as to induce the efficient amount of contacting activity by each side.[5]

Some internalization obviously is accomplished by intermediaries in the labor market, such as employment agencies, university placement services, newspapers, and trade associations; as well as by retail and wholesale firms, auction houses, jobbers, specialist traders, financial intermediaries, real estate agents, etc., in other markets. But the scope of such intermediation in labor markets is limited by the problems of heterogeneity and asymmetry of information, which tend to render large-scale intermediation uneconomical. Even in other markets there is no reason to think a priori that intermediation eliminates all substantial externalities.

An example of a formal model of this kind of externality was provided by Jones (1976), who based his explanation of the emergence of monetary exchange upon a search model in which the expected time required to contact a trading partner depended inversely upon the number of such potential partners actively in the market.

Diamond has shown, using this kind of search model, how the externality can explain 'low-level' equilibria in very special models, which are suggestive of fixed-price excess-supply equilibria but without the fixed prices. In these models, a widespread expectation of high costs of contacting trading partners can be self-fulfilling. It will discourage production, thereby resulting in a low volume of trade, and thereby bringing about the expected high cost by thinning out markets.

10.4 AN EXAMPLE

The example of this section can be seen as recasting into more familiar macroeconomic terms the basic results of Diamond.[6] Rather than focus exclusively upon one of the many informational, logistical, institutional, or strategic factors underlying transaction costs I shall model such costs in the less explicit but more general manner of such writers as Hahn (1971), and Niehans (1971).

Specifically, assume that traders are convened by an auctioneer (or a set of specialist auctioneers) able to find market-clearing wages and prices at no cost, but unable to arrange the trades costlessly. There are unspecified trading institutions in place that reduce but do not eliminate the trading costs faced by households and firms. In addition to the usual budget constraint, there is a transaction-cost constraint requiring each trader to use up resources in order to execute his planned transactions.

There are only two markets, labor and output; and two types of traders, identical households and identical firms. Let $\bar{y}$, $\bar{s}_y$, and $\bar{b}_y$ denote the quantity of output traded in the market, the amount of output used up by all firms in selling output (their 'marketing effort'), and the amount of output used up by households in buying output (their 'buying effort'), all measured as aggregate quantities per firm. Each firm takes these quantities as given and faces the transaction-cost constraints:

$$s_y = \bar{\sigma}(\bar{s}_y, \bar{b}_y)y \tag{1}$$

where s_y is his own marketing effort, y is the quantity he plans to sell, and[7]

$$\bar{\sigma} > 0, \qquad \bar{\sigma}_1 > 0, \qquad \bar{\sigma}_2 < 0 \tag{2}$$

Equation (1) asserts that his selling cost must be incurred in the form of output used up, and that this cost is proportional to the volume of his transactions.[8] The negative dependency upon households' buying effort asserted in (2) represents the externality described in the previous section. The positive dependency upon the marketing effort of the firm's rivals represents an external diseconomy that might reasonably be supposed to counteract that external economy. For example, more advertising and product promotion by rivals might require the firm to increase its own efforts to avoid losing customers.[9]

Averaging (1) across all firms yields

$$\bar{s}_y = \bar{\sigma}(\bar{s}_y, \bar{b}_y)\bar{y} \tag{3}$$

Assume that households' transaction-cost constraints require a buying effort proportional to the quantity bought. Thus $\bar{b}_y = \beta_y\bar{y}$ for some constant $\beta_y \in (0,1)$. By specifying β_y as a constant, this example is ignoring the external economy conferred upon buyers when firms spend more upon marketing. Substituting for $\bar{b}_y$ in (3) produces the equation:

$$\bar{s}_y = \bar{\sigma}(\bar{s}_y, \beta_y\bar{y})\bar{y} \tag{4}$$

Assume that for any $\bar{y} > 0$ there is some $\bar{s}_y$ satisfying (4), and that

$$\bar{\sigma}_1(\bar{s}_y, \beta_y\bar{y})\bar{y} < 1 \qquad \text{for all } (\bar{s}_y, \bar{y}) \tag{5}$$

Inequality (5) asserts that a firm does not have to match an increase in its rivals' marketing effort in order to maintain constant sales. These two assumptions imply that (4) can be expressed as: $\bar{s}_y = \bar{s}_y(\bar{y})$, with

$$\bar{s}_y'(\bar{y}) = (\bar{\sigma} + \beta_y \bar{y} \bar{\sigma}_2)/(1 - \bar{\sigma}_1 \bar{y}) \tag{6}$$

Thus the per-unit selling cost faced by each firm will be

$$\sigma(\bar{y}) \equiv \frac{\bar{s}_y(\bar{y})}{\bar{y}} \equiv \bar{\sigma}(\bar{s}_y(\bar{y}), \beta_y \bar{y}) \tag{7}$$

Assume that the external economy dominates the congestion externality, in the sense that a proportional increase in both marketing efforts and buying efforts will reduce the per unit selling cost:

$$d\bar{\sigma}(\theta s, \theta b)/d\theta < 0 \tag{8}$$

Then an increase in the market quantity will cause a decrease in the per unit cost of selling:

$$\sigma'(\bar{y}) = (1/\bar{y})(\bar{s}_y'(\bar{y}) - \bar{s}_y(\bar{y})/\bar{y})$$

$$= (1/\bar{y})(\bar{y}\bar{\sigma}\bar{\sigma}_1 + \bar{y}\beta_y\bar{\sigma}_2)/(1 - \bar{y}\bar{\sigma}_1)$$

$$= (1/\bar{y})(1/(1 - \bar{y}\bar{\sigma}_1)) \frac{d}{d\theta}\bar{\sigma}(\theta\bar{s}_y(\bar{y}), \theta\beta_y\bar{y})\big|_{\theta=1} < 0 \tag{9}$$

(from equations (5)–(8)).

Finally, assume that

$$1 + \bar{\sigma} + \bar{y}(\beta_y\bar{\sigma}_2 - \bar{\sigma}_1)\big|_{(\bar{s}_y, \bar{b}_y) = (\bar{s}_y(\bar{y}), \beta_y\bar{y})} > 0 \tag{10}$$

Assumption (10) is hard to interpret directly. Obviously it implies a limitation on the extent of externalities, since $\beta_y\bar{\sigma}_2 - \bar{\sigma}_1 < 0$. It would be implied, given assumption (5), if we assumed that an increase in market demand, accompanied by a corresponding increase in buying effort by households, would not generate so large an external benefit on firms that they could meet this increase without an increase in selling effort; that is, if we assumed that $\bar{s}_y' > 0$. For, in that case, (5) and (6) would imply that

$$1 + \bar{\sigma} + \bar{y}(\beta_y\bar{\sigma}_2 - \bar{\sigma}_1) = (1 - \bar{y}\bar{\sigma}_1) + (\bar{\sigma} + \bar{y}\beta_y\bar{\sigma}_2)$$

$$= (1 - \bar{y}\bar{\sigma}_1)(1 + \bar{s}_y'(y)) > 0.$$

It follows from (5), (9), and (10) that

$$1 + \sigma(\bar{y}) + \bar{y}\sigma'(\bar{y}) = \frac{1 + \sigma + \bar{y}(\beta_y\bar{\sigma}_2 - \bar{\sigma}_1)}{1 - \bar{y}\bar{\sigma}_1} > 0 \tag{11}$$

An example satisfying all the above conditions is the function:

$$\bar{\sigma}(s, b) \equiv (1 + \beta_y s/b)e^{-(\mu/\beta_y)b}, \qquad \mu > 0 \tag{12}$$

which yields

$$\sigma(\bar{y}) \equiv e^{-\mu y}/(1 - e^{-\mu y}) \tag{13}$$

An analogous treatment of the costs of buying and selling labor leads to the per unit cost of selling, $\tau(\bar{n})$, where $\bar{n}$ is the quantity of labor services traded in the market, and τ is measured in units of labor. Assume that all transaction costs in the labor market are incurred in the form of labor services used up. Unemployment is interpreted as labor services used up in the selling of labor services. The market quantity of unemployment is $\bar{s}_n = \tau(\bar{n})\bar{n}$, and the rate of unemployment is the fraction of all labor services used in selling labor:[10]

$$u(\bar{n}) \equiv \frac{\bar{s}_n}{\bar{s}_n + \bar{n}} = \frac{\tau(\bar{n})}{1 + \tau(\bar{n})} \tag{14}$$

As with σ, the per-unit cost of selling labor satisfies

$$\tau(\bar{n}) > 0, \qquad \tau'(\bar{n}) < 0$$
$$1 + \tau(\bar{n}) + \bar{n}\tau'(\bar{n}) > 0 \tag{15}$$

Therefore the rate of unemployment and the level of employment are inversely related:

$$u'(\bar{n}) = \tau'(\bar{n})/(1 + \tau(\bar{n}))^2 < 0 \tag{16}$$

The cost of buying n units of labor is $b_n = \beta_n n$, for some constant $\beta_n \in (0, 1)$.

To sell y a firm must produce $y(1 + \sigma(\bar{y}))$. If it hires n it can use $n(1 - \beta_n)$ in production. It therefore chooses n to maximize its profit:

$$f(n(1 - \beta_n))/(1 + \sigma(\bar{y})) - wn$$

where w is the real wage and f a production function satisfying

$$f'(x) > 0; f''(x) < 0 \qquad \text{for all } x > 0$$
$$\lim_{x \to 0} (f(x), f'(x)) = (0, \infty)$$
$$\lim_{x \to \infty} (f(x), f'(x)) = (\infty, 0) \tag{17}$$

Given any $(w, \bar{y})$ the firm's demand for labor is uniquely determined by the first-order condition:

$$w = \frac{1 - \beta_n}{1 + \sigma(\bar{y})} f'(n(1 - \beta_n)) \tag{18}$$

which can be solved for the demand-for-labor function $n^d(w, \bar{y})$, with

$$n^d > 0, \quad n_1^d < 0, \quad n_2^d > 0 \tag{19}$$

Note that this demand function depends not only upon the real wage, but also upon the realized quantity of aggregate demand, $\bar{y}$. This is because, in order to formulate its plans, the firm must know the per-unit cost of selling output, which depends upon aggregate demand; as in the Barro–Grossman model, the firm must receive quantity signals as well as price signals.

As Clower pointed out, this dependency of demand upon realized quantities is what distinguished Keynes' concept of effective demand from the Walrasian concept of notional demand. But the present derivation of the effective demand for labor does not require firms to make unrealistically pessimistic conjectures. Although they take the quantity demand per firm as given, they see themselves as able to sell more if they wish at the going price, as long as they are willing to pay the marketing cost. An increase in aggregate demand for output raises the demand for labor even with no change in the real wage, not because it raises the maximum amount a firm can sell, but because it makes any given amount of output easier to sell.[11]

Each household's utility function has the form $U(z, m) - c(l)$, where z is consumption, m is demand for real money balances, and l is supply of labor. Assume that U is homogenous of degree one with indifference curves that do not touch the axes. Assume also that there is an upper limit $\bar{l} > 0$ to each household's potential labor supply and that the cost function c is defined over the interval $(0, \bar{l})$, with

$$c'(l) > 0 \text{ and } c''(l) > 0 \qquad \text{for all } l \in (0, \bar{l}) \tag{20}$$

$$c'(0) = 0 \text{ and } \lim_{l \to \bar{l}} c'(l) = \infty$$

The assumptions of homogeneity and additivity eliminate income effects from labor supply and permit a diagrammatic analysis similar to Figure 10.1.

The household that buys y and sells n gets to consume $y(1 - \beta_y)$ and must supply $n(1 + \tau(\bar{n}))$. Thus the household's decision problem is to choose y, m and n so as to maximize $U(y(1 - \beta_y),m) - c(n(1 + \tau(\bar{n})))$ subject to the budget constraint $y + m = wn + \pi + M/P$, where π is the household's profit income, M the supply of money, and P the price level, all of which the household takes as given. In equilibrium, $m = M/P$ so that y and M/P must satisfy the marginal condition

$$U_1(y(1 - \beta_y), M/P)(1 - \beta_y) = U_2(y(1 - \beta_y), M/P) \tag{21}$$

Given any $(w, \bar{n})$ the household's supply of labor is uniquely determined by the marginal condition

$$w = c'(n(1 + \tau(\bar{n})))(1 + \tau(\bar{n}))/\lambda \tag{22}$$

where λ is the value of U_2 when (21) is satisfied. Homogeneity implies that λ is a constant. Equation (22) can be solved for the 'effective' supply-of-labor function $n^s(w, \bar{n})$, with

$$n^s > 0, \quad n_1^s > 0 \quad n_2^s > 0 \tag{23}$$

The dependency of labor supply upon the realized demand for labor, $\bar{n}$, arises because an increase in $\bar{n}$ reduces the per unit cost of selling labor. Since $\bar{n}$ is inversely related to the rate of unemployment (16), the dependency of labor supply upon $\bar{n}$ is operationally the same as the 'discouraged worker' effect.

An equilibrium is defined as a triple (w, n, y) such that

$$n^d(w, y) = n^s(w, n) \tag{24}$$

$$n = n^s(w, n) \tag{25}$$

$$y(1 + \sigma(y)) = f(n(1 - \beta_n)) \tag{26}$$

Equation (24) is the usual labor market equilibrium condition. But equilibrium requires also that the quantity signals to which the agents are responding correspond to the actual market quantities. Thus (25) requires the quantity of labor taken as given by the household to equal the equilibrium quantity, and (26) requires the sales quantity taken as given by firms to equal the equilibrium quantity; that is the amount produced $f(n(1 - \beta_n))$ minus the amount used up in marketing $y\sigma(y)$. (Bars are now omitted from market quantities.) Given the equilibrium values of these variables, the price level satisfying (21) will equate y with the demand for output.

The equilibrium condition (26) can be rewritten in the following way. First define the function $q(y) \equiv (1 + \sigma(y))y$. This function indicates the amount of production required to market any given quantity of sales. By (9) and (11),

For all $y > 0$, $q(y)$ is continuous,
strictly increasing, with $q(y) > y$ (27)

Next, define $\underline{q} \equiv \lim_{y \to 0} q(y) \geq 0$, and $\underline{n} \equiv (1 - \beta_n)^{-1} f^{-1} (\underline{q}) \geq 0$ (where $f^{-1}(0) \equiv 0$). Then $\underline{q}$ is the minimal amount of output needed to market any sales at all, and $\underline{n}$ the corresponding amount of employment. Note that $\underline{q}$ is well defined, by (27), that $\underline{n}$ exists, by (17), and that $\underline{n} = 0$ if and only if $\underline{q} = 0$, by (17).

Next it is shown that given n, (26) has a solution $y > 0$ if and only if $n > \underline{n}$. To show this suppose first that $n \leq \underline{n}$. Then, by (17) and (27) $f(n(1 - \beta_n)) \leq f(\underline{n}(1 - \beta_n)) \equiv \underline{q} < q(y)$ for all $y > 0$, so (26) has no such solution. Next suppose that $n > \underline{n}$. Then by (17) and (27):

$$\lim_{y \to 0} q(y) \equiv f(\underline{n}(1 - \beta_n)) < f(n(1 - \beta_n))$$
$$< \infty = \lim_{y \to \infty} q(y)$$

So, by Rolle's theorem and the continuity of $q(\cdot)$, there is a solution to (26) with $y > 0$.

Finally note that, since $q(\cdot)$ is strictly increasing, the implicit function theorem implies that (26) defines a function $\bar{y}(n)$ for all $n > \underline{n}$ and that

$$\bar{y}'(n) = (1 - \beta_n)f'/q'$$
$$= \frac{(1 - \beta_n)f'}{1 + \sigma + y\sigma'} > 0 \tag{28}$$

$$\lim_{n \to \underline{n}} \bar{y}(n) = \lim_{n \to \underline{n}} q^{-1}(f(n(1 - \beta_n)))$$
$$= \lim_{x \to \underline{q}} q^{-1}(x) = 0 \tag{29}$$

The function $\bar{y}(\cdot)$ indicates the level of sales that can feasibly be marketed given any amount of employment greater than the minimal amount $\underline{n}$. Condition (26) is equivalent to the condition: $y = \bar{y}(n)$.

The definition of equilibrium can now be reduced to one involving a single equation in n. From the definitions of n^d and n^s, (w, n, y) is an equilibrium if and only if n satisfies

$$\frac{1 - \beta_n}{1 + \sigma(\bar{y}(n))} f'(n(1 - \beta_n)) = (1 + \tau(n))c'(n(1 + \tau(n)))/\lambda \tag{30}$$

w equals the common value of either side of (30), and $y = \bar{y}(n)$. The two sides of (30) are the demand price and supply price for n units of labor, represented by D and S in Figure 10.2.

Because of the externalities, the equilibrium will not generally be unique. To see this suppose first that there were no externalities – that σ and τ were constant. Then the usual labor market equilibrium condition (24) would be sufficient to determine the equilibrium level of employment, without the quantity equations (25) and (26), because n^s and n^d would depend only upon w. This equilibrium condition would be equivalent to (30) with σ and τ constant. Equilibrium would be unique because the assumptions of declining marginal product (17) and rising marginal disutility (20) of labor would guarantee that the demand price was decreasing and the supply price increasing in n. This is illustrated by D' and S' in Figure 10.2 along which σ and τ equal $\sigma(\bar{y}(n_H))$ and $\tau(n_H)$. But, with the externality, D can be upward sloping because as employment increases, the unit cost of selling output $\sigma(\bar{y}(n))$ decreases (from (9) and (28)), which tends to increase the demand price. Likewise S can be downward sloping because as employment increases, the unit

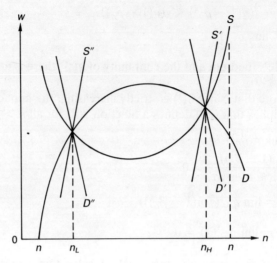

Figure 10.2 The multiple equilibria account of unemployment.

cost of selling labor decreases (from (15)), which tends to lower the supply price. These effects of externalities make it possible for D and S to intersect more than once in nonpathological cases.

Indeed it is possible to specify boundary conditions that guarantee multiplicity except in razor's-edge cases. For example, suppose that in order to sell any output at all, firms must produce at least some positive critical mass of output; that is, that $\underline{q} > 0$ and $\underline{n} > 0$. Under this assumption the unit cost of selling rises to infinity as sales fall to zero, and rises so fast that the total cost $y\sigma(y)$ is bounded away from zero. The example (12) specified above satisfies this assumption.

In order for n to be the equilibrium level of employment, all the expressions in the equilibrium condition (30) must be well defined. This implies that $n \geq \underline{n}$. It also implies that $n(1 + \tau(n))$ must be less than the upper limit on labor supply $\bar{l}$. From (15) the function $l(n) \equiv n(1 + \tau(n))$ is strictly increasing and positive valued for all $n > 0$, with a range $(\underline{l}, \infty)$ for some $\underline{l} \geq 0$. Assume that $\underline{l} < \bar{l}$. Then $\bar{n} \equiv l^{-1}(\bar{l})$ is well defined and the restriction imposed by the limit on labor supply is that n be less than $\bar{n}$.

If $\underline{n} \geq \bar{n}$, then no equilibrium is possible. So suppose that $\underline{n} < \bar{n}$. Then the equilibrium level of employment must lie in the interval $(\underline{n}, \bar{n})$; there must be enough to get the output market started but no more than can feasibly be supplied. Therefore, to show generic multiplicity, it suffices to show that the supply price exceeds the demand price for values of n close enough to $\underline{n}$ and for values close enough to $\bar{n}$. If this is so, then in terms of Figure 10.2 the only way that D and S can have a unique point of intersection is for them to be tangent at that point. But this is obviously a razor's-edge case. Generically there will exist an even number of intersections, so that if equilibrium exists it will be nonunique.

To show this, consider first what happens as n approaches $\bar{n}$. Because $\bar{n} > \underline{n} > 0$, the demand price remains bounded. But $n(1 + \tau(n)) \equiv l(n)$ approaches $l(\bar{n}) \equiv \bar{l}$ so that, by (20), the supply price becomes infinite. Next suppose $n \to \underline{n}$. Because $\underline{n} > 0$, (15) and (20) imply that the supply price remains bounded away from zero. Also, from (17), $f(n(1 - \beta_n)) \to f(\underline{n}(1 - \beta_n)) > 0$; but from (29), $\lim_{n \to \underline{n}} (1 + \sigma(\bar{y}(n))) = \lim_{y \to 0} (1 + \sigma(y)) = \infty$, so the demand price approaches zero. Therefore the demand price is less than the supply price as n approaches either limit.

A similar demonstration of generic multiplicity goes through under the alternative assumption that $\underline{l} \equiv \lim_{n \to 0} (1 + \tau(n))n > 0$. Even with both $\underline{l}$ and $\underline{q}$ equal to zero a similar demonstration can be constructed under the assumption that

$$\lim_{n \to 0} [(1 + \tau(n))c'(n(1 - \tau(n))) (1 - \sigma(\bar{y}(n)))]/$$

$$[\lambda(1 - \beta_n)f'(n(1 - \beta_n))] > 1$$

Another consequence of the externalities is that not all gains from trade are fully exploited in an equilibrium even if it is unique. Specifically, suppose firms were to hire a small amount more labor at the same wage, and the price level were to adjust so as to allow the resulting increase in output to be sold. Consider what would happen to the typical firm's profit: $f(n(1 - \beta_n))/(1 + \sigma(\bar{y}))) - wn$. If there were no externalities (i.e., if σ were constant) then the firm's marginal condition (18) would imply that profit would remain unchanged. But, with the externalities, σ would fall, so profit would increase. Next, consider the level of household utility. If σ, τ, and m were constant, then according to (28) y would change at the rate $dy/dn = (1 - \beta_n)f'/(1 + \sigma)$, which by the firm's marginal condition equals the wage w; the change in household utility would therefore be $(1 - \beta_y)U_1w - (1 + \tau)c'$, which, by the marginal condition (22) and the definition of λ, equals zero. But, with the externality, σ and τ would decrease. The decrease in σ would make y increase by more than w. The decrease in τ would make the disutility of labor rise by less than $(1 + \tau)c'$. Furthermore, the change in the price level would have to keep the marginal condition (21) satisfied, which by homogeneity would require real balances m to equal $k\bar{y}(n)$ for some constant k. Therefore m would increase. Thus taking into account the externalities and the change in m, utility would increase. Both firms and households would gain.

The following argument shows that, if there are multiple equilibria, household utility will be strictly greater whenever employment is greater. Consider any two equilibria, n_0 and n_1, each satisfying (30), with $0 < n_0 < n_1$. Define

$$\phi(n) \equiv U[\bar{y}(n)(1 - \beta_y), k\bar{y}(n)] - c[n(1 + \tau(n))]$$

It will be shown that $\phi(n_0) < \phi(n_1)$. Next, define

$$\Psi(n) \equiv \max_{\{x\}} U\left(f(x(1 - \beta_n)) \frac{1 - \beta_y}{1 + \sigma(\bar{y}(n))}, k\bar{y}(n)\right) - c(x(1 + \tau(n)))$$

The first-order condition uniquely defining the solution to this problem is

$$U_1\left(f(x(1 - \beta_n)) \frac{1 - \beta_y}{1 + \sigma(\bar{y}(n))}, k\bar{y}(n)\right) f'(x(1 - \beta_n)) \frac{(1 - \beta_y)(1 - \beta_n)}{1 + \sigma(\bar{y}(n))}$$
$$- c'(x(1 + \tau(n)))(1 + \tau(n)) = 0$$

which is satisfied by $x = n$ whenever n satisfies (30). Thus $\Psi(n) = \phi(n)$ whenever n satisfies (30). Furthermore, for all $n > 0$,

$$\Psi'(n) = -[\sigma'\bar{y}'f(1 - \beta_y)/(1 + \sigma)^2]U_1 + k\bar{y}'U_2 - \tau'xc' > 0$$

Therefore, $\phi(n_0) = \Psi(n_0) < \Psi(n_1) = \phi(n_1)$.

By (16) the rate of unemployment will be lower whenever employment is greater. But what happens to the total amount of unemployment $n\tau(n)$ as employment increases cannot be predicted.

10.5 COMPARISON TO THE KEYNESIAN ACCOUNT

The preceding example shows how transaction costs and the externality of thin markets might account for persistently high rates of unemployment. Under any of the boundary conditions discussed, or more generally whenever multiple equilibria exist, the economy could shift permanently from one equilibrium to another with a lower level of employment and a higher rate of unemployment. How such shifts might be initiated and what course they would take cannot be analyzed with this static model. But the model predicts that increases in unemployment can persist indefinitely.

The example has several Keynesian features, all of which are attributable to the fact that each agent is affected directly by the quantities $\bar{n}$ and $\bar{y}$ chosen by others. First, as we have seen, these direct effects are the reason why the example exhibits Keynesian 'effective' demand and supply functions for labor.

Second, in the case of multiple equilibria the model exhibits a reciprocal feedback between labor and output markets similar to that involved in the Keynesian multiplier process. Consider a shift from n_H to n_L in Figure 10.2. This can be described as leftward shifts in the 'constant-selling-cost' demand and supply functions to D'' and S''. The level of aggregate demand declines because of the decline in employment (from $\bar{y}(n_H)$ to $\bar{y}(n_L)$). Conversely, employment declines at least in part because of the leftward shift in labor demand, which is caused by the decline in aggregate demand $\bar{y}$.

The case of multiple equilibria highlights another Keynesian feature;[12] namely, that the example is consistent with no discernible cyclical pattern to real wages. It is obviously possible for the real wage to be the same in the two equilibria of Figure 10.2, in which case employment can fluctuate (between n_L and n_H) with no change in the real wage.

Another Keynesian feature is the result that not all gains from trade will be fully exploited in equilibrium. We saw that, as in the Keynesian account, firms would willingly hire more workers if they thought that aggregate demand would go up by as much as the net supply of output; but they have no incentive to do so because they take the level of aggregate demand as given.

Finally, it can be argued that the unemployment exhibited by the model is involuntary, as in Keynesian economics, despite the flexibility of wages. As Patinkin (1965: 313–15) has argued, 'involuntary' must mean chosen subject to an 'unusually severe' constraint. By this criterion the unemployment in our example is involuntary in two distinct senses. First, in addition to the 'usual' budget constraint workers are subject to a constraint requiring so much time to be spent in unemployment for every hour worked. Although each household is choosing to incur the amount $n\tau(\bar{n})$ of employment, this choice is not being made as a substitute for employment as it would be if there were only the budget constraint. In this sense all unemployment in the example is involuntary.

In principle there is, however, no reason to think of the constraints imposed by transaction costs as being any less 'usual' than the budget constraint. Still there is a sense in which at least some of the unemployment in a low-level equilibrium (n_L in Figure 10.2) fits Patinkin's criterion of involuntariness. For, in this equilibrium, the transaction-cost constraint could be regarded as 'unusually severe.' In order to sell n_L units of labor, the household is required to spend the amount $n_L\tau(n_L)$ in unemployment instead of the smaller amount $n_L\tau(n_H)$ that would be required to sell this much if the economy were at its high-level equilibrium. Thus the amount $n_L(\tau(n_L) - \tau(n_H))$ might be regarded as involuntary. If we interpret these increased costs along the lines suggested by Okun's analysis as the increased difficulty of finding potential employers who are actively hiring, then they are indeed what observers of labor markets in depression refer to when describing the rise in unemployment as involuntary.

The example thus shows that it is possible to develop an account of unemployment with several Keynesian features, based upon the externalities of transaction costs, without some of the shortcomings of the Keynesian account. Specifically, the example does not require an assumption of unrealistically pessimistic sales conjectures as a foundation for its concept of effective demand, and it avoids the dilemma of basing a theory of 'involuntary' unemployment on the refusal of the unemployed to work for less than the going wage.

This is not to say that the example provides a restatement of Keynesian economics. Among the Keynesian elements missing from it is any role of the marginal propensity to consume in the multiplier process. Nor is the model as it stands able to explain how changes in the level of aggregate demand, whether exogenous or induced by monetary or fiscal policy, could affect the level of output. In particular, money is neutral in the model, in the sense that all equilibria remain invariant in real terms to changes in M. Such changes might propel the economy from one real equilibrium to another, but the model as it stands has no dynamics with which to address the question. Nor is the model consistent with the Keynesian implication that, within some interval, any level of employment is consistent with equilibrium under the same tastes and technology. Furthermore the assumption of perfectly flexible wages and prices makes it inconsistent with Keynesian explanations of the slow adjustment of nominal wages and prices.

10.6 CONCLUSIONS

Quantity adjustments are often seen as substitutes for price-adjustments in Keynesian economics. If prices were perfectly flexible, transactors would not have to be informed of realized quantities in order to formulate mutually consistent trading plans; they would just need to observe prices that had been adjusted to their equilibrium values. If prices were inflexible transactors would also have to know realized quantities, which would have to be adjusted to their fixed-price equilibrium values. Patinkin (1976, especially pp. 65–66) has identified the essential contribution of Keynes's *General Theory* as the analysis of the equilibrating role of such quantity adjustments.

The example presented in this chapter suggests that if there are significant external economies operating through transaction costs, quantity and price adjustments may be complements, not substitutes.

Even with perfectly flexible prices, transactors must know the equilibrium values of realized quantities in order to formulate mutually consistent plans. The quantity signals to which they respond must satisfy the consistency conditions (25) and (26). Because many of the essential features of the Keynesian account of persistent unemployment follow from this need for quantity adjustment, they will be exhibited even in models with fully flexible prices.

None of this implies that perfect price flexibility is a good assumption, or that the issue of price flexibility has little quantitative importance for understanding fluctuations in unemployment. But it suggests that the issue of price flexibility is not crucial to many Keynesian results. When the transaction costs that are implicit in Keynesian analysis are made explicit, these results go through regardless of the degree of price flexibility. It also suggests, therefore, that from a Keynesian perspective a deeper understanding of unemployment will come from paying more attention to these transaction costs rather than attaching to 'sticky prices' the blame for all communication problems in the economy.[13]

Future research along these lines will obviously require a more explicit treatment of price formation, along with a more explicit account of the institutional arrangements underlying the cost of transacting.

NOTES

1. The model of Azariadis (1975) implies a fixed real wage rather than the (temporarily) fixed nominal wage of Keynesian theory. However, McCallum (1978) has pointed out that the important qualitative implications of a natural-rate model with rational expectations and the Lucas aggregate-supply schedule, from which presumably all Keynesian elements of market failure are absent, would go through unaffected even if nominal wages and prices were preset by contractual agreements.
2. This problem was pointed out by Patinkin (1965: 323, fn. 9).
3. See, however, the attempt by Iwai (1981) to develop a general theory of nonclearing markets upon a micro foundation that makes explicit the institutional restrictions according to which firms set their prices. See also Woglom's (1982) macro model, in which the failure of firms to engage in competitive price reductions whenever they face prices in excess of marginal cost is based upon Stiglitz's (1979) analysis of markets with costly communication. Woglom's analysis is similar to the conjectural equilibrium analysis of Hahn (1978), which provides another possible approach to resolving this difficulty.
4. How this can happen and why searching workers are affected by this change in recruiting behavior independently of its effects on wages is described graphically by Okun's analysis of 'No-Help-Wanted signs' (1981: 56–61).

5. Such arrangements are analyzed by Mortenson (1982b). As he points out, they are most likely to occur in markets intermediated by brokers who have dealt with each other in the past, either directly or through their common membership in some organized institution, and have thus had the occasion to reach some understanding prior to their current contacting activities. The brokers also need to have an expectation that their mutual dealings will continue in the future in order to have an incentive to adhere *ex post* to agreements that do not have the force of law.

6. The differences between this model and Diamond's are that: (a) Diamond's model has essentially one kind of agent and one kind of good, rather than firms and households and labor and output; (b) his production technology is described by an exogenous Poisson process rather than a usual short-run production function; (c) his model has no congestion externalities; (d) he describes unemployment as waiting for a production opportunity and employment as searching for a trading partner, which on the face of it seems to get it the wrong way around, whereas this model has more conventional descriptions; (e) his model is explicitly dynamic whereas this one is static; and (f) his model is more explicit about the institutional arrangements underlying transaction costs.

7. All functions are assumed to be smooth. Partial derivatives are denoted by subscripts. Unless otherwise indicated the domain of each function introduced consists of all strictly positive values of its arguments, and unqualified statements like (2) are understood to hold over the entire domain of the functions involved. All prices and quantities are understood to be strictly positive unless otherwise indicated.

8. This assumes away the important phenomenon of setup costs.

9. Such diseconomies are made explicit in the context of hiring labor, rather than selling output, by the analysis of Chapter 11 below.

10. Interpreting (14) as the rate of unemployment requires one to identify $\bar{n}$ as not only the quantity traded but also the quantity employed. This is required again when n is used as the argument of a production function. I am thus abstracting from one of the most important implications of Okun's 'Toll' model, namely that the costly trades in the labor market are new matches. Thus transaction costs would perhaps better be described as a function of the rate of increase in employment. This timeless model might be interpreted as describing stationary quantities chosen by households and firms who realize that more employment will, in the stationary state, imply more turnover (because, say, job separations occur at some exogenous proportional rate), and hence more new matches to be formed. Obviously a fuller treatment of time is required to analyze this issue.

11. In this sense the model is similar to the stochastic manipulable rationing model of Svensson (1980), in which the cost to an agent of trying to exceed his allocated ration is that he might be forced to make the proposed trade. The difference is that, in Svensson's model, the rationing process uses up no resources whereas in this model it is costly to propose trades. In both cases one ends up with an alternative concept of effective demand.

12. 'Keynesian' in the sense of the account described in Figure 10.1. Keynes's *General Theory* actually implies countercyclical wages.
13. Ostroy (1973) gives a graphic description of the communication problems that would remain even if an auctioneer costlessly computed and announced equilibrium prices.

11 · COSTLY SEARCH AND RECRUITING

11.1 INTRODUCTION

This chapter provides a simple model of market exchange, which, while stylized, possesses constructs that can plausibly be interpreted in terms of a typical labor market. The process of hiring a worker involves frictions, and both workers and firms may expend effort to overcome these frictions. All of the model's agents optimize. In this single framework, effects found by Diamond (1982b), Mortensen (1982a), Pissarides (1984), and Negishi (1976) exist. In addition, the model is simple enough that a wide variety of market structures and institutions may be incorporated into the model with varying degrees of difficulty. These include: take it or leave it wage offers, wages determined by the Raiffa bargaining solution, advertising, variation in the disutility of work, raiding by firms of other firms' workers, word-of-mouth information transfer, variety in initial information, and some assumptions about intermediaries in the job/worker matching process. A second use of the model involves comparative statics in a multiple equilibrium world. Limited comparative statics exercises can be performed in this model, despite an inherent indeterminacy, because the set of equilibria move in a uniform way.

Recent contributions by Peter Diamond (1982b, 1984a) have shown how search theory might be used to explain abnormally low levels of economic activity. The key to Diamond's analysis is an externality related to the common idea that trading is more costly the thinner the

The authors wish to thank, without implicating, John McMillan, Hans-Werner Sinn, an anonymous referee and reader, and the participants of the Western Ontario theory workshop for useful comments.

Written jointly with R. Preston McAfee. Reprinted from *International Economic Review* (1987), **28**, February, 89–107.

market. Specifically, the more activity there is on one side of the market, the lower the costs faced by those on the other side wanting to contact a trading partner. Thus the expectation of an abnormally low level of economic activity can lead to the expectation of thin markets and high contacting costs, and thus discourage people from engaging in trading activities, thereby fulfilling the original expectation. People might all be willing to trade at higher levels, but the fact that no one else is doing so dissuades each trader from communicating a willingness to do so himself.

Diamond's contributions suggest a possible explanation for the phenomenon of persistent large-scale unemployment. However, they are cast in terms of models that are hard to relate to every day labor-market phenomena.[1] The present chapter examines an explicit model of the labor market, in which Diamond's thin-markets externality is present. Both workers and firms actively engage in contacting activities; namely search and recruiting. Successful contacts result in lifetime wage contracts being signed. Workers find it equally costly to search whether they are currently employed or unemployed.

The thin-markets externality is embodied in the function that depicts the contacting institutions and technology. This function gives the rate of new hiring per unit of time in the economy as a function of the number of active participants on each side of the market and of their respective intensities of contacting activity. Rather than take this function as given we derive it from an explicit description of the underlying institutions and technology.

Under appropriate conditions there exist a continuum of stationary perfect-foresight equilibria, with different wages and rates of unemployment. Also, for almost each equilibrium wage rate there exist at least two equilibrium (natural) rates of unemployment; likewise for each equilibrium value of the typical firm's recruiting intensity. All equilibria are Pareto inefficient.

The nonuniqueness obtains for two separate reasons. The first reason has to do with externalities in the recruiting process. There is the thin-markets externality whereby more recruiting by firms raises the optimal rate of job search by unemployed workers, which in turn makes recruiting more attractive. But there is also an external diseconomy: more recruiting by firms will reduce the pool of unemployed from which the firms recruit, thereby reducing the incentive to recruit. This 'common-property' externality has been analyzed by Mortenson (1982a), Diamond (1982a) and Pissarides (1984). The two externalities interact so as to yield some equilibria with active search and recruiting and others with less active search and recruiting.

The second reason has to do with a fundamental indeterminacy of wages in the model. Because of contacting costs, all bargaining will be in a situation of bilateral monopoly. The opportunity cost of signing a contract will be less than the market wage to the worker, who would have to recommence costly search to get that wage elsewhere, and greater than the market wage to the firm, who would have to pay extra recruiting costs to find an alternative worker. The indeterminacy of the solution to the bilateral monopoly problem induces an indeterminacy in the equilibrium market wage.

The inefficiency of equilibria is similar to the inefficiency in Diamond's (1984a) model, in which the indeterminacy of bilateral monopoly is eliminated by imposing the Raiffa bargaining solution. The related work of Mortenson (1982a) suggests that there might be some alternative solution that will yield an efficient equilibrium. But our results imply that in the present model no such solution exists.[2]

11.2 THE MODEL

The economy is populated by a large number n of identical firms, located uniformly through space, and a continuum of identical workers. There are two tradable objects: goods and labor services; neither of which is storable. Firms produce goods using labor, with a constant average product, $f > 0$. Firms live forever and have no endowments other than their technology. Each worker dies according to a Poisson process with a death rate of $\delta > 0$; during his life he has an endowed flow of one unit of labor services per unit of time. The flow rate of new births at each instant is an exogenous constant $L > 0$.

Each worker is born at a random location in space. In order to trade he must first seek to contact a firm. Until such a contact has been made no communication is possible with a potential trading partner. Until he has made contact he travels through space at the speed α. He has no prior information concerning the location of firms, and thus chooses his direction at random. Alternatively, he can choose his speed of search but not his direction. As he searches he gains no new information that would help him better to direct his search, until he finally contacts a firm. Speed is costly. The rate of disutility from search is given by the function $c(\cdot)$, which satisfies:

$$c(0) = c'(0) = 0; c''(\alpha) > 0 \qquad \text{for all } \alpha \geqslant 0, \qquad c'(\alpha) \rightarrow \infty \text{ as } \alpha \rightarrow \infty$$

$$(1)$$

This concept of search emphasizes the importance of finding an appropriate match, which involves searching for the right trading partner rather than for the right price. Otherwise it would make little sense to suppose that the searching worker doesn't know the location of any firms. It is best to think of the model as applying to a representative 'subsector' of a bigger labor market, where 'false' contacts with trading partners of the wrong type are not explicitly represented.

A firm can also contribute to the contacting process, by increasing its visibility, or casting a recruiting net about itself. Consider Figure 11.1. The firms are represented by dots, and the circles represent their recruiting nets, the places from which they are visible. When a worker runs into a recruiting net, a contact has taken place. Firms can vary the size θ of their recruiting nets.[3] The cost of θ, measured in units of the consumption good, is given by the function $G(\cdot)$, which satisfies

$$G'(\theta) > 0, \, G''(\theta) > 0 \qquad \text{for all } \theta \geq 0 \tag{2}$$

This recruiting activity is the only means available to the firm for communicating with prospective trading partners. Because there is no way that a firm can send messages to a worker that has not yet fallen into its net it therefore cannot in any way influence the direction in which the workers search.

We shall restrict our attention to symmetric equilibria, in which all firms recruit at the same intensity θ and all households search at the same intensity α. In such an equilibrium each searching worker will find that the time elapsed before he contacts a firm is homogenous of degree -1 in α, because doubling the speed halves the time to reach any given goal. In addition, because firms are identical and uniformly located, the time to meeting the first firm follows a Poisson process, with rate proportional to α.

Each recruiting firm will find its flow of contacts is proportional to the size of its net θ, because the identical searchers are uniformly located in

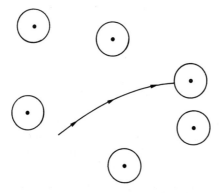

Figure 11.1 A contact occurs when a worker's path intersects a firm's net.

space.[4] In fact it will find this flow proportional to $a\theta u$, where u is the number of searching workers, because doubling any one of these variables doubles the rate of contacting. Furthermore, because there is a continuum of workers per firm, this flow is deterministic. In addition, the workers obtain contacts at a rate proportional to $an\theta$, and by choosing appropriate units for time and θ, we may make both constants of proportionality equal to unity.

It follows that the aggregate rate of contacting will be equal to the product $a\theta nu$. This contacting technology embodies the thin-markets external economy discussed earlier. The marginal product of the speed of search α in producing contacts is $n\theta u$, which is proportional to the recruiting intensity θ; likewise the marginal product of recruiting intensity is proportional to the speed of search. The technology also embodies the 'common-property' diseconomy. A reduction in the number of searchers u will lower the marginal product of the firms' recruiting intensity.[5]

11.3 WAGE BARGAINS

Each contact will result in the firm and worker agreeing to a lifetime contract according to which the worker will supply his services until he dies, at a negotiated wage payed in the form of goods. We shall suppose that all negotiations will result in a constant wage over the lifetime of the match, and that each contract results in the same wage $w > 0$. For simplicity we assume the household has no value of leisure.[6] Thus as long as w is less than f, there will be no quitting or firing once a contract has been made. This is because a worker's best alternative upon quitting would be to recommence a costly search for the same contract, and a firm who fires a worker will be giving up the flow of net marginal products $f - w > 0$ from that worker. Likewise there will be no on-the-job search because it is costly and cannot result in a higher wage.

As we have already mentioned, each wage negotiation takes place in a situation of bilateral monopoly. Furthermore we assume that each agent is risk-neutral,[7] with the same rate of time preference r. The total expected discounted utility to be divided by the bargainers is $f/(r + \delta)$. Any contract that resulted in no quitting or firing would yield this total. Any other contract would yield a strictly smaller total. If the two parties agree to a contract at the market wage there will be no quitting or firing and hence the agreement will be privately efficient. Thus, any wage in the interval $(0, f)$ will be privately efficient.

In the same situation there will be many alternative agreements that would also be privately efficient. Because of this it seems that other equilibria (with wages varying across contracts and with contracts specifying a time-varying wage) will probably exist. Because we get a surfeit of symmetric constant-wage equilibria we are not interested in these other equilibria.

11.4 THE WORKER'S DECISION PROBLEM

In the interest of simplicity we shall restrict attention to stationary equilibria, in which not only w but also α, u, and θ are constant. The individual worker makes no choices if he is employed. If he is unemployed his only decision is to choose the optimal speed α with which to look for a job. He makes this choice knowing the market value of w and θ.

If he makes a contact he will receive a contract worth $w/(r + \delta)$ in expected discounted utility. The probability of making such a contact over the next instant is $\alpha n\theta$. Thus V, the value of searching, must satisfy the equation

$$rV = \alpha n\theta \left(\frac{w}{r + \delta} - V \right) - \delta V - c(\alpha)$$

or

$$V = \frac{\alpha n\theta \left(\dfrac{w}{r + \delta} \right) - c(\alpha)}{r + \delta + \alpha n\theta} \tag{3}$$

Equation (3) has a straightforward interpretation. The value of a 'ticket to search' is the discounted value of the flow of expected net returns to the ticket. The flow is the expected payoff per unit time $\alpha n\theta w/(r + \delta)$ minus the cost $c(\alpha)$. The appropriate discount factor includes not just the rate of time preference but also the rate at which the ticket can be expected to 'depreciate' because of search termination due to death or contact, $\delta + \alpha n\theta$.

The searching worker chooses α to maximize (3). The first-order condition for this problem is:

$$c'(\alpha) = n\theta(w + c(\alpha))/(r + \delta + \alpha n\theta) \tag{4}$$

It follows easily from (1) that a unique optimum exists to this problem, which we denote by the function $\alpha^*(w, \theta)$, and that, '

(a) $\alpha^*(0, \theta) = \alpha^*(w, 0) = 0$ for all w, $\theta \geqslant 0$

(b) $\alpha^*(w, \theta) > 0$ for all w, $\theta > 0$

(c) $a_w^*(w, \theta) = 1 \Big/ \left(\dfrac{r + \delta}{n\theta} + a \right) c''(a) > 0 \qquad$ for all $w \geq 0, \theta > 0$

(d) $a_\theta^*(w, \theta) = c'(a)(r + \delta)/(r + \delta + an\theta)\theta c''(a) > 0$

$\qquad$ for all $w > 0, \theta \geq 0$

(e) $\lim\limits_{w \to \infty} a^*(w, \theta) = \infty \qquad$ for all $\theta > 0.$ \hfill (5)

The result (5d) shows one aspect of the thin-markets externality. An increase in recruiting intensity will induce workers to increase their speed of search even with no change in the wage.[8]

The number of searchers u is the number of unemployed young people who have yet to make their first contact. The flow of people into the pool of unemployed is the rate of birth of new workers L. The flow out is the flow of deaths δu plus the flow of new contacts: $an\theta u$. In a stationary equilibrium, the inflow and outflow must be equal. Therefore the number of unemployed searchers will be given by the function:

$$u = u^*(w, \theta) = L/(\delta + a^*(w, \theta)n\theta) \qquad (6)$$

11.5 THE FIRM'S DECISION PROBLEM

Each firm must decide its recruiting intensity knowing that there are u workers each searching at the rate a, and knowing that each contact will result in the wage w. The firm takes a as given, even though according to (4), a depends upon θ, because it conjectures that a unilateral increase in its own individual recruiting intensity would be too insignificant to influence household search behavior. Likewise it takes u as given. It takes w as given because it rationally anticipates that this wage is the best it can get from any negotiation.

The expected discounted utility attributable to the firm's current recruiting activities is $\theta au(f - w)/(r + \delta) - G(\theta)$ where θau is the flow of hiring and $(f - w)/(r + \delta)$ is the expected present value to the firm of each new hire. It chooses θ so as to maximize this amount; i.e. so that:

$$G'(\theta) - au\left(\frac{f - w}{r + \delta}\right) \geq 0, \text{ with equality unless } \theta = 0. \qquad (7)$$

It follows from (2) that for any $u > 0$ and any $w \in [0, f]$ there is a unique solution $\theta^*(a, u, w)$ to this problem. The dependence of θ^* on a again reflects the thin-market externality. According to (6) and (7), θ affects and is in turn affected by u. This is the common-property externality.

11.6 EQUILIBRIUM

An equilibrium is a symmetric, stationary situation in which each firm chooses the same $\theta > 0$, each household chooses the same $\alpha > 0$ and the level of u is constant. By substituting for α and u in (7) using (4) and (6) we can define it equivalently as a pair (w, θ), with $w \in (0, f)$ and $\theta > 0$, such that:

$$G'(\theta) = \sigma(w, \theta) \left(\frac{f - w}{r + \delta} \right) \tag{8}$$

where $\sigma(w, \theta)$ is the arrival rate of workers to a firm, per unit of θ:

$$\sigma(w, \theta) \equiv \alpha^*(w, \theta)u^*(w, \theta)$$
$$= \alpha^*(w, \theta)L/(\delta + \alpha^*(w, \theta)n\theta) \tag{9}$$

Equation (8) just equates the marginal cost and benefit from recruiting, where the marginal benefit itself depends upon the recruiting intensity through effects that are external to the firm choosing θ; i.e. through its effects on α^* and u^*.

It is easy to derive conditions under which an equilibrium will exist (see Howitt and McAfee, 1984a). In general, when one equilibrium exists a continuum exists, because it is defined as a pair of variables satisfying a single equation. This indeterminacy is a result of the bilateral monopoly indeterminacy.[9]

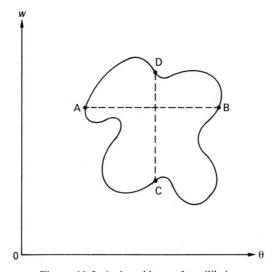

Figure 11.2 A closed loop of equilibria.

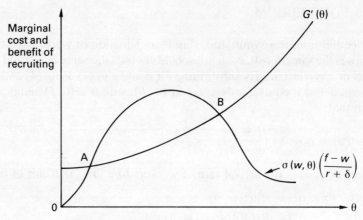

Figure 11.3 Multiple equilibrium values of θ.

Furthermore, the set of equilibria will generally consist of closed loops, as in Figure 11.2, because for every equilibrium with a given wage there will exist another with the same wage. Also, for every equilibrium with a given recruiting intensity there will generally exist another with the same recruiting intensity.

The reason for these closed loops is the interaction of the externalities. As Figure 11.3 illustrates, when θ falls towards zero so does the marginal benefit from recruiting, because the fall in θ induces households to slow down their search through the thin-market externality, which makes the arrival rate σ fall towards zero (recall (5a) and (9)). Because of (2) the marginal cost of recruiting does not fall all the way to zero. Therefore for any given w and small enough θ, marginal cost will exceed marginal benefit. But the same will be true for large enough θ, because as θ goes to infinity the common-property external diseconomy makes the number of searchers and hence the arrival rate σ fall to zero (note that (5b) and (9) imply $\sigma < L/n\theta$). Thus if marginal benefit equals marginal cost for some (w, θ) it will generally do so for at least one other θ and the same w. As in Diamond's models there will be equilibria with a lot of activity (θ) and others with not so much.[10]

Likewise, as Figure 11.4 shows, if we hold θ fixed then the marginal benefit will fall below the marginal cost for wage rates that are too high, or too low. High wages reduce the incentive to hire for obvious reasons. Low wages reduce it because they discourage search, and that reduces the arrival rate σ.

Note that the result of multiple values of θ for a given w depends upon our assumption that $G'(0) > 0$. This assumption could easily be replaced with others. For example, if $G'(0) = 0$ but $G''(0)$ is greater than

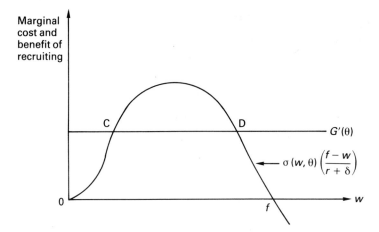

Figure 11.4 Multiple equilibrium values of w.

$$\sigma_\theta(w,\, \theta) \left(\frac{f-w}{r+\delta}\right)$$

then the same reasoning goes through. Alternatively, as in an earlier version of the paper (1984a) we could assume that there is a distribution of entry costs across households that makes the participation rate fall continuously to zero as θ falls to a positive lower limit $\bar{\theta}$ at which the optimized value of V has fallen to equal the lowest entry cost. At that point, the arrival rate of searchers to a firm will fall to zero, and hence the marginal benefit of recruiting will fall to zero.

The indeterminacy of equilibrium implies an indeterminacy of the rate of unemployment. The steady-state labor force is L/δ. Thus, the rate of unemployment is $u^*(w,\, \theta)\delta/L$, which is decreasing in both w and θ. As you move up an upward-sloping part of the closed loop the rate of unemployment will be continuously decreasing.

11.7 PARETO INEFFICIENCY OF EQUILIBRIA

Because of the externalities, equilibria are inefficient. This can be shown in two different senses. First, consider as welfare criteria the expected utility of the unborn worker and the expected discounted profits of each firm. It follows from (3) and (4) that the former equals:

$$V^*(w,\, \theta) = \frac{1}{r+\delta} \int_0^{a^*(w,\theta)} xc''(x)\mathrm{d}x$$

which is increasing in w and θ. The latter is

$$[(f - w)(L/\delta - u^*(w, \theta))/n - G(\theta)]/r$$

where $L/\delta - u^*(w, \theta)$ is total employment (labor force minus those employed). By (9), total employment also equals $n\theta\sigma(w, \theta)/\delta$. Thus by (8), the firm's expected profits can also be expressed as:

$$W^*(\theta) = [(r + \delta)\theta G'(\theta)/\delta - G(\theta)]/r$$

which, by (2) is a strictly increasing function of θ.

It follows that some equilibria Pareto-dominate others in terms of these criteria. Specifically, as you move to equilibria with higher w and/or higher θ, expected utility of workers goes up and that of firms does not go down.

This concept of inefficiency ignores any transitional gains or losses in moving from one stationary state to another. But the following argument shows that even taking these dynamic considerations into account, all equilibria are inefficient.

Consider the social problem of maximizing the discounted sum of total utility of all workers and firms:

$$\max_{\{\alpha,\theta,u\}} \int_0^\infty e^{-rt}\{f(L/\delta - u) - uc(\alpha) - nG(\theta)\}dt$$

subject to $\dot{u} = L - (\delta + \alpha n\theta)u$

given an initial value of unemployment. The necessary conditions to this problem are:

$$-uc'(\alpha) - \theta nu\lambda = 0$$
$$-nG'(\theta) - \alpha nu\lambda = 0$$
$$\dot{\lambda} = r\lambda + (f + c(\alpha)) + (\delta + \alpha n\theta)\lambda$$

Thus if u, α, θ provide a stationary solution to the problem they must satisfy:

$$c'(\alpha) = \theta n(f + c(\alpha))/(r + \delta + \alpha n\theta) \tag{10}$$

$$G'(\theta) = \alpha u(f + c(\alpha))/(r + \delta + \alpha n\theta) \tag{11}$$

Comparison of (10) and (4) reveals that the equilibrium can coincide with this stationary social optimum only if $w = f$. But, by the private optimality condition (7) and condition (2) the equilibrium must have $w < f$. Thus there is no wage compatible with an equilibrium that maximizes the sum of discounted utilities. In this sense, all equilibria are Pareto-inefficient.

The economic interpretation of this last result is straightforward. The efficient speed of search is one that equates the marginal cost $c'(\alpha)$ to the marginal social benefit. The latter is the marginal product of α in producing contacts, $n\theta$, times the social value of a contact. But the only way to induce a household to search that intensively is to promise him the entire social value f, if he makes a contact, i.e. to pay him a wage equal to his marginal product. But if firms must pay a wage equal to the marginal product there is no gain to recruiting and hence they will not recruit.

Mortenson (1982a) found that there was an efficient wage in a related model. The key difference in this model preventing the existence of such a wage is that the contacting rate $\alpha n\theta u$ exhibits increasing returns in the contacting intensities α and θ, whereas in Mortenson's model there were constant returns in the intensities α and θ. An efficient wage would be one that paid contacting activities at rates equal to their respective marginal value products. With constant returns such payments would be possible. But with increasing returns they would more than exhaust the economy's total output.

11.8 COMPARATIVE STATICS RESULTS

Even with all this indeterminacy our model yields comparative statics predictions if we are willing to treat the wage and recruiting intensity as exogenous variables. Thus, for example, (6) implies that a *ceteris paribus* increase in w or θ will reduce the equilibrium number unemployed. By the same token such a change will reduce the equilibrium rate of unemployment, which is just $u^*(w, \theta)\delta/L$, and will also reduce the equilibrium value of the average duration of unemployment, which is just $1/(\alpha^*(w, \theta)n\theta + \delta)$, and increase the equilibrium level of employment $L/\delta - u^*(w, \theta)$. The admissibility of such *ceteris paribus* changes is guaranteed by our earlier result that equilibria come in closed loops, although they must generally be discrete changes. Analogous results for continuous variations in w and θ can be derived under the assumption that w and θ vary together. Thus as w and θ rise together along an upward-sloping part of a closed loop, with no other exogenous variable changing, the equilibrium values of the number unemployed, the rate of unemployment and the duration of unemployment will all decrease while equilibrium employment increases.

Comparative-statics effects of changes in other exogenous variables can be derived in the following way. An increase in, say, the marginal product of labor, will cause each closed loop of equilibria to expand outward. This can be seen from Figures 11.3 and 11.4. The rise in f will shift the marginal benefit curve up in both diagrams, causing the larger value of θ (resp. w) to increase and the smaller one to decrease. Suppose we hold w fixed. Then whether the equilibrium recruiting intensity increases or decreases depends upon which side of the loop the equilibrium is on.

Assume that:

$$\frac{\alpha c''(\alpha)}{c'(\alpha)} \cdot \frac{\theta G''(\theta)}{G'(\theta)} > 1 \qquad \text{for all } \theta, \alpha \qquad (12)$$

Condition (12) asserts that the increasing returns in contacting that come about from the fact that the rate of contacting is proportional to $\alpha\theta$ are outweighed by the increasing marginal cost of producing the intensities α and θ, in the sense that the solution to the social welfare-maximization problem of the preceding section does not involve making α and θ infinite for an instant. More precisely, (12) is easily seen to be a necessary second-order condition for α and θ to provide an interior maximum to the Hamiltonian of that problem.

Under condition (12) our earlier paper (1984a) shows that all points on the left-hand face of the closed loop are unstable. Intuitively this is because at point A in Figures 11.2 and 11.3 an increase in θ by all other firms would induce a firm to raise its own θ by even more. Thus if we restrict attention to stable equilibria the rise in f can be seen to cause a rise in the equilibrium value of θ. Because of this and our previous comparative-statics results it also causes a decrease in the equilibrium number of unemployed.

By similar reasoning it can be shown that the same effects on θ and u would be produced by a reduction in the marginal cost of recruiting; i.e. by a shift from the cost function $G(\theta)$ to the function $\hat{G}(\theta) = \gamma G(\theta)$ where $0 < \gamma < 1$. Likewise for an analogously defined reduction in the marginal cost of search, which can be shown to cause an increase in $\alpha^*(w, \theta)$ for given values of (w, θ) and thus, according to (9), shifts the marginal benefit curve up in Figure 11.3. It follows immediately that any of these changes would also decrease the equilibrium rate and duration of unemployment and increase equilibrium employment.

None of these results is surprising or difficult to derive. Nevertheless, they show that the model is capable of providing a simple account of several important labor-market variables while yielding falsifiable implications that are not obviously false.

11.9 VARYING THE ASSUMPTIONS

In this section, we consider how our results would be affected by altering some key assumptions. First, we consider applying different solution concepts to the bilateral monopoly situation faced by each matched pair. The concept we consider initially is the Raiffa bargaining solution used by Diamond (1984a), which splits the gains from trade evenly between the two parties. With this solution, workers and firms will still take the equilibrium wage as given when choosing their contacting intensities; thus equilibria will still have to solve the condition (8) defining the closed loops. But the requirement that the wage split the gains from trade evenly will impose a second condition on w and θ.

The gain to the worker is the difference between the expected discounted value of his lifetime wage $w/(r + \delta)$ and the value of recommencing search at the optimal rate. By using the first-order condition (4) to substitute for $c(\alpha)$ in (3) we can write this difference as $c'(\alpha^*(w, \theta))/n\theta$. The gain to the firm is $(f - w)/(r + \delta)$. The condition that these two gains be equal describes a positively sloped arc in (w, θ) space. Equilibria will consist of the points of intersection of this arc with the closed loops.

Thus the Raiffa solution generally reduces our continuum of equilibria to a discrete set. There will generally be an even number of equilibria, as in our earlier model with any fixed wage. Our previous welfare and comparative-statics results will still apply. Furthermore if we generalize the solution to allow the gains to be split in fixed proportions other than one to one, the result will be qualitatively the same. As we vary the proportion going to the workers from zero to one, the upward-sloping arc will vary continuously and the set of equilibria will trace out the original closed loops.

One complication is added by these solution concepts, however; workers might engage in on-the-job search, knowing that they can attract a higher wage from the second firm they contact. This is because a worker's best alternative to concluding a bargain will be better in his second contact than it was in his first; in the second contact he can always return to working at the market wage with no additional search cost. Unless this is ruled out by supposing, for example, that there is no way that a second-time searcher can distinguish himself in the bargaining process from a first-time searcher, or that search is more costly on the job than off, our single-wage equilibria are no longer equilibria under one of these bargaining solutions. Of course, a policy by the firm of matching best offers would further encourage this on-the-job search.

Another solution to the bargaining problem is that firms might make take-it-or-leave-it wage offers to newly contacted workers. Under the assumption that all offers must take the form of a constant lifetime wage, workers will search as before, and the first-order condition (7) will still govern the firm's choice of θ. Thus equation (8) will still have to be satisfied in equilibrium. But now the market wage will also have to satisfy the condition that the typical firm not find it optimal to offer some other wage.

Suppose a firm decides to offer Δ below the market wage. Then its wage bill will be reduced. But its newly hired workers will engage in on-the-job search, at the rate $\alpha^*(\Delta, \theta)$, and hence will quit at the rate $\alpha^*(\Delta, \theta)n\theta$ at which they encounter other firms. Workers will continue to arrive at the same rate $\sigma(w, \theta)$ as before because the individual firm's wage offers cannot be made until a worker has been contacted, by which time it is too late to influence his search behavior.

If a firm decides to offer above the market wage the only effect on its profits will be to raise its wage bill. The quit rate of its employees will not be affected because that is already zero.

Thus the firm's profits from its current recruiting activities will be:

$$\begin{cases} \theta\sigma(w, \theta)(f - w + \Delta)/(r + \delta + \alpha^*(\Delta, \theta)n\theta) - G(\theta) & \text{if } 0 \leq \Delta \leq w \\ \theta\sigma(w, \theta)(f - w + \Delta)/(r + \delta) - G(\theta) & \text{if } \Delta < 0 \end{cases} \tag{13}$$

It follows from (5c) that this function always has a kink at $\Delta = 0$, reflecting the asymmetric reaction of quits to an increase or decrease in the wage offer. Furthermore, it is strictly increasing for $\Delta \leq 0$. Thus the firm will never offer above the market wage.

Assume that $c'''(\alpha) \geq 0$ for all $\alpha \geq 0$. Then it can be shown using (5) that the profit function (13) is convex in Δ on the interval $[0, w]$. Thus the firm will choose either $\Delta = 0$ or $\Delta = w$, and the further condition on the market wage is that:

$$\frac{f - w}{r + \delta} \geq \frac{f}{r + \delta + \alpha^*(w, \theta)n\theta} \tag{14}$$

This condition requires (w, θ) to lie to the right of an arc that goes from $(0, 0)$ to (∞, f) with a strictly increasing wage (see Figure 11.5). Equilibria consist of the intersection of this set with the closed loops. If any exist there will generally be a continuum. Again, our previous welfare and comparative-statics results will go through.

Equilibrium can be shown to exist under this solution concept if, for example, the marginal product of labor is large enough (Howitt and McAfee, 1984a). However, this existence is precarious. For if (1) were modified to assert that $c'(0) > 0$ no equilibrium could exist. It would always pay a firm to offer below the market wage because a small differential will not induce on-the-job search.[11] Likewise, even *if* $c'(0) = 0$ no equilibrium would exist if firms were allowed to offer non-constant wage profiles. It would pay a firm to offer a profile of zero for an initial period of length ε then equal to the market profile with a fixed delay of ε.

The gain to the firm in the form of a reduced wage bill per new recruit would be of the order ε. But the cost would be of the order ε^2 because the new recruits would search at a slow speed for a short time. Thus some such undercutting of the market profile would always be optimal.[12]

We now consider the question of how robust our results are to modifications that would relax the very severe limitations we have imposed on agents' ability to communicate with one another.

It seems that a limited form of price advertising could be introduced at little cost. Consider the take-it-or-leave-it version of the model. Suppose that a firm that offers above the market wage (i.e. a negative Δ) finds it easier to cast a net of given size because news of the extraordinary wage travels by word of mouth. Specifically, let the recruiting cost be given by the convex function $G(\Delta, \theta)$, with $G_1, G_2 > 0$. Then equilibria will still have to solve equation (8) with $G_2(0, \theta)$ replacing $G'(\theta)$, and inequality (14). But they will also have to satisfy the condition that lowering Δ below zero cannot raise the firm's profits. By the convexity of G this condition is that:

$$G_1(0, \theta) \leq \frac{\sigma(w, \theta)\theta}{r + \delta}$$

Suppose that increasing the net size reduces the marginal cost of lowering the wage; i.e. that $G_{12} < 0$. Then solutions to this inequality are describable as the set of points lying to the left of a downward-sloping line. As shown in Figure 11.5 this means that equilibria, if they exist, still occur in continua, with no substantive change in our results. Economically, some indeterminacy remains in this model because

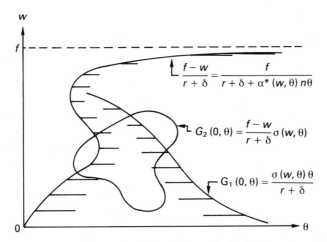

Figure 11.5 Equilibria with wage advertising.

allowing advertising does not remove the asymmetric quitting behavior that kinks the profit function. This kink produces indeterminacy of the equilibrium wage for the same reason as in the models of Negishi (1976) and Woglom (1982).

It might also seem reasonable to allow agents to begin life with more information than they have here; to know the location, for example, of at least some firms. In this case each searcher would head straight for the nearest known firm, at a speed that is optimal given the known wage, the known distance to the firm, and the known probability of encountering a closer firm on the way. One equilibrium in this model would be $(\theta, w) = (0, f)$. The probability of encountering an unknown firm would be zero. Households would travel at a speed that was socially optimal for the closest known firm, given that $\theta = 0$. But if each worker knew few enough locations this equilibrium would not be efficient; it would be socially worthwhile to have some recruiting to catch workers headed to more distant firms. Likewise, unless households began by knowing all the locations the externalities that made equilibria in our earlier model come in closed loops would still exist. A bigger θ would induce faster search, which would tend to make recruiting more profitable up to some point, but would also deplete the stock of searchers and therefore tend to make recruiting less profitable. Likewise the same bilateral monopoly problem would continue to make the equilibrium indeterminate.

The implication of our model that all search is pointless if $\theta = 0$ seems overly restrictive. Surely a diligent enough job searcher should be able to communicate an offer to a firm that is not actively in the market. This possibility could be allowed for by setting $G(\theta) = 0$ for all θ in some interval $[0, \bar{\theta}]$. Thus all firms would always have a net size of at least $\bar{\theta}$, and a searcher's probability of encountering a firm would never fall to zero unless he stopped moving. All that this would affect in our analysis is the result that at least two equilibrium values of θ will exist for each equilibrium w. As Figure 11.3 shows that result would no longer follow. But it is equally clear from Figure 11.3 that the result would still be possible; it would just require the marginal benefit and cost curves to intertwine in the region where marginal benefit was increasing. Furthermore, the result would follow by necessity if we also added the assumption discussed earlier that there is a distribution of participation costs with a positive lower bound. For at least some values of the wage, the value $\bar{\theta}$ at which the optimized value of search equals the lowest participation cost would be greater than $\bar{\theta}$, and hence the marginal benefit curve would first intersect $G'(\theta)$ from below in Figure 11.3, yielding more than one equilibrium θ.

Another implication that ought to be relaxed is that of no raiding.

Surely it ought to be less costly for a firm to recruit by sending messages to the employees of other firms, whose locations can be identified, than by sending them aimlessly into space. If we allowed raiding that was costless to the raiding firm it seems that equilibrium would no longer exist in our model. No firm would cast a recruiting net. Instead they would send offers to employees of existing firms. The only equilibrium offer would be a wage equal to the marginal product. But with no recruiting nets no contacts would ever get made.

However, as long as raiding were costly we would get the same equilibria as before, provided that we allowed firms to adopt a policy of matching any offers their employees received from a raiding firm (which they would find optimal to do) and provided that in the case of a matched offer the employee always decided to remain. Under these assumptions no raiding would ever be attempted, because it would produce positive costs and no benefits.

A final restrictive assumption is that of no intermediaries. If everyone could costlessly communicate with one of a number of competitive intermediaries then the model would have no indeterminacy and no externalities, because people would, in effect, be costlessly communicating with one another, and all remaining costs of hiring would be internalized by the intermediaries. What would happen with intermediaries that were costly to find, and who themselves had to advertise their location, would require a more complicated model to deal with. But as long as the communication costs remained, so would the basis for our major results; the contacting intensities of the intermediaries would interact with those of the primary agents in the same qualitative manner as do the search and recruiting intensities in the present model.

Intermediation could solve the externalities problems if there were private ownership of the space through which workers search and firms broadcast. For example, a single owner could charge an entry fee to firms and households. These entry fees could be set high enough to appropriate all the economy's surplus. In order to maximize its profit the intermediary would promise households a rebate of $(f - w)/(r + \delta)$ for having found a job, and it would rebate to firms the amount

$$\frac{c'(\hat{\alpha})}{n\hat{\theta}} - \frac{f}{r + \delta}$$

for each hire, where $\hat{\alpha}$ and $\hat{\theta}$ are the socially optimal values that satisfy (10) and (11). This scheme would induce workers and firms to set $\alpha = \hat{\alpha}$ and $\theta = \hat{\theta}$, resulting in a unique, socially optimal outcome.

Of course the problem with such schemes is that they would require a very large firm with a great deal of information to act as the intermediary. Such a large firm might be uneconomical for reasons of internal diseconomies. It would also be subject to misrepresentation of contacting activities by the other firms and households. And if there were differences across agents it would also be subject to misrepresentation of the agent-specific parameters that enter the fee/rebate schedule. Our own view is that one can reasonably model the labor market on the assumption that this kind of centralized organization is prohibitively costly.

11.10 CONCLUSION

According to Leijonhufvud (1968), persistent, large-scale unemployment is best understood as a communication failure. Sellers who receive few messages of a willingness to buy will themselves be discouraged from communicating a willingness to buy, in a self-reinforcing manner. Leijonhufvud argued that these failures could not be accounted for in conventional competitive equilibrium theory where the auctioneer handled all communications problems costlessly. Diamond's recent work promises a method for making this view operational. In this chapter we have tried to show that the method can be applied to models in which there are identifiable counterparts to real-world labor-market phenomena. Multiple equilibria exist with different rates of unemployment. Both high and low unemployment rates can exist at the same real wage rate for reasons that are related to the communication failures analyzed by Leijonhufvud; the expectation of a low level of labor-market communication can be self-fulfilling. Although barriers to communication are at the heart of these results we have argued that the specific barriers assumed in the present chapter could be relaxed considerably without changing the essential message of the analysis.

NOTES

1. More specifically: (a) production, instead of using hired inputs through a continuous production function, consists of the random arrival at discrete points in time of opportunities to produce one unit of output, at a random subjective cost to the agent; (b) each agent's ability to store goods is limited to exactly one unit, which requires him to forgo any possibility of producing while attempting to sell goods that have already been produced; (c) no agent can attempt to sell goods unless he has already produced them, which, in combination with (b) comes close to an assumption that many have argued discredits search theory as a vehicle for explaining unemployment, namely that work and job search are mutually exclusive activities; (d) it isn't clear which activity in the model ought to be interpreted as unemployment

and which as employment. (Diamond interprets waiting for a production opportunity as unemployment, whereas this kind of waiting is presumably a necessary input into production and ought to be interpreted as employment. The activity of looking for a trading partner seems to us analogous to job search, but he calls it employment.); and (e) after each act of production search begins anew with no possibility of recalling the previous trading partner, in contrast to the long-term bilateral relationships typical of real-world labor markets.

2. Pissarides (1984) also finds that no efficient solution exists in a related model, although his efficiency criterion is a steady-state criterion that ignores costs of transitions. His model embodies a more general matching technology than the present study, but lacks the treatment of multiple equilibria.

3. For an informal example, consider workers travelling on a maze of roads. Firms place signs around, informing workers of job opportunities at the firm. If the workers travel twice as fast, they will double the number of signs they see on average. Alternatively, if the firms double the number of signs posted, this will double the number of people seeing their sign. The 're-cruiting net,' θ, is the proportion of the roads from which a sign is visible, while the search rate, a, is the speed searchers travel. Observe that one can increase θ either by erecting more signs, or by placing them up higher.

4. This assumes implicitly that the firms are far enough apart that their nets do not overlap. This assumption of sparsely located firms is consistent with our emphasis on the difficulties of contacting. If it were relaxed then the model would have to deal with a congestion externality, as one firm's increase in θ would, beyond some point, reduce the hiring by other firms whose area it was invading. Such externalities would obviously be important for the present analysis. However, as we have observed, there is already a dynamic version of that externality (the common-property externality) in the present model, which becomes increasingly important as θ increases. (More specifically, that externality is the reason why the marginal benefit of recruiting, as shown in Figure 11.3, eventually falls below the marginal cost.)

5. There are other, potentially important, labor-market externalities that we do not consider. For example, an increase in the flow of applicants to a firm with given net size might increase his costs by making him have to sort through more applications. Likewise, an increase in the flow of applicants might raise the cost to any given applicant by making him wait longer in line. We rule out these phenomena by assuming that all transaction costs are those implied by the spatial considerations that we wish to focus on. Once a contact has been made there are no further transaction costs.

6. This implies that the search cost c is an effort cost, not a forgone leisure cost. Our earlier (1984a) paper deals with the case where leisure is valuable and must be given up entirely if the worker wishes either to search or to work; the main results of that paper were the same as of the present chapter with the exception that workers faced a nontrivial decision whether or not to enter the labor force.

7. That is, his utility is linear in the flow of real income at each date.

Assumption (1) implies that a worker is averse to risk in the speed of search, but search is a bygone when a contract is being negotiated.

8. To verify (5e) note that if $w \rightarrow \infty$ and α remains finite then the right-hand side of (4) will eventually exceed the left-hand side.

9. This indeterminacy might be taken to imply nothing more than that we have an incompletely specified model. We do, however, have a complete description of tastes and technology, the classical determinants of economic variables. Thus, one can also take our indeterminacy to imply that the classical determinants are not sufficient in a world such as the one we have described. In Section 11.8 below we discuss how to eliminate the indeterminacy by imposing various bargaining solutions. Even without imposing such a solution we show in Section 11.7 how our 'incomplete' model yields meaningful comparative-statics propositions.

10. One might wonder how the economy could get started from an initial position of zero employment, since no firm will find it worthwhile to start recruiting until others start recruiting. Actually this positive interdependence of recruiting decisions poses a problem no matter what the initial position. Even if the economy had been forever in a stationary equilibrium with positive employment, if everyone suddenly formed the belief that θ would equal zero from now on, that would be a self-fulfilling belief. No worker would search, no firm would recruit, and employment would fall to zero through attrition at the rate δ. This alerts us to the fact that starting at any given initial employment level there may be more than one perfect-foresight equilibrium path. Starting from a nondegenerate stationary equilibrium one such path stays there and another converges on zero employment. There is more than one set of self-fulfilling beliefs. But by the same token if we start at zero employment there will generally exist paths that converge to a 'high-level' equilibrium. Remember that starting with low employment is itself an inducement to high recruiting because it lowers the cost of hiring. The dynamic version of this model presented in our earlier (1984a) paper shows that if the wage is fixed then there will generally exist an equilibrium path starting at zero employment, along which θ *exceeds* the highest level stationary equilibrium value $\hat{\theta}$ associated with the fixed wage, and falls asymptotically to $\hat{\theta}$ as employment rises to its stationary value. The phenomenon of multiple stationary solutions in similar models is examined more fully in chapter 13 below.

11. A similar argument for nonexistence has been proposed by Stiglitz (1979).

12. A formal demonstration of this result is given by Howitt and McAfee (1984a).

12 · BUSINESS CYCLES WITH COSTLY SEARCH AND RECRUITING

12.1 INTRODUCTION

Macroeconomic theories are distinguished to a large extent by their different treatments of labor markets. New Classical theories and real business-cycle theories model them as rapidly clearing auction markets, and seek to explain fluctuations in employment as movements along a supply-of-labor schedule. Keynesian theories assume that wages are slow to clear labor markets, so that fluctuations in employment are movements off the supply curve.

Both of these approaches have been subject to well-known criticisms. New Classical theories require what many regard as an implausibly large elasticity of labor supply (or of intertemporal substitution of labor) in order to be consistent with the relatively small movements of real wages over the business cycle. They also cannot explain the apparently involuntary character of unemployment.

The Keynesian approach has been criticized by Barro (1979) and others for failing to explain clearly why potential gains from trade remain unexploited. The logical underpinnings of wage (price)-setting behavior are unclear, but from what we know of them, they do not imply that quantities will be demand determined as in Keynesian economics. They also seem to imply stickiness of relative prices, whereas

An earlier version of this paper was originally presented at a conference on macroeconomics at McMaster University in October 1983. Useful comments and suggestions were received from the participants there, as well as from Olivier Blanchard, John Burbidge, Joel Fried, David Laidler, Preston McAfee, Hans–Werner Sinn, Aman Ullah, Michael Veall, and two anonymous referees.

Reprinted from *Quarterly Journal of Economics* (1988), **103**, February, 147–65.

Keynesian economics postulates stickiness of nominal prices. Further, in order to account for persistent unemployment, the Keynesian approach must explain why potential workers without contracts do not succeed in underbidding those with contracts, whereas contract theory assumes that everyone who wants one always has a contract.

Elsewhere (Chapter 10 above) I have argued that many of the conclusions of Keynesian economics can be derived without having to rely upon sticky wages or prices, by recognizing explicitly the high cost of transacting in some markets, the factor stressed by such writers as Leijonhufvud (1968), Okun (1981), and Laidler (1982), as well as the external economy of scale implicit in the notion that trading is more costly the thinner the market, an idea embodied in the recent contribution of Peter Diamond (1982b). Preston McAfee and I (Chapter 11 above) have developed an explicit model of labor markets along these lines with costly job search and recruiting, in which there exists a continuum of natural rates of unemployment.

The present chapter develops a model of the business cycle based upon a simplified version of the Howitt–McAfee model, rather than upon clearing labor markets or sticky wages. One purpose of the model is to suggest by example that this alternative conception of labor markets may permit a business-cycle theory that avoids some of the shortcomings of standard approaches. In particular, the model exhibits persistent involuntary unemployment, even though expectations are rational, no nominal wage or price rigidity exists, and no privately attainable gains from trade are left unexploited. It also allows output and employment to fluctuate with only small movements in aggregate real wages, but without invoking an implausibly large elasticity of labor supply. Indeed the household sector is specified in such a way that the usual measure of labor supply elasticity is zero.

Another purpose of the model is to argue by example that one cannot infer from the ability or inability of New Classical business-cycle models to account for cyclical co-movements in aggregate output and price time series anything about the welfare propositions often associated with such models. In particular, a linear approximation to the present model yields a relationship between output and price surprises identical to the Lucas (1973) aggregate-supply relationship except for a time delay. Such a relationship is derived by Sargent (1979, ch. 16) from a model in which observed equilibria would be Pareto optimal except for agents' inability to observe the current money supply. But in the present model equilibria would generally not be optimal, because of externalities in the labor market.

A third purpose of the model is to show how this approach to labor markets can yield implications concerning the aggregate effects of relative price shocks. The externalities in the labor market imply a nonlinearity in the response of employment in each sector to perceived changes in relative output prices. It is shown that because of this nonlinearity an increase in either the variability or persistence of relative price shocks causes both an increase in the natural rate of unemployment and an increase in the initial impact upon employment of a monetary shock.

In order to focus upon the effects of costs of trading in labor markets, this chapter makes a number of simplifying assumptions that severely limit the ability of agents to communicate offers to buy and sell labor. For the same reason, and to facilitate comparison with New Classical models, the specification of output markets follows closely the elementary treatment of Lucas (1973). The model is thus intended as no more than an example of the kind of results that can follow from this alternative conception of labor markets. In particular, the fact that it embodies (to a linear approximation) a Lucas aggregate-supply relationship leaves it open to the criticism that the price-surprise mechanism at the heart of that relationship is too weak to account for the observed cyclical variability of output. It is clear, however, that many of the insights of the present chapter can be incorporated into richer models with more complex patterns of labor-market interaction and with alternative mechanisms and features such as nominal contracts, intertemporal substitution, or productivity shocks to account for output fluctuations.[1]

12.2 BASICS

There are J sectors in the economy, each with F identical firms and L identical workers. Firms remain always in the same sector. Each worker is temporarily attached to one sector, but is constantly subject to exogenous relocation (no voluntary mobility is permitted). The probability that a worker will be relocated to a randomly chosen sector during the current period is a constant, $\delta \in (0, 1)$. Relocations always leave an equal number of workers remaining in each sector.[2]

Trading in the labor market of each sector is organized around a set of contact points distributed through space. Firms that wish to hire leave offers at these points, and workers wishing an offer must sample the points to find one. To emphasize the difficulty of finding a job, assume that a worker can sample only one point per period, and the only situation in which it is technically feasible for a worker and firm to communicate is that in which the worker has sampled a point at which the firm has left an offer that period. Once such a contact has been made, the two parties can bargain over a contingent real-wage contract.

It is possible for the worker to remain working for the firm he has contacted, with no additional contacting activities required by either side, until he is relocated. Indeed in the equilibrium described below he will choose to remain.

Output of each sector is sold in an auction market that clears in the usual Walrasian sense. Each period the quantity supplied is determined by the amount of employment, which has already been determined by previous contacting activities. Demand is determined by an exogenous stochastic process. As buyer of output, each agent can observe all output prices. But as buyer or seller or labor, he can observe only the nominal price of his own sector's output. This gives rise to the familiar Lucas signal-extraction problem that permits unanticipated monetary disturbances to have real effects.

The marginal cost of hiring by a firm in sector j at date t depends positively on the number of workers hired h_t^j, as in other dynamic factor-demand models. It also depends negatively upon the number of workers searching for a job, because the more searchers there are, the fewer offers the firm will have to make to contact another worker.[3] The number of searchers in turn equals the number unemployed in that sector, U_t^j, because the employed have no incentive to search and face a positive cost of search, whereas this cost is assumed to be small enough that all the unemployed choose to search.

Specifically, the expected number of contacts that a firm will make is equal to the fraction of all contact points at which it has left an offer, multiplied by the number of searchers who are each sampling one contact point. Thus, a firm that expects h_t^j workers must leave offers at the fraction h_t^j/U_t^j of all contact points. Assume that the marginal cost of hiring is proportional to this fraction.[4] Then the firm will hire up to the point where marginal cost equals the marginal benefit, λ_t^j:

$$Gh_t^j/U_t^j = \lambda_t^j \qquad (1)$$

where $G > 0$.

The firm takes as given the stochastic process driving the relative price π_t^j of its output and the real wage w_t^j that will result from the bargaining process. Given the positive discount factor β and the constant marginal product of labor, $f > 0$, the marginal benefit of hiring is

$$\lambda_t^j = E_t^j \sum_{i=1}^{\infty} \beta^i (1 - \delta)^i (\pi_{t+i}^j f - w_{t+i}^j) \qquad (2)$$

where E_t^j denotes the rational expectation conditional on information available in sector j at the time of hiring.

Assume that the cost of leisure is zero. Then the total surplus to be shared by a worker and his employer each period is $\pi_t^j f$. Assume that each time a contact is made the ensuing bargain results in an agreement for the worker to be paid a proportion ξ of that surplus each period:

$$w_t^j = \xi \pi_t^j f, \qquad 0 < \xi < 1 \tag{3}$$

The proportion is assumed to be constant across time and across firms.

Under the assumption that firms and workers share the same pure rate of time preference, that both are risk-neutral, and that π_t^j is always positive, the contract (3) is privately efficient. If both parties to the bargain take it as given that all other bargains will result in the same contract, then no alternative contract could make both better off. Because the worker will choose to remain working until exogenous relocation, without engaging in costly on-the-job search, nothing could increase the total surplus to be shared. Alterations in the contracted wage would merely affect the distribution of that surplus. This does not mean, of course, that the contract is socially efficient, as will be discussed below in Section 12.5.

The relative price π_t^j is assumed to follow a first-order autoregressive process, with coefficient ϱ, and unit mean. Also, $\Sigma_{j=1}^{J} \pi_t^j = 1$ in all realizations. Following Lucas, we take this process as exogenously given, and independent of all other elements of the agents' information sets. Thus, (2) can be rewritten, using (3), in the form

$$\lambda_t^j = \bar{\lambda} + \alpha E_t^j (\pi_t^j - 1) \cdot \tag{4}$$

where $\bar{\lambda} > 0$ and

$$\alpha = f(1 - \xi)\beta(1 - \delta)\varrho[1 - \beta(1 - \delta)\varrho]^{-1} > 0 \tag{5}$$

As in Lucas (1973) the information conditioning the expectation in (4) does not include the current relative price π_t^j. Instead it consists of last period's relative price and the current nominal price in that sector. The nominal price is assumed to inform the observer of the sum of the current white-noise innovations to the relative price process in that sector and to the economy-wide level of aggregate demand: $v_t^j + m_t$. Assume that agents form expectations using least-squares projections,[5] and that v_t^j and m_t are statistically independent. Then the marginal benefit of hiring is

$$\lambda_t^j = \bar{\lambda} + \alpha(\varrho(\pi_{t-1}^j - 1) + \eta(v_t^j + m_t)) \tag{6}$$

where η is the usual variance ratio: $\sigma_v^2/(\sigma_v^2 + \sigma_m^2)$.

The parameters and distributions in the model are assumed to be restricted so that the following inequalities are always satisfied:

$$\pi_t^j > 0, \lambda_t^j > 0, \qquad FG^{-1}\lambda_t^j < 1 \tag{7}$$

The first inequality has already been asserted. The second follows from the first. The third is equivalent to restricting the number hired to be less than the number unemployed, by (1).

12.3 EQUILIBRIUM

Our assumptions concerning exogenous relocation imply that a firm's employment n_t^j will evolve according to

$$n_{t+1}^j = (1 - \delta)(n_t^j + h_t^j) \tag{8}$$

From (1) and (8),

$$n_{t+1}^j = (1 - \delta)n_t^j + (1 - \delta)G^{-1}U_t^j\lambda_t^j \tag{9}$$

To understand the model's dynamics, consider first an isolated firm that takes as given the stochastic behavior of both U_t^j and λ_t^j. That firm's employment will vary according to the stochastic difference equation (9). Thus, an increase in the monetary shock m_t will increase λ_t^j through the Lucas price-surprise mechanism, which will increase the hiring rate and thereby increase next period's employment.

Note that the effect of a monetary shock is greater, the greater is unemployment. This nonlinearity is the source of the effects to be analyzed below in Section 12.6. It arises because the marginal cost of hiring depends upon the number unemployed. A firm in a tight labor market will be relatively unresponsive to a perceived increase in the marginal value of hiring because of the difficulty of finding recruits.

The stochastic difference equation (9) is stable because $\partial n_{t+1}^j/\partial n_t^j = (1 - \delta) \in (0, 1)$. To interpret this derivative, note that according to (1) an increase in the isolated firm's employment this period will not affect its hiring. Thus, for each additional worker this period there will be $(1 - \delta)$ more workers next period after relocation.

Next, note that, because $\partial n_{t+1}^j/\partial n_t^j > 0$, the positive effect of a monetary shock will persist into future periods, being embodied each period in a higher value of current employment, despite the fact that the future values of λ_t^j will be unaffected by the shock.

To pass from the dynamics of the isolated firm to the equilibrium dynamics of the model, substitute for U_t^j in (9) using the definition: $U_t^j = L - Fn_t^j$. This results in

$$n_{t+1}^j = (1 - \delta)(n_t^j + G^{-1}(L - Fn_t^j)\lambda_t^j) \tag{10}$$

The equilibrium of the model is defined by the solution to the two equations (6) and (10). In this equilibrium firms are all acting optimally, with rational expectations (subject to the qualification of note 5).

Workers are also acting optimally, although their choices have been severely limited by the setup of the model. Those who are working are optimally choosing to continue working, and those who are unemployed are optimally searching for an offer at the maximum allowable speed of one contact point per period.

According to (10), the impact effect of a monetary shock upon the equilibrium value of next period's employment is exactly as described above for the isolated firm. The increase in employment comes about not because workers are fooled or in any way induced to offer more labor for sale, but because the increase in hiring allows them to find offers more rapidly. The supply side of the labor market affects this impact effect only in the sense that, as described above, the effect will be greater the more unemployed workers there are.

Next note that, according to (7) and (10),

$$\frac{\partial n^j_{t+1}}{\partial n^j_t} = (1 - \delta)(1 - G^{-1} F\lambda^j_t) \in (0, 1)$$

Thus the deterministic counterpart to the difference equation (10) is stable, and the effect of a monetary shock will persist. To interpret this derivative, note that if an increase in this period's employment is shared by all firms, then it will be accompanied by a decrease in the number unemployed this period, and through the nonlinearity described earlier in this section, will cause each firm to reduce its hiring. Therefore, the change in each firm's employment next period will be less than it would have been if the firm had been the only one to experience the increase. Assumption (7) limits the extent of the reduction in hiring and guarantees that the overall effect upon next period's employment is still positive.

In order to demonstrate the existence of an ergodic solution to (6) and (10), and also in order to conduct the comparative dynamics exercises of Section 12.6 below, it helps to transform (10) in the following way. First note that if λ^j_t were always equal to its average value $\bar{\lambda}$, then employment would converge on the equilibrium value $\bar{n}$, where

$$\bar{n} \equiv \frac{(1 - \delta)G^{-1} L\bar{\lambda}}{\delta + (1 - \delta)G^{-1} F\bar{\lambda}} \in \left(0, \frac{L}{F}\right) \tag{11}$$

Next, define the autocorrelated zero mean random variable:

$$\varepsilon^j_t = (1 - \delta)G^{-1} (L - F\bar{n})(\lambda^j_t - \bar{\lambda}) \tag{12}$$

Then (10) can be rewritten in terms of the deviations $x^j_t \equiv n^j_t - \bar{n}$ as

$$x^j_{t+1} = ax^j_t - bx^j_t\varepsilon^j_t + \varepsilon^j_t \tag{13}$$

where

$$a = (1 - \delta)(1 - G^{-1}F\bar{\lambda}) \in (0, 1) \tag{14}$$

and

$$b = F/(L - F\bar{n}) > 0 \tag{15}$$

Except for the fact that the error term ε_t^j is not white noise, the transformed equation (13) is a bilinear time series model of the sort studied by Granger and Andersen (1978). Appendix A uses a slightly modified version of the theorem of Quinn (1982) to show that, under a mild additional assumption, (13) has a strictly stationary, ergodic solution, which can be written as

$$x_t^j = \varepsilon_{t-1}^j + \sum_{k=2}^{\infty} \Pi_{l=1}^{k-1} (a - b\varepsilon_{t-1}^j)\varepsilon_{t-k}^j \tag{16}$$

By substituting from the definition of ε_t^j and x_t^j into (16), we can express employment as a function of all past shocks:

$$n_t^j = \hat{n}(\{m_r, v_\tau^j\}_{-\infty}^{t-1}) \tag{17}$$

12.4 THE LUCAS AGGREGATE SUPPLY FUNCTION

This model is very close to that of Lucas (1973). The predictions of the two models concerning the interrelationships between price surprises and aggregate output are almost identical. Specifically, a linear approximation to (10) around the point $(\bar{n}, \bar{\lambda})$ yields, after summing across sectors,

$$n_{t+1} \simeq n^* + a(n_t - n^*) + b'\eta m_t$$

where $n^* \equiv J\bar{n}$ and $b' \equiv a\delta n^*/\bar{\lambda} > 0$. Changing variables from employment to aggregate output ($y_t = fn_t$) transforms this into

$$y_{t+1} \simeq y^* + a(y_t - y^*) + b''\eta m_t \tag{18}$$

where $y^* \equiv fn^*$ and $b'' \equiv fb'$. Note that, because aggregate supply at date t is predetermined, m_t is also the innovation in the aggregate price level. Therefore, (18) is the Lucas aggregate-supply relationship except that, because it takes one period for newly hired workers to be put to work, the price surprise in period t becomes the innovation in y_{t+1} rather than y_t.

The present model derives this aggregate supply relationship from an approach similar to Sargent (1979, ch. 16). In both cases the persistence term $a(y_t - y^*)$ comes from costs of changing employment. As far as the demand for labor is concerned, the present model is almost a special case of Sargent's. What distinguishes the two approaches is the manner in which changes in a demand for labor induce changes in the equilibrium quantity of employment. As discussed above, these changes do not represent movements up and down and supply-of-labor schedule in the present approach as they do in Sargent's.

The model is also close to the empirical model used by Barro (1977a) to account for unemployment. Another change of variables from the linear approximation to (10), together with a Koyck transformation, yields

$$u_t \simeq u^* - b''' \eta \sum_{i=0}^{\infty} a^i m_{t-i-1}$$

where the rate of unemployment is $u_t = 1 - Fn_t/JL$, the natural rate of unemployment is $u^* \equiv 1 - Fn^*/JL$, and $b''' \equiv Fb'/JL > 0$.

Even without any linear approximations the model yields the policy-invariance prediction usually associated with New Classical models. The solution (17) expresses employment in each sector as a function of monetary surprises and relative price shocks, but these functions do not depend upon the systematic component of nominal aggregate demand, which we have not even had to specify.

Because of the assumed lag involved in putting a newly hired worker to work, employment in any sector will depend upon last period's monetary shock, even given employment in past periods. Thus, the model implies that money will 'cause' employment, in Granger's sense. Likewise the linear approximation to (10) yields the same causality prediction with respect to aggregate employment or output. Without such a lag the usual Lucas aggregate-supply relationship does not yield this policy prediction. Whether Sargent's derivation could easily be modified to incorporate a similar time delay or whether it is a fundamental distinguishing feature of the present approach is not clear.

Although the present model bears these resemblances to New Classical models, it avoids the specific shortcomings attributed in the introduction to such models. First, it permits output in each sector to vary in the same direction in response to monetary shocks without large fluctuations in aggregate real wages (the average wage across all sectors is the constant ξf) and also without assuming an unrealistically large elasticity of labor supply. Indeed we have specified household preferences in such a way that if each labor market were always in a competitive equilibrium, the supply and demand for labor would always be equal at a real wage (π_t^j/f), where the supply schedule was completely inelastic.

Second, the model exhibits unemployment that is involuntary in the everyday sense of the word. Unemployed workers would always prefer to be employed. They are doing everything in their power to become employed. They remain unemployed because it takes time to find a job.[6]

The story we have told also avoids the specific shortcomings attributed above to Keynesian models. No contractual rigidity of nominal prices is invoked. All contracts are privately efficient, so no privately attainable gains from trade are being left unexploited. The impediments that prevent unemployed workers from underbidding employed workers are made explicit as part of the technology of exchange. (Specifically, no one can communicate with a potential employer in any way except by finding a contact point at which an offer has been made, and only one contact point per period can be sampled.) One might object that the impediments are *ad hoc* in the sense that they are specified exogenously rather than being explained on the basis of even more primitive notions, but to eliminate this kind of 'ad hocery' would require either the assumed absence of all impediments or else an infinite regress.

12.5 SOCIAL EFFICIENCY

Although the model implies that all privately attainable gains from trade will be exploited, it does not generally yield an efficient outcome, because of the presence of two sorts of externalities. The first is the external economy of scale stressed by Diamond. Specifically, the greater the recruiting effort by firms, the more quickly will the average unemployed worker find a job. This external effect is what transmits the impulses of monetary shocks into employment fluctuations with no change in aggregate real wages.

The second sort of externality is a common-property externality. Each firm takes as given the stochastic process driving unemployment in its sector. Therefore, it fails to take into account the effect of its current recruiting activities in depleting the stock of unemployed workers and hence in raising future costs of hiring. This external effect is what produces the nonlinearity pointed out in Section 12.3.

Suppose that a social planner could costlessly take over all hiring decisions and make unlimited lump-sum transfers. Then social efficiency would require the hiring rates that maximize the expected present value of output net of the costs of recruiting and search. Suppose, as before, that all workers who have made a contact work until relocation, and all unemployed workers search. (Either the government can force this behavior on workers, or the transfer scheme is designed like the wage contract (3) to induce the behavior.) Then the socially optimal rate of hiring must solve the stochastic dynamic-programming problem with the Lagrangean:

$$E_t^j \mathcal{L} \equiv E_t^j \sum_{i=0}^{\infty} \beta^i \{\pi_{t+i}^j f \hat{n}_{t+i}^j - (G/2) (\hat{h}_{t+1}^j)^2/(L - F\hat{n}_{t+i}^j)$$
$$- \sigma(L - F\hat{n}_{t+i}^j)/F + \lambda_{t+i}^j [\hat{h}_{t+i}^j + \hat{n}_{t+i}^j$$
$$- \hat{n}_{t+i+1}^j/(1 - \delta)]\}$$

where σ is the cost of search, and where each Lagrangean multiplier λ_{t+i}^j can be interpreted as the expected marginal *social* value of hiring.

In order to compare the social optimal rate of hiring with the *laissez-faire* equilibrium rate, note that the latter solves the problem with the Lagrangean:

$$E_t^j \mathcal{L} \equiv E_t^j \sum_{i=0}^{\infty} \beta^i \{(1 - \xi)\pi_{t+i}^j f n_{t+i}^j$$
$$- (G/2)h_{t+i}^{j\,2}/U_{t+i}^j + \lambda_{t+i}^j [h_{t+i}^j + n_{t+i}^j - n_{t+i+1}^j/(1 - \delta)]\}$$

where U_t^j is taken as given.

The common-property externality shows up as a difference between these two problems. Specifically, the private firm takes unemployment as given, whereas the social planner takes into account that unemployment is determined by its hiring decisions. Because of this externality the private firm tends to hire too much in any given situation – it tends to overharvest the common property stock of unemployed searchers.

Similarly, the thin-market externality shows up in a difference between the two problems in how the gain from employment is represented. In the social problem that gain is

$$\beta^i(\pi_{t+i}^j f + \sigma)$$

whereas in the private problem it is just that part of the social gain accruing to the firm:

$$\beta^i(1 - \xi)\pi_{t+i}^j f$$

Because the wage cannot be negative, a firm in *laissez-faire* cannot capture all the social gains from its marginal hiring decisions. Instead it must share some of the gain with the worker. For this reason, the firm tends to hire too little.

The interaction between these eternalities and their effects on recruiting have been studied by Mortenson (1982a) and Pissarides (1984) in the context of similar search models. Because the externalities distort the hiring decision in opposite directions, it can be shown by examples that the *laissez-faire* rate of hiring may be more or less than the socially optimal rate.[7] The inefficiency is hardly surprising, but it is interesting that it can be exhibited by a model that is almost identical in its output price predictions to New Classical models in which no such inefficiency exists.

12.6 THE AGGREGATE EFFECTS OF RELATIVE PRICES

The nonlinearity of the model implies that the stochastic structure of relative price shocks will affect output, employment, and unemployment in ways not found in linear business-cycles models. In the linear approximation to (10) that yields the Lucas aggregate-supply relationship, the variability of relative price shocks has a positive effect on η and hence on the impact upon unemployment of a monetary shock. In the nonlinear model this variability also has a positive effect upon the natural rate of unemployment, $Eu_t \equiv 1 - (F/JL)En_t$, under the additional assumption that

v_t^j is distributed symmetrically about its mean of zero (19)

Furthermore, the degree of persistence of relative price shocks has these same two effects. An increase in ϱ raises the impact effect of a monetary shock and raises the natural rate of unemployment.

The effect of relative price variability upon the natural rate of unemployment is similar to, and hence suggests an alternative explanation of the empirical finding by Lilien (1982) to the effect that given any history of monetary shocks, the expected rate of unemployment is positively affected by the dispersion of hiring rates across sectors.

This effect is similar to that described by Lipsey (1960) and analyzed further by Archibald (1969) whereby an increase in the dispersion of unemployment across markets shifts the aggregate Phillips curve to the right if the Phillips curve in each market is convex to the origin, i.e., in the terms of the present model, if the absolute effect upon unemployment of a price shock is positively related to the amount of unemployment. Most of the added complications in the present formulation of this effect arise because of lags, i.e., because a price shock affects unemployment only next period, and with an absolute effect that is positively related not to next period's rate of unemployment but to this period's rate:

$$\left| \frac{\partial u_{t+1}^j}{\partial m_t} \right| = \left(\frac{F}{L} \right) \frac{\partial n_{t+1}^j}{\partial m_t} = \left(\frac{F}{L} \right) (1 - \delta) G^{-1} (L - Fn_t^j) a\eta$$

$$= \left(\frac{F}{G} \right) (1 - \delta) u_t^j a\eta$$

The nonlinearity arises because of the externality according to which the cost of hiring depends inversely upon the existing amount of unemployment.[8]

The rest of this section is devoted to demonstrating these effects. Appendix B shows that the mean of the stationary distribution of n_t^j can be expressed as

$$En_t^j = \bar{n} + \sum_{\substack{k=2}}^{\infty} \sum_{\substack{r=2 \\ (r \text{ even})}}^{k} a^{k-r}(-b)^{r-1}\gamma^r \sum_{c\in C(r,k)} \sum_{i(\cdot)\in I(c)} (\Pi_{l\in c}d_{i(l)})$$

$$(\Pi_{s-1}^r \mu_s^{\psi(s,i(\cdot))})$$

$$(20)$$

where

$$\gamma = (1 - \delta)G^{-1}(L - F\bar{n})a > 0$$

$$d_i = \begin{cases} \eta & \text{if } i = 0 \\ \varrho^i & \text{if } i \geqslant 1 \end{cases}$$

$C(r, k)$ is the set of subsets of the integers $\{1, \ldots, k\}$ containing exactly r elements, all distinct and one of them being k,

$I(c)$ is the set of all functions mapping c into the nonnegative integers,

μ_s is the sth moment of v_t^j, and

$\psi(s, i(\cdot))$ is a nonnegative integer, equal to the number of distinct values of ϕ for which $l - i(l) = \phi$ for exactly s elements l of c.

(By convention, $0^0 = 1$.) Note that, by (19), $\mu_s = 0$ for all odd values of s. Because of this, and because a, b, γ, and all d_i's are positive, each term in the infinite sum in (20) is nonpositive, and some of these terms are strictly negative.

Consider first the effects of an increase in the variability of relative price shocks. Specifically, suppose that all the even moments μ_s were to increase. Because $\mu_2 = \sigma_v^2$, η would also increase. Note that the parameters a, b, and γ in equation (20) are unaffected by this change, as is d_i for each $i > 0$. So in terms of (20) the change can be represented by an increase in d_0 and μ_s for each even s. By inspection of (20) the effect on En_t^j of these increases is negative.

An increase in the degree of persistence of relative price shocks, ϱ, would leave a, b, d_0, and each μ_s unchanged but would increase γ and d_i for all $i \geqslant 1$. The same line of reasoning as above shows that the overall effect on En_t^j of this change is strictly negative.

The effects upon the initial impact of a monetary shock are relatively simple to analyze. From (6) and (10),

$$\frac{\partial n_{t+1}^j}{\partial m_t} = (1 - \delta)G^{-1}(L - Fn_t^j)a\eta$$

$$(21)$$

Given n_t^j this is increasing in the variability of relative price shocks (which affects η positively) and in the degree of persistence of relative price shocks (which affects α positively).[9] Taking expected values of both sides of (21) produces

$$E\left\{\frac{\partial n_{t+1}^j}{\partial m_t}\right\} = (1 - \delta)G^{-1}(L - FEn_t^j)\alpha\eta$$

Thus, the expected value of the initial impact of a monetary shock is also increasing in the variability and persistence of relative price shocks, each of which has not only a positive effect upon the coefficient $\alpha\eta$ but also, as we have shown, a negative effect upon En_t^j.

APPENDIX A

A slightly modified version of the theorem by Quinn (1982) states that if for some subsets X_1 and X_2 of the real numbers, the following conditions hold:

ε_t^j has a strictly stationary ergodic distribution on X_2 (A.1)

$ax_t^j - bx_t^j\varepsilon_t^j + \varepsilon_t^j \in X_1$ for all $(x_t^j, \varepsilon_t^j) \in X_1 \times X_2$ (A.2)

$Eln\,|a - b\varepsilon_t^j| < 0$ (A.3)

$E\,|\,ln\,|x + \varepsilon_t^j|\,| < \infty$ for all $x \in X_1$ (A.4)

then (13) has a strictly stationary, ergodic solution on X_1, which can be written as (16).

Let X_1 be the interval $(-\bar{n}, L/F - \bar{n})$, and X_2 be the interval $(-(1 - \delta)G^{-1}(L - F\bar{n})\bar{\lambda}, (1 - \delta)G^{-1}(L - F\bar{n})(F^{-1}G - \bar{\lambda}))$. Assume that (A.4) holds. The following argument shows that (A.1)–(A.3) also hold, and hence that such a solution to (13) exists.

From (7) and (11),

$$-(1 - \delta)G^{-1}(L - F\bar{n})\bar{\lambda} < (1 - \delta)G^{-1}(L - F\bar{n})(\lambda_t^j - \bar{\lambda})$$
$$< (1 - \delta)G^{-1}(L - F\bar{n})(F^{-1}G - \bar{\lambda}) \quad \text{(A.5)}$$

From (A.5) and the definition (12) of ε_t^j it follows that $\varepsilon_t^j \in X_2$. Also, it follows directly from the fact that m_t and v_t^j are white noise that ε_t^j is strictly stationary and ergodic. Thus, (A.1) holds.

The proof of (A.2) uses the untransformed difference equation (10). Given (A.1), (A.2) is equivalent to

$$(1 - \delta)(n_t^j + G^{-1}(L - Fn_t^j)\lambda_t^j) \in (0, L/F) \quad \text{if } n_t^j \in (0, L/F)$$

But (A.2′) follows directly from (7). To prove (A.3), note that, by definition,

$$a - b\varepsilon_t^j = (1 - \delta)(1 - G^{-1}F\bar{\lambda}) - [F/L - F\bar{n}](1 - \delta)G^{-1}$$
$$\times (L - F\bar{n})(\lambda_t^j - \bar{\lambda})$$
$$= (1 - \delta)(1 - G^{-1}F\lambda_t^j) \tag{A.6}$$

It follows from (A.6) and (7) that

$$a - b\varepsilon_t^j \in (0, 1) \tag{A.7}$$

Condition (A.3) follows directly from (A.7).

APPENDIX B

This appendix derives equation (20). From (16) and the fact that $E\varepsilon_t^j = 0$,

$$En_t^j = \bar{n} + \sum_{k=2}^{\infty} E\Pi_{l=1}^{k-1} (a - b\varepsilon_{t-l}^j)\varepsilon_{t-k}^j \tag{B.1}$$

By expanding products and using the fact that $E\varepsilon_t^j = 0$,

$$E\Pi_{l=1}^{k-1} (a - b\varepsilon_{t-l}^j)\varepsilon_{t-k}^j$$
$$= a^{k-1}E\varepsilon_{t-k}^j - a^{k-2}b \sum_{l=1}^{k-1} E\ \varepsilon_{t-l}^j\varepsilon_{t-k}^j + \ldots + a(-b)^{k-2}\sum_{i=1}^{k-1}$$
$$E(\Pi_{l=1(l\neq i)}^{k-1}\ \varepsilon_{t-l}^j)\varepsilon_{t-k}^j + (-b)^{k-1}E\Pi_{l=1}^{k-1}\varepsilon_{t-l}^j)\ \varepsilon_{t-k}^j$$
$$= \sum_{r=2}^{k} a^{k-r}(-b)^{r-1} \sum_{c \in C(r,k)} E\Pi_{l \in c}\varepsilon_{t-l}^j;\ k = 2, 3, \ldots, \infty \tag{B.2}$$

Take any $k \geqslant 2$, any $r \in \{2, \ldots, k\}$, and any $c \in C(r, k)$. Then, from (6) and (12),

$$E\Pi_{l \in c}\ \varepsilon_{t-1}^j = \gamma^r E\Pi_{l \in c}\left(\sum_{i=1}^{\infty} \varrho^i v_{t-l-i}^j + \eta v_{t-1}^j + \eta m_{t-1}\right)$$

Because this product is linear in each m_{t-l}, we can rewrite it as

$$E\Pi_{l \in c}\varepsilon_{t-l}^j = \gamma^r E\Pi_{l \in c}\left(\sum_{i=1}^{\infty} \varrho^i v_{t-l-i}^j + \eta v_{t-1}^j\right) = \gamma^r\ E\Pi_{l \in c}\left(\sum_{i=0}^{\infty} d_i v_{t-l-i}^j\right)$$

Next, we can expand this product to write

$$E\Pi_{l \in c}\ \varepsilon_{t-l}^j = \gamma^r \sum_{i(\cdot) \in I(c)} E\Pi_{l \in c}\ d_{i(l)}v_{t-l-i(l)}^j \tag{B.3}$$

For any $i(\cdot) \in I(c)$ we have

$$E\Pi_{l \in c}d_{i(l)}v_{t-l-i(l)}^j = (\Pi_{l \in c}\ d_{i(l)})\Pi_{s=1}^r\ \mu_s^{\psi(s,i(\cdot))} \tag{B.4}$$

Note that

$$\sum_{s=1}^{r} s\psi(s, i(\cdot)) = r$$

Therefore, if r is odd, there is at least one odd value of s such that $\psi(s, i(\cdot)) \geq 1$. But, by (19) $\mu_s = 0$ for all odd s. Therefore,

$$\Pi_{s=1}^{r}\mu_s^{\psi(s,i(\cdot))} = 0 \text{ for all odd } r \tag{B.5}$$

Equation (20) follows immediately from (B.1)–(B.5).

NOTES

1. Recent papers by Pissarides (1985a,b) construct business-cycle models on similar search foundations. In (1985a) the aggregate shocks are real productivity shocks. In (1985b) anticipated monetary policy generates aggregate effects on hiring via a Tobin effect on real interest rates. Wright (1986) develops a search-theoretic business-cycle model in which signal extraction problems produce serially correlated aggregate effects, similar to those generated by unanticipated money in the present model. However, Wright's search model, like that of Lucas and Prescott (1974), has no externalities.
2. Relocations can also be interpreted as the death of old workers and their replacement by newly born workers. In either case the people who are unemployed in the model will always be the new entrants to their labor market, a prediction that seems roughly consistent with the observed high incidence of unemployment among the young and unskilled.
3. If there were congestion externalities through which one firm's hiring was interfered with by other firms' efforts to hire the same workers, then the marginal cost might also depend negatively on the number hired by other firms. This is ruled out by assuming that the number of contact points is so large that no two firms ever leave offers simultaneously at the same point. However, the model does imply a dynamic congestion externality in the form of the common property externality to be discussed below in Section 12.5.
4. It would be more natural to assume that the total cost of hiring was proportional to the square of this fraction, in which case the marginal cost would be proportional to $h_t^j/(U_t^j)^2$. This would result in no substantive change in the analysis up to Section 11.6. However, it would greatly complicate the analysis of Section 11.6, because the equilibrium would no longer be given by a bilinear model with a known closed-form solution.
5. This would be equivalent to rational expectations if all variables were normally distributed, but the fact that π_t^j must remain positive rules out normality.
6. Involuntary unemployment also exists in the sense of Keynes (1936: 15). If the price level were to rise (because of a monetary shock) and the money wage contract were not to adjust (i.e., if the real wage in each contingency

were reduced equiproportionately), then both firms and workers in each market would want the rate of hiring to be greater than what it would have been in the absence of that exogenous change.

7. In the model of Pissarides (1984) the overall effect of the two externalities is unambiguously to make firms hire too little in *laissez-faire*. His formulation of the search technology differs from the present setup in several ways. He also assumes free entry of firms. Mortenson (1982a) found that efficiency could be attained if the sharing rule assigned a different share to each party depending upon who initiated the contact. No such imputation of responsibility seems possible in the present setup. Hosios (1986) presents a useful general framework in which to study the efficiency of entry and job acceptance as well as search and recruiting when the two sorts of externalities are present in a broad class of models. He also shows a formal equivalence in this class between the constant-returns-to-scale-in--production model of the present chapter and the one-firm-one-vacancy model employed by Mortenson and Pissarides.

8. Lilien (1982) interprets his findings as evidence that an increased pace of labor reallocation requires an increase in unemployment as an input into a search technology, as in the Lucas–Prescott (1974) model. Davis (1986) also provides an interpretation of Lilien's and other evidence using this assumption. According to Davis, fluctuations in the pace of labor reallocation are caused not by exogenous changes in the dispersion of relative prices but by aggregate shocks that induce intertemporal substitution of labor mobility. Abraham and Katz (1986) also interpret the evidence as reflecting aggregate shocks. Topel and Weiss (1985) provide an interpretation according to which increases in the degree of uncertainty concerning relative prices induce people to substitute unemployment for the accumulation of sector-specific human capital. The present interpretation differs from all of the above in assuming a constant pace of labor reallocation between sectors, attributing unemployment fluctuations to exogenous changes in the dispersion of relative prices, and treating all increases in unemployment as involuntary.

9. The analogous role of ϱ in inducing a positive effect of monetary surprises on investment in physical capital was noted by Lucas (1975: 1135).

13 · STABILITY OF EQUILIBRIA WITH EXTERNALITIES

13.1 INTRODUCTION

Recent contributions by Diamond (1982b), Howitt (Chapter 10 above), Howitt and McAfee (Chapter 11 above), and others have shown how externalities in the transactions technology of an economy can generate various Keynesian phenomena without any of the price rigidities typical of Keynesian analysis. In particular, these papers show how there can exist multiple stationary equilibria, with different levels of unemployment. The low-level equilibria are in many respects similar to the persistent states of unemployment depicted by Keynes. The present chapter addresses the question of the dynamic stability of these equilibria.

In well-behaved one-dimensional dynamic systems with multiple equilibria, successive equilibria alternate between locally stable and locally unstable. The analog to this result in well-behaved dynamic optimization models with one state variable is the result of Liviatan and Samuelson (1969) that the two-dimensional system describing the motion of the system has equilibria that alternate (as the equilibrium value of the state variable changes) between saddlepoint stable and unstable. If one can argue that there is a unique equilibrium trajectory starting from any initial value of the state variable, then the saddlepoints are locally stable in the economic sense because the second dimension of the dynamic system is a co-state variable, or a rate of change of the state variable, whose initial value is not given by history but can adjust to put

---

This paper is a revision of our earlier discussion paper (1984b). We are grateful to Paul Romer for suggesting a reformulation of the analysis of that paper.

Written jointly with R. Preston McAfee. Reprinted from *Quarterly Journal of Economics* (1988), **103**, May, 261–77. © 1988 the President and Fellows of Harvard College and the Massachusetts Institute of Technology.

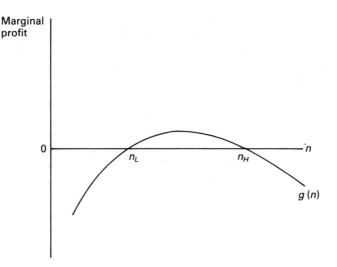

Figure 13.1 Multiple equilibria.

the economy on the unique stable trajectory passing through the given initial value of the state variable.

If this usual result were true in trade-externality models, then in the simplest case (e.g. Figure 13.1 above) of two nondegenerate equilibria only one would be observable under occasional perturbations, the other being unstable. Furthermore, intuition suggests that the low-level equilibrium would be the unstable one. If true, this would obviously reduce the empirical importance of the multiplicity result. The result could perhaps be used to explain the complete shutting down of the economy because the origin in Figure 13.1 may be a (degenerate) saddlepoint equilibrium. But to explain an observable low-level equilibrium short of this catastrophe (in the economic sense), one would have to rule out the simple configuration of Figure 13.1.

Recent papers on price-level dynamics (e.g. Calvo, 1979) show that the stability properties of dynamic optimization models do not carry over to perfect-foresight equilibrium models. These papers have shown how the equilibrium trajectories in a perfect-foresight model of an economy with a single-state variable can be characterized by a two-dimensional dynamic system that bears a superficial resemblance to the Euler equation of an analogous optimization model. But they exhibit stationary equilibria that can be locally stable under this system, a phenomenon ruled out in optimization models by the Liviatan–Samuelson result.

The present chapter examines a perfect-foresight equilibrium model of an economy with trade externalities and with a single state variable. The main result is that every other stationary equilibrium is a saddlepoint, as in the Liviatan–Samuelson result, but the nonsaddle stationary equilibria can be locally stable, as in the Calvo model. In the case illustrated by Figure 13.1, the high-level equilibrium will be the saddlepoint. Thus, the low-level equilibrium of Figure 13.1 may be locally stable, and hence may be observable under perturbations.

More specifically, we show that one can get local stability of the nonsaddle equilibria if, in addition to the external economy emphasized by Diamond and others, there is also a diseconomy of scale, according to which the marginal adjustment cost faced by a firm trying to expand its activity level at a given rate is positively related to the activity level already attained by its rivals. An example of this diseconomy is the effect analyzed in our earlier paper (Chapter 11 above), whereby an increase in aggregate employment raises a firm's recruiting cost by reducing the rate at which unemployed job searchers contact the firm. Furthermore, we show that this diseconomy is necessary for our result because without it the model's trajectories can be characterized as solutions to the Euler equation of a social planning problem, to which the Liviatan–Samuelson local result applies.[1]

As in the price-level-dynamics literature, this local stability result implies an indeterminacy of equilibrium when the economy begins in the neighborhood of a low-level equilibrium. The penultimate section of this chapter discusses the implications of the indeterminacy and points out how it can apply even in the neighborhood of the high-level equilibrium.

Most of the chapter is motivated by the macroeconomic questions addressed by the trade-externality literature. But the abstract formal model that we use admits of several microeconomic interpretations, which we discuss in the final section.

13.2 THE MODEL

We postulate a model with a large number of identical firms, and an even larger number of identical households, all risk neutral and all with the same constant rate of pure time preference. There are three tradable objects: output, homogeneous labor services, and money. The money is a pure accounting device. A firm's receipts are instantaneously transferred to its workers and owners and must be used for purchasing output from other firms during the current period. No credit market is assumed to exist, but that is no restriction in a world of risk neutrality and identical rates of time preference.

The output market is perfectly competitive, in that all firms and households perceive a perfectly elastic demand schedule, and aggregate demand always equal aggregate output. But, as in the analyses of Hahn (1971), Niehans (1971), and others, firms must incur a transaction cost to operate in the market. This transaction cost takes the form of output used up in the selling process. Thus, a firm employing n units of labor will have a gross revenue of $f(n)$, where f is its production function, and will pay a total transaction cost of $\sigma(n, \bar{n})$, where $\bar{n}$ is aggregate employment (per firm).

This transaction cost depends upon the firm's own employment because the more it sells, the greater the required cost. It depends upon aggregate employment (per firm) $\bar{n}$ because of the trade externality. The larger is $\bar{n}$, the greater is the equilibrium level of aggregate demand, and by assumption, the less the cost of selling a given quantity. This effect may be rationalized in a number of different ways. For example, as aggregate demand goes up, the rate of arrival of buyers to a store may increase, thereby reducing the costs of advertising, or the size of the average customer's purchase may go up, thereby allowing the same quantity to be sold with fewer individual sales. Rather than be specific about the source of the externality, we shall merely take the function σ as given.

The typical firm's wage bill will be $w(n, \bar{n})$. This function can be derived in a number of different ways: for example, if the labor market is perfectly competitive then $w(n, \bar{n}) = w^s(\bar{n}) \cdot n$, where w^s is the supply price of $\bar{n}$ units of labor (per firm). On the other hand, if the labor market is a search market as in Diamond (1982b) or Chapter 11 above, then $w(n, \bar{n})$ will represent the predictable outcome of a bargaining process that takes place between a firm and n workers (each inelastically supplying one unit) when aggregate employment is $\bar{n}$.

The firm also faces costs of hiring – costs which it incurs in the form of output used up. The costs are given by the function $\gamma(\dot{n} + \delta n, \bar{n})$, where δ can be interpreted as either the death rate of workers or the exogenous rate at which job separations occur for noneconomic reasons. The expansion-cost function γ is written as depending upon $\dot{n} + \delta n$ because under the assumption that employed workers do not search for a job elsewhere (which makes sense in a symmetric equilibrium with homogeneous firms and workers), this will be the firm's gross rate of hiring. It is written as depending upon $\bar{n}$ to allow for the diseconomy referred to earlier. This diseconomy can be thought of as arising from the common-property nature of the pool of unemployed job searchers. As $\bar{n}$ increases, the size of the pool from which the typical firm draws its new recruits is thereby reduced.[2] This makes it more difficult for the firm to find any given number of new recruits. Thus, if this externality is present, $\gamma_2 > 0$, and $\gamma_{12} > 0$. We shall also be interested in the limiting case where the externality is absent, defined by the conditions $\gamma_2 = \gamma_{12} = 0$.

The flow of instantaneous profits to a firm is given by the function

$$L(\dot{n}, n, \bar{n}) \equiv \Pi(n, \bar{n}) - \gamma(\dot{n} + \delta n, \bar{n})$$
$$\equiv f(n) - \sigma(n, \bar{n}) - w(n, \bar{n}) - \gamma(\dot{n} + \delta n, \bar{n}) \qquad (1)$$

where $\Pi(n, \bar{n})$ is its gross profit function (gross of expansion costs). Assume that

L is almost everywhere twice continuously differentiable,

and for any $\bar{n}$ it is concave in $(\dot{n}, n)$, with $L_{11} = -\gamma_{11} < 0$ \qquad (2)

The properties of stationary equilibria depend upon the function

$$g(n) \equiv L_2(0, n, n) + rL_1(0, n, n)$$
$$\equiv \Pi_1(n, n) - (r + \delta)\gamma_1(\delta n, n)$$
$$\equiv f'(n) - \sigma_1(n, n) - w_1(n, n) - (r + \delta)\gamma_1(\delta n, n) \qquad (3)$$

where r is the rate of time preference. This function describes the steady-state marginal profit of employment, i.e., the marginal contribution of a unit of labor to the stationary flow of profits: $L_2 = \Pi_1 - \delta\gamma_1$, minus the interest cost of the initial recruiting outlay: $-rL_1 = r\gamma_1$. Note that g describes only the private component of this marginal profit. We make two assumptions on g:

$g(n) < 0$ for all n in some interval $(0, n_1)$ \qquad (4)

$g(n) < 0$ for all $n > n_2$, where $n_2 > n_1$ \qquad (5)

Assumption (4) is a generalization of the notion in the models of Diamond (1982b) and Chapter 10 above, that, because of the trade externality, if the entire economy is operating at too low a level, then the transaction cost of selling even a single unit outweighs the benefit. It would follow under normal assumptions if, for example, $\sigma(n, \bar{n})$ were proportional to $f(n)$ but inversely proportional to the level of aggregate demand $f(\bar{n})$, as in the example (15) below. Assumption (4) is the only place in the formal analysis where the external economy in trading is invoked.

Assumption (5) asserts that eventually some combination of the rising cost of expansion, decreasing returns, and the finiteness of the economy's endowment of labor overcome the external trade economy and reduce the marginal profit below zero. It could be derived under very general assumptions on f, σ, and w if, for example, the cost of hiring approached infinity as $\bar{n}$ approached the economy's endowment of labor. But it is important to note that the external diseconomy of expansion which this would require is not necessary for any of the above assumptions. Thus, (5) could be derived by assuming a competitive labor market in which the supply price of labor goes to infinity as employment approaches the economy's total endowment, or by assuming an infinitely elastic supply of labor but a marginal expansion cost that goes to infinity with the gross rate of hiring. We shall provide examples in Section 13.5, both with and without the external diseconomy. The latter illustrates the importance of the external diseconomy in achieving stability of all stationary equilibria.

13.3 EQUILIBRIA

We analyze symmetric perfect foresight equilibrium trajectories for the economy. Each firm can foresee perfectly the time path of aggregate employment $\{\bar{n}(\tau)\}_{\tau=0}^{\tau=\infty}$. Given this path and an initial employment level $n(0)$, the firm chooses the time path of its own employment so as to

$$\max \int_0^\infty e^{-rt} L(\dot{n}, n, \bar{n}) \, dt \tag{6}$$

It follows from well-known results that, given (2), a path $n(t)$ solves the firm's decision problem only if it satisfies the Euler equation:

$$L_2(\dot{n}, n, \bar{n}) + r L_1(\dot{n}, n, \bar{n}) = \frac{d}{dt} L_1(\dot{n}, n, \bar{n}) \tag{7}$$

and that it provides a solution to the problem if it satisfies the Euler equation and the transversality condition:

$$\lim_{t \to \infty} e^{-rt} L_1(\dot{n}, n, \bar{n}) = 0 \tag{8}$$

An equilibrium trajectory for the economy is defined as a piecewise differentiable time path for employment such that if each firm takes it as the given path of aggregate employment, then it will also choose it as the path of its own employment. Thus, along an equilibrium trajectory the Euler equation must be satisfied with $n(t) \equiv \bar{n}(t)$; that is, for $n(t)$ to be an equilibrium trajectory, it must solve the second-order differential equation:

$$L_2(\dot{n}, n, n) + r L_1(\dot{n}, n, n) = \frac{d}{dt} L_1(\dot{n}, n, n) \tag{9}$$

Furthermore, any solution to the 'Euler' equation (9) is necessarily an equilibrium trajectory if it also satisfies the 'transversality' condition:

$$\lim_{t \to \infty} e^{-rt} L_1(\dot{n}, n, n) = 0 \qquad (10)$$

The stationary equilibria of the model are equilibrium trajectories with constant employment. They correspond to the rest points of the system (9) because any rest point obviously satisfies (10). They are thus defined by (9) together with the condition $\dot{n} = \ddot{n} = 0$. It follows immediately that at any rest point n^*, the marginal profit of employment just equals zero:

$$g(n^*) = L_2(0, n^*, n^*) + rL_1(0, n^*, n^*) = 0 \qquad (11)$$

It follows also that any n^* satisfying (11) is a rest point because where $n = n^*$ and $\dot{n} = 0$, then according to (9), $\ddot{n} = L_{11}^{-1} \cdot g(n^*) = 0$. Thus, stationary equilibria correspond to the solutions to (11).

Assumptions (4) and (5) guarantee that if there is a nonzero stationary equilibrium, it must occur between n_1 and n_2, and if there exists one such equilibrium, then there will exist at least one other, except in the razor's edge case where $0 = \max g(n)$. The simplest case of two nonzero stationary equilibria is shown in Figure 13.1.

13.4 LOCAL STABILITY AND OBSERVABILITY

Except in razor's edge cases that we ignore, the local stability properties of a stationary equilibrium n^* under the system (9) are determined by the linear approximation to (9) (a complete derivation is given in the appendix):

$$0 = L_{11}\ddot{n} + (L_{13} - rL_{11})\dot{n} - (L_{22} + L_{23} + rL_{12} + rL_{13}) \times (n - n^*)$$

$$= -\gamma_{11}\ddot{n} + (r\gamma_{11} - \gamma_{12})\dot{n} - g'(n^*)(n - n^*) \qquad (12)$$

where all partial derivatives are evaluated at $(0, n^*, n^*)$. The roots of this system, (λ_1, λ_2) must satisfy

$$\lambda_1 + \lambda_2 = r - (\gamma_{12}/\gamma_{11}) \qquad (13)$$

$$\lambda_1\lambda_2 = g'(n^*)/\gamma_{11} \qquad (14)$$

Saddle-stability will occur if there are two real roots: one positive, and the other negative. This is equivalent to the condition $\lambda_1\lambda_2 < 0$. By (14) and (2) this is equivalent to the condition $g'(n^*) < 0$. Since $g(n^*) = 0$, our first result is that every other stationary equilibrium, i.e., each one at which the curve $g(n)$ cuts the horizontal axis from above, will be a saddlepoint, and that the intervening equilibria, at which $g'(n^*) > 0$, will not be saddlepoints. Furthermore, the assumptions (4) and (5) guarantee that the lowest-level equilibrium will be one at which $g'(n^*)$

> 0 and the highest-level equilibrium will have $g'(n^*) < 0$. Thus, the lowest-level equilibrium will not exhibit saddle-stability but the highest-level equilibrium will.

According to (13), the nonsaddle equilibria will be locally stable or unstable, depending upon the sign of $r - \gamma_{12}/\gamma_{11}$. From this follows our next result, that if there is no external diseconomy in expansion, i.e., $\gamma_{12} = 0$, then the nonsaddle equilibria must all be locally unstable, because $\lambda_1 + \lambda_2 = r > 0$. In this case, the 'usual' result holds, and the low-level equilibrium of Figure 13.1 is unobservable under perturbations. There is no equilibrium trajectory starting anywhere other than at the low-level equilibrium itself that converges to it.

If (9) were the Euler equation to an optimization model with concave maximand, our result in the absence of expansion diseconomies would be a direct consequence of the Liviatan–Samuelson result. This is almost the case, because (9) is indeed the Euler equation for the problem of maximizing

$$\int_0^\infty e^{-rt}\{H(n) - \gamma(\dot{n} + \delta n)\}\,dt, \qquad \text{where } H(n) \equiv \int_0^n \Pi_1(x, x)dx$$

But in the neighborhood of any nonsaddle equilibrium, where $g'(n^*) > 0$, the integrand of this problem is not concave, since at the equilibrium,

$$\frac{\partial^2}{\partial n^2}\{H(n) - \gamma(\dot{n} + \delta n)\} = \frac{d}{dn}\{\Pi_1(n, n) - \delta\gamma_1(\delta n)\}$$

$$= \frac{d}{dn}\{g(n) + r\gamma_1(\delta n)\}$$

$$> g'(n)$$

$$> 0$$

The main result of this chapter is that in the presence of the expansion diseconomy the nonsaddle equilibria like n_L of Figure 13.1 may be locally stable. By our previous results this will happen if at these equilibria, $\gamma_{12}/\gamma_{11} > r$. Obviously, this will hold in the limiting case of no discounting. By continuity it will also happen with a small enough rate of discount. An example with positive discounting is provided in the following section.

The local stability of n_L means that it is observable under occasional perturbations. For any n in a neighborhood of n_L, there will be a continuum of solutions of the 'Euler' equation (9) that converge upon n_L, one for each initial value of $\dot{n}$ in the neighborhood of zero. Any such convergent solution will obviously satisfy the 'transversality' condition (10) and will thus be an equilibrium trajectory. Thus, even if n is displaced a little from n_L, there will be equilibrium trajectories that return asymptotically to n_L.

More generally, any stationary equilibrium that is either a saddlepoint or has $\lambda_1 + \lambda_2 < 0$ is observable under perturbations. A saddlepoint is observable because starting at any initial n in its neighborhood there will be a unique solution to (9) converging monotonically to it. Thus, contrary to the 'usual' result, it is possible for all stationary equilibria to be observable under perturbations.

It is useful to contrast this outcome, the local stability of stationary equilibria, with the more conventional models featuring multiple equilibria. In these models a slight increase in activity at a low-level equilibrium makes marginal profit positive, encouraging further expansion toward the high-level equilibrium.

By contrast, in our model the value of expansion depends on future levels of activity of the other agents. Thus, if the activity level n is increased beyond the low-level equilibrium n_L, this increases only the instantaneous gains to expansion. However, since current expansion produces a stream of returns, the marginal value of n increases only if the future value of activity will be high enough, which depends on the discount rate r. Effectively, if a firm believes that the other firms will not expand farther, that firm will not be induced to undertake further expansion. Around the low-level equilibrium, there are generally at least two sets of perfect foresight beliefs about other firms' activity levels: one in which all firms expand to a high level of activity, and one in which the activity level returns to the low level. Believing the latter to be true drastically reduces the gains to expansion, even when returns are (instantaneously) higher than at n_L which supports the stability of the low-level equilibrium.

13.5 EXAMPLES

An example of the economy satisfying (2), (4), and (5) with an external diseconomy of expansion is

$$
\left\{
\begin{array}{l}
f(n) = fn, f > 0; \ \sigma(n, \bar{n}) = n \cdot \min\left(f, \sigma/\bar{n}\right), \ \sigma > 0 \\[2mm]
w(n, \bar{n}) = n\left(\dfrac{\bar{n}}{\xi - \bar{n}}\right), \ \xi > \dfrac{\sigma}{f} \\[2mm]
\gamma(\dot{n} + \delta n, \bar{n}) = \left(\dfrac{\dot{n} + \delta n}{a(\xi - \bar{n})}\right)^2, \ a > 0 \\[2mm]
L \text{ defined on } RX(0, \xi)^2
\end{array}
\right. \tag{15}
$$

In this example ξ represents the economy's endowment of labor. As aggregate employment approaches ξ, the example assumes that both the wage and the marginal cost of hiring at any given rate go to infinity.

Note that, from (3) and (15),

$$g(n) = f - \min(f, \sigma/n) - n/(\xi - n) - 2(r + \delta)\delta n/\alpha^2(\xi - n)^2 \quad (16)$$

Thus, $g(n) < 0$ for $n < \sigma/f$, implying that the example satisfies (4), and $\lim_{n \to \xi} g(n) = -\infty$, implying that it also satisfies (5).

The expansion-cost function of (15) might be derived as follows. Suppose, as in our earlier paper (Chapter 11 above) that for a firm to hire workers, it must first attract them into their 'recruiting net,' and that the rate at which searching workers enter a net of unit size is proportional to α, their speed of search, and U, the number of unemployed searchers. Assume a zero value of leisure. Then $U = \xi - \bar{n}$, where ξ is the constant exogenous size of the labor force (all employment magnitudes are per firm). Assume that the speed of search is a constant. Assume that the firm has no way of influencing the search activity of workers that have not yet fallen into its net and that the rate at which it attracts workers into the net is proportional to the size of the net θ. Then the firm's gross rate of hiring will equal the rate at which searching workers enter the firm's net, which can be written as (by normalizing):

$$\dot{n} + \delta n = \theta \cdot \alpha(\xi - \bar{n}) \quad (17)$$

because it would be privately inefficient for each 'contact' not to result in a job match. Assume that the firm may vary its net size according to the quadratic cost function, $\gamma = \theta^2$; then the expansion cost function in (15) follows directly from (17).

An example of an economy satisfying (2), (4), and (5) without the external diseconomy is constructed by replacing the expansion-cost function in (15) with the pure quadratic function, $\gamma = (\dot{n} + \delta n)^2$.

To construct an example in which there are exactly two nondegenerate stationary equilibria, as in Figure 13.1, with the two-level equilibrium being locally stable under the 'Euler' equation, take the special case of (15) with $\alpha = \delta = \xi = \sigma = 1$, $f = 8$, and $r = \frac{1}{5}$. From (16),

$$g(n) = \begin{cases} 8 - \dfrac{1}{n} - \dfrac{n}{1 - n} - \dfrac{2(\frac{6}{5})n}{(1 - n)^2}; & \dfrac{1}{8} < n < 1 \\[4mm] -\dfrac{n}{1 - n} - \dfrac{2(\frac{6}{5})n}{(1 - n)^2}; & 0 < n \leqslant \dfrac{1}{8} \end{cases} \quad (18)$$

A stationary equilibrium is an n in the interval $(0, 1)$ with $g(n) = 0$. By (18) such an n must lie in the subinterval $(\frac{1}{8}, 1)$ because $g(n) < 0$ on

$(0, \frac{1}{8})$. But within that subinterval it is easily verified that g is strictly concave, that $g < 0$ at each end of the subinterval, and that g attains positive values inside the subinterval (because $g(\frac{1}{2}) = \frac{1}{5}$). Hence there are exactly two stationary equilibria, as in Figure 13.1: the lower one $n_L \in (\frac{1}{8}, \frac{1}{2})$, and the higher one $n_H \in (\frac{1}{2}, 1)$. To verify that n_L is locally stable, note that because $n_L > \frac{1}{8}$, therefore $\gamma_{12}(\delta n_L, n_L)/\gamma_{11}(\delta n_L, n_L) = 2n_L/(1 - n_L) > \frac{2}{7} > \frac{1}{5} = r$.

13.6 ECONOMIC STABILITY AND INDETERMINACY

The local stability properties of the 'Euler' equation (9) are sufficient to derive our main observability results, which address the question of whether there exist equilibrium trajectories that converge upon the stationary equilibrium in question. But a positive answer to this observability question does not guarantee that every time the economy begins in a neighborhood of a stationary equilibrium employment will in fact converge to that stationary equilibrium. That is, it does not guarantee that each stationary equilibrium is stable in the economic sense.

Consider, for example, the phase diagram Figure 13.2, corresponding to Figure 13.1, in the case where n_L is locally stable. The economy could

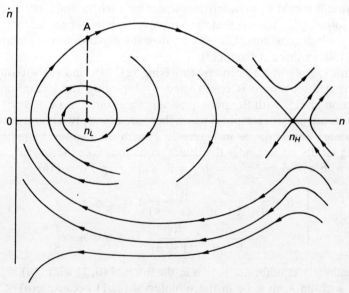

Figure 13.2 Local stability.

start with employment equal to n_L yet follow the trajectory starting at point A that approaches n_H. Likewise every time initial employment was near n_L, it could follow this same path to n_H. Because it converges to n_H, any trajectory that follows this path is an equilibrium trajectory. Furthermore, if, as drawn, this convergent path bends down underneath n_L, then there will be two equilibrium trajectories starting at such an initial point that converge to n_H; one that starts with $\dot{n} < 0$, the other with $\dot{n} > 0$. By the same token there may be an equilibrium trajectory starting at such an initial point that converges upon the degenerate equilibrium at the origin. Thus, even though n_L is locally stable under the 'Euler' equation (9), it may not be economically stable.

Similar qualifications must be made with respect to the saddlepoint equilibria. As in Figure 13.2 there may be an equilibrium path that goes through n_H and converges to the origin. Furthermore, if, as shown in Figure 13.3, the stable path leading to n_H bends back under n_H as well as under n_L, there can be a continuum of equilibrium trajectories starting from any n in the neighborhood of n_H and converging upon n_L; specifically any trajectory starting in the shaded open loop of Figure 13.3 formed by the stable path.[3] (All paths diverging to the northeast violate 'transversality.')

Thus, although a stationary equilibrium that is either a saddlepoint or

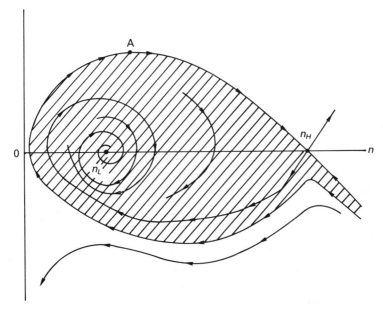

Figure 13.3 Perfect foresight paths.

locally stable will be potentially observable, the economy may never approach it no matter how close it starts to it. It all depends upon which of the equilibrium trajectories is selected, and our analysis says nothing about how the equilibrium trajectory is selected.[4]

There is one consideration that makes the locally stable low-level equilibrium more likely to be observed than the high-level saddlepoint. As Figures 13.2 and 13.3 illustrate, starting from any initial position that has some trajectories converging to n_L and some to n_H there will generally be a finite number converging on n_H but a continuum converging on n_L. Thus, a mechanism that selected an equilibrium trajectory at random would almost never select one converging on n_H.

We hasten to add, however, that the existence of a continuum of equilibrium trajectories raises the question of whether any of the trajectories will be followed. Along each of these trajectories every firm has perfectly predicted the employment decisions of every other firm. But in the absence of some mechanism for coordinating firms' predictions, there seems to be no way that an isolated firm could make such a prediction. It seems more likely that the firms would have to follow some trial-and-error procedure, which at most would converge asymptotically upon one of the equilibrium trajectories that we have described.[5] Our main point is just that, in the absence of any such trial-and-error analysis, we cannot rule out the possibility that the low-level equilibrium of Figure 13.1 will be stable in an economically meaningful sense.

13.7 OTHER APPLICATIONS

The general form of our model (i.e. the differential equation (9) with the assumptions (2), (4), and (5)) is obviously applicable to a variety of problems other than the aggregate employment problem that has motivated our analysis. The important characteristic of such a problem is that it can be described as the outcome of firms' intertemporal maximization, with current profits subject to an external economy sufficiently strong to make (4) hold, and eventually subject to diseconomies, either internal or external, that make (5) hold. What we have shown is that in such a context all stationary equilibria may be potentially observable, provided that there is an external diseconomy of expansion. Specifically, the equilibria at which $g'(n) < 0$ will exhibit the usual saddlepoint stability and each of the nonsaddle equilibria will be the limit of a continuum of perfect foresight trajectories going through the same initial activity level if $\gamma_{12}/\gamma_{11} > r$.

One context where the analysis might apply is that of the growth of a city. Agglomeration economies coexist with the natural limits imposed by the availability of land. Thus, not only might there be multiple equilibrium sizes to the city but each one might be observable.

Another example might be the market for any new product whose demand is ultimately limited by the availability of potential customers. The economy of scale could arise for a variety of reasons. Imitators can free-ride on the increasing familiarity that raises demand when other firms operate on a larger scale, as IBM has been accused of doing with several products (see, for example, Burstein, 1984). There is the likelihood that a service network or an auxiliary product market will develop for propane gas, for quadraphonic hi-fis that require special tapes, or for turbo-engined cars that require servicing by specially trained mechanics.[6] In all these cases the analysis suggests that one is likely to find observable low-level equilibria.

The analysis may also be applicable to the development of the standard arrangement of keys in typewriters. As David (1985) has argued, the standard arrangement is demonstrably inferior to known alternatives, yet it persists. Here we have a case of an equilibrium with a low level of quality. David argues that external economies of scale have been important in explaining the stability of that low level. Manufacturers do not find it profitable to raise the quality until typists begin to learn on an improved arrangement, and typists do not find it worthwhile to learn until manufacturers change.

As a final example, consider the process of economic growth, which, according to countless writers from Adam Smith through Schumpeter, is intimately connected with external economies of scale. Romer (1983) has analyzed this problem with a model similar to ours. His model, however, does not have the diseconomies of expansion required to render all stationary equilibria observable. Our analysis suggests that combining the limitations of finite natural resources together with the external economies considered by Romer can give rise to stable low-level equilibria.

In all these examples, including the unemployment example of the previous sections, the multiplicity of equilibria obviously depends upon the firms' inability to internalize the external economy of scale. Similarly, the local stability of low-level equilibria depends on the firms' inability to internalize the diseconomy of expansion. Such inability seems to make most sense in the macro examples of unemployment and economic growth, where internal diseconomies are likely to discourage the large-scale organization of the market in question under a few entrepreneurs. Casual empiricism suggests that internalization does occur in some of the micro examples cited, as where computer companies pay others to write software for their microcomputers. Still there is no a priori reason to believe that it is so extensive as to completely vitiate our analysis.

APPENDIX: DERIVATION OF EQUATION (12)
Define

$$\phi(\ddot{n}, \dot{n}, n) = L_2(\dot{n}, n, n) + rL_1(\dot{n}, n, n) - L_{11}(\dot{n}, n, n)\ddot{n}$$
$$- L_{12}(\dot{n}, n, n)\dot{n} - L_{13}(\dot{n}, n, n)\dot{n}$$

Equation (9) forces $\phi(\ddot{n}, \dot{n}, n) = 0$. Note that

$$\phi_1(0, 0, n) = - L_{11}(0, n, n)$$

$$\phi_2(0, 0, n) = L_{12}(0, n, n) + rL_{11}(0, n, n) - L_{111}(0, n, n)\ddot{n}$$
$$- (L_{12}(0, n, n) + L_{13}(0, n, n))$$
$$- (L_{121}(0, n, n) + L_{131}(0, n, n))\dot{n}$$

$$= rL_{11}(0, n, n) - L_{13}(0, n, n)$$

$$\phi_3(0, 0, n) = L_{22}(0, n, n) + L_{23}(0, n, n) + rL_{12}(0, n, n)$$
$$+ rL_{13}(0, n, n) - \ddot{n}(L_{112} + L_{113})$$
$$- \dot{n}[L_{122} + L_{123} + L_{132} + L_{133}]$$

$$= L_{22}(0, n, n) + L_{23}(0, n, n) + r(L_{12}(0, n, n) +$$
$$L_{13}(0, n, n))$$

Now use a first-order Taylor expansion around an equilibrium n^*, so that

$$\phi(0, 0, n^*) = 0$$

$$0 = \phi(\ddot{n}, \dot{n}, n) \simeq \phi(0, 0, n^*) + \phi_1(0, 0, n^*)(\ddot{n} - 0)$$
$$+ \phi_2(0, 0, n^*)(\dot{n} - 0) + \phi_3(0, 0, n^*)(n - n^*)$$

$$= - L_{11}(0, n, n)\ddot{n} + [rL_{11}(0, n, n) - L_{13}(0, n, n)]\dot{n}$$
$$+ [L_{22}(0, n, n) + L_{23}(0, n, n) + r(L_{12}(0, n, n)$$
$$+ L_{13}(0, n, n))](n - n^*)$$

Multiplying both sides by (-1), we obtain (12).

NOTES

1. Diamond and Fudenberg (1989) also show the possibility that the lower of two nondegenerate stationary equilibria can be a sink in the Diamond (1982b) model of trade externalities. Their analysis, which is directed toward

showing the existence of deterministic cycles, does not show the dependence of this result on an expansion diseconomy.

2. We are assuming here that if there is an 'encouraged worker' effect on participation rates, a unit increase in $\bar{n}$ raises the labor force by less than one unit. For a more detailed discussion of this diseconomy, see Section 13.5 below.

3. Guckenheimer and Holmes (1983: 290 ff.) give examples of second-order systems with configurations like those of Figures 13.2 and 13.3. Generally, there may be only one path to n_H.

4. Efficiency aspects of equilibrium trajectories are complicated by the presence of both external economies and external diseconomies. Furthermore, in the search interpretation of the labor market, the wage-setting rule will generally induce inefficiencies, as shown by Mortensen (1982a). But we can be sure that when $\gamma_{12} > 0$ the equilibrium trajectories do not maximize any intertemporally additive social welfare function with a rate of discount r, for that would require the roots of (9) to sum to r. In the specific example analyzed in the previous version of this chapter (1984b), the trajectory that led monotonically to n_H Pareto-dominated every other trajectory from the same initial value of n.

5. Mussa (1984) points out other problematic aspects of models with a continuum of convergent solutions, most notably that they lack a dependency of current endogenous variables upon predictable future variations in exogenous variables. Whether this lack is a defect of such models, as Mussa asserts, or an empirical prediction that may be hard to reject in some contexts remains to be seen.

6. Markusen (1984) analyzes several examples of this sort.

REFERENCES

Abraham, Katharine, and Lawrence Katz (1986), 'Cyclical unemployment: Sectoral shifts or aggregate disturbances?' *Journal of Political Economy* **94**, June 507–22.

Akerlof, George A. and Janet L. Yellen (1985a), 'Can small deviations from rationality make significant differences to economic equilibria?' *American Economic Review* **75** September, 708–21.

Akerlof, George A., and Janet L. Yellen (1985b), 'A near-rational model of the business cycle, with wage and price inertia,' *Quarterly Journal of Economics* **100** (Supplement); 823–38.

Archibald, G. Christopher (1969), 'The Phillips curve and the distribution of unemployment,' *American Economic Review Proceedings* **59**, May, 124–34.

Archibald, G. Christopher, and Richard G. Lipsey (1958), 'Monetary and value theory: a critique of Lange and Patinkin,' *Review of Economic Studies* **26**, October, 1–22.

Arrow, Kenneth J., H.D. Block and L. Hurwicz (1959), 'On the stability of the competitive equilibrium II,' *Econometrica* **27**, January, 82–109.

Arrow, Kenneth J., and Frank H. Hahn (1971), *General Competitive Analysis*. San Francisco: Holden-Day.

Arrow, Kenneth J., and Leonid Hurwicz (1958), 'On the stability of the competitive equilibrium I,' *Econometrica* **26**, October, 522–52.

Azariadis, Costas (1975), 'Implicit contracts and underemployment equilibria,' *Journal of Political Economy*, **83**, December, 1183–202.

Azariadis, Costas (1981), 'Self-fulfilling prophecies,' *Journal of Economic Theory* **25**, December, 380–96.

Barro, Robert J. (1976), 'Rational expectations and the role of monetary policy,' *Journal of Monetary Economics* **2**, January, 1–32.

Barro, Robert J. (1977a), 'Unanticipated money growth and unemployment in the United States,' *American Economic Review* **67**, March, 101–15.

Barro, Robert J (1977b), 'Long-term contracting, sticky prices, and monetary policy,' *Journal of Monetary Economics* **3**, July, 305–16.

Barro, Robert J. (1979), 'Second thoughts on Keynesian economics,' *American Economic Review Proceedings* **69**, May, 54–9.

Barro, Robert J., and Herschel I. Grossman (1971), 'A general disequilibrium model of income and employment,' *American Economic Review* **61**, March, 82–93.

Barro, Robert J., and Herschel I. Grossman (1976), *Money, Employment, and Inflation*. New York: Cambridge University Press.

Baumol, William J. (1952), 'The transactions demand for cash: An inventory theoretic approach,' *Quarterly Journal of Economics* **66**, November, 545–56.

Baumol, William J., Robert W. Clower, Meyer L. Burstein, Frank H. Hahn, R.J. Ball, R. Bodkin, G. Christopher Archibald and Richard G. Lipsey, (1960), 'A symposium on monetary theory,' *Review of Economic Studies* **28**, October, 29–56.

Blanchard, Olivier J. (1986), 'The wage–price spiral,' *Quarterly Journal of Economics* **101**, August, 543–65.

Blanchard, Olivier J., and Nobuhiro Kiyotaki (1987), 'Monopolistic competition and the effects of aggregate demand,' *American Economic Review* **77**, September, 647–66.

Blanchard, Olivier J., and Mark Watson (1982), 'Bubbles, rational expectations, and financial markets.' In Paul Wachtel (ed.), *Crises in the Economic and Financial Structure*. Lexington, Ma.: Lexington Books.

Bliss, Christopher J. (1975), 'The reappraisal of Keynes' economics: An appraisal.' In A.R. Nobay and Michael Parkin (eds.), *Current Economic Problems: The Proceedings of the A.U.T.E., Manchester, 1974*. New York: Cambridge University Press.

Boschen, John F. and Herschel I. Grossman (1982), 'Tests of equilibrium macroeconomics using contemporaneous monetary data,' *Journal of Monetary Economics* **10**, November, 309–33.

Brainard, William C. (1967), 'Uncertainty and the effectiveness of policy,' *American Economic Review Proceedings* **57**, May, 411–25.

Brechling, Frank (1975), *Investment and Employment Decisions*. Manchester: Manchester University Press.

Brock, William A. (1975), 'A simple perfect foresight monetary model,' *Journal of Monetary Economics* **1**, April, 133–50.

Burstein, Meyer L. (1984), 'Diffusion of knowledge-based products,' University of Western Ontario Centre for Economic Analysis of Property Rights, Paper No. 84–05, February.

Bushaw, Donald W., and Robert W. Clower (1957), *Introduction to Mathematical Economics*. Homewood, Ill.: Irwin.

Cagan, Phillip (1956), 'The monetary dynamics of hyperinflation.' In Milton Friedman (ed.), *Studies in the Quantity Theory of Money*. Chicago: University of Chicago Press.

Calvo, Guillermo A. (1979), 'On models of money and perfect foresight,' *International Economic Review* **20**, February, 83–103.

Caskey, John and Steve Fazzari (1985), 'Monetary contractions with nominal debt commitments: Is wage flexibility stabilizing?' Unpublished paper, Washington University.

Clapham, J.H. (1944), *The Bank of England*, vol. 2. Cambridge: Cambridge University Press.

Clower, Robert W. (1963), 'Permanent income and transitory balances: Hahn's paradox,' *Oxford Economic Papers* **15**, June, 177–90.

Clower, Robert W. (1965), 'The Keynesian counter–revolution: A theoretical appraisal.' In Frank H. Hahn and Frank P.R. Brechling (eds.), *The Theory of Interest Rates.* London: Macmillan.

Clower, Robert W. (1967), 'A reconsideration of the microfoundations of monetary theory,' *Western Economic Journal* **6**, December, 1–9.

Clower, Robert W. (1969), 'Introduction,' *Readings in Monetary Theory.* Harmondsworth: Penguin.

Clower, Robert W. (1971), 'The microfoundations of monetary theory: Reply,' *Western Economic Journal* **9**, September, 304–5.

Clower, Robert W. (1975), 'Reflections on the Keynesian perplex,' *Zeitschrift für Nationalökonomie*, July, 1–24.

Clower, Robert W. (1984), 'Afterward' to Donald A. Walker (ed.), *Money and Markets.* New York: Cambridge University Press.

Clower, Robert W. (1986), 'What's left of the General Theory?' Paper presented to meetings of Eastern Economics Association, Philadelphia, April.

Clower, Robert W., and Peter W. Howitt (1978), 'The transactions theory of the demand for money: A reconsideration,' *Journal of Political Economy* **86**, June, 449–66.

Clower, Robert W., and Bruce Johnson (1968), 'Income, wealth, and the theory of consumption.' In J.N. Wolfe (ed.), *Value, Capital and Growth.* Chicago: Aldine.

Coddington, E.A., and N. Levinson (1955), *Theory of Ordinary Differential Equations.* New York: McGraw–Hill.

Cooley, T.F., S.F. LeRoy and N. Raymon (1984), 'Econometric policy evaluation: Note,' *American Economic Review* **74**, June, 467–70.

Cooper, Russell, and Andrew John (1988), 'Coordinating coordination failures in Keynesian models,' *Quarterly Journal of Economics* **103**, August, 441–63.

David, Paul (1985), 'Clio and the Economics of QWERTY,' *American Economic Review Proceedings* **75**, May, 332–7.

Davis, Steven (1986), 'Fluctuations in the pace of labor reallocation,' unpublished, University of Chicago, October.

DeLong, J. Bradford, and Lawrence H. Summers (1986a), 'The changing cyclical variability of economic activity in the United States.' In Robert J. Gordon (ed.), *The American Business Cycle: Continuity and Change.* Chicago: University of Chicago Press.

DeLong, J. Bradford, and Lawrence H. Summers (1986b), 'Is increased price flexibility stabilizing?' *American Economic Review* **76**, December, 1031–44.

Diamond, Peter A. (1982a), 'Wage determination and efficiency in search equilibrium,' *Review of Economic Studies* **49**, April, 217–27.

Diamond, Peter A. (1982b), 'Aggregate demand management in search equilibrium,' *Journal of Political Economy* **90**, October, 881–94.

Diamond, Peter A. (1984a), 'Money in search equilibrium,' *Econometrica* **52**, January, 1–20.

Diamond, Peter A. (1984b), *A Search Equilibrium Approach to the Micro Foundations of Macroeconomics.* Cambridge, Ma.: MIT Press.

Diamond, Peter A. (1987), 'Equilibrium without an auctioneer.' In Truman Bewley (ed.), *Advances in Economic Theory*. New York: Cambridge University Press.

Diamond, Peter A., and D. Fudenberg (1989), 'Rational–expectations business cycles in search equilibrium,' *Journal of Political Economy* **97**, June, 606–19.

Dold, A. and B. Eckmann (eds.) (1976), *Structural Stability, the Theory of Catastrophies, and Applications in the Sciences*. New York: Springer–Verlag.

Dubey, P., and J.D. Rogawski (1982), 'Inefficiency of Nash equilibria: I,' Cowles Foundation Discussion Paper #662, Yale University.

Edgeworth, F.Y. (1881), *Mathematical Psychics*. London: Kegan Paul.

Elster, Jon (1979), *Ulysses and the Sirens*. New York: Cambridge University Press.

Evans, George (1985), 'Expectational stability and the multiple equilibria problem in linear rational expectations models,' *Quarterly Journal of Economics* **100**, November, 1217–34.

Fane, G. (1977), 'Stabilization policy in models with rational expectations and uncertainty,' Mimeographed, Australian National University

Feige, Edgar L., and Douglas K. Pearce (1976), 'Economically rational expectations: Are innovations in the rate of inflation independent of innovations in measures of monetary and fiscal policy?' *Journal of Political Economy* **84**, June, 499–522.

Fischer, Stanley (1977), 'Long–term contracts, rational expectations, and the optimal money supply rule,' *Journal of Political Economy* **85**, February, 191–206.

Fisher, F.M. (1972), 'On price adjustment without an auctioneer,' *Review of Economic Studies* **39**, January, 1–15.

Fisher, Irving (1931), *Booms and Depressions*. New York: Adelphi.

Fisher, Irving (1933), 'The debt–deflation theory of great depressions,' *Econometrica* **1**, October, 337–57.

Frenkel, Jacob A. (1975), 'Inflation and the formation of expectations,' *Journal of Monetary Economics* **1**, October, 403–21.

Frevert, Peter (1970), 'On the stability of full employment equilibrium,' *Review of Economic Studies* **37**, April, 239–51.

Friedman, Benjamin M. (1979), 'Optimal expectations and the extreme information assumptions of "rational expectations" macromodels,' *Journal of Monetary Economics* **5**, January, 23–41.

Friedman, Milton (1953), 'The effects of a full–employment policy on economic stability: A formal analysis.' In *Essays in Positive Economics*. Chicago: University of Chicago Press.

Friedman, Milton (1968), 'The role of monetary policy,' *American Economic Review* **58**, March, 1–17.

Friedman, Milton (1970a), *The Counter-Revolution in Monetary Economics*. London: International Economics Association.

Friedman, Milton (1970b), 'A theoretical framework for monetary analysis,' *Journal of Political Economy* **78**, March/April, 193–238.

Friedman, Milton (1971), 'A monetary theory of nominal income,' *Journal of Political Economy* **79**, March/April, 323–37.

Friedman, Milton, and David Meiselman (1963), 'The relative stability of monetary velocity and the investment multiplier in the United States, 1898–1958.' In Commission on Money and Credit, *Stabilization Policies.* Englewood Cliffs, N.J.: Prentice–Hall.

Friedman, Milton, and Anna Schwartz (1963), *A Monetary History of the United States 1867–1960.* Princeton: Princeton University Press.

Frydman, Roman, and Edmund S. Phelps (eds.) (1983), *Individual Forecasting and Aggregate Outcomes.* New York: Cambridge University Press.

Gantmacher, F.R. (1959), *The Theory of Matrices,* vol. II. New York: Chelsea.

Geary, Patrick T. and John Kennan (1982), 'The employment–real wage relationship: An international study,' *Journal of Political Economy* **90**, August, 854–71.

Gordon, Robert J. (1982), 'Price inertia and policy ineffectiveness in the United States, 1890–1980, *Journal of Political Economy* **90**, December, 1087–117.

Grandmont, Jean-Michel (1977), 'Temporary general equilibrium theory,' *Econometrica* **45**, April, 535–72.

Granger, C.W.J., and A.P. Andersen (1978), *An Introduction to Bilinear Time Series Models.* Gottingen: Vandenhoeck and Ruprecht.

Grossman, Herschel I. (1971), 'Money, interest, and prices in market disequilibrium,' *Journal of Political Economy* **79**, September/October, 943–61.

Grossman, Herschel I. (1972a), 'Was Keynes a 'Keynesian'?: A review article,' *Journal of Economic Literature* **10**, March, 26–30.

Grossman, Herschel I. (1972b), 'A choice–theoretic model of an income–investment accelerator,' *American Economic Review* **62**, September, 630–41.

Grossman, Herschel I. (1974), 'Effective demand failures: A comment,' *Swedish Journal of Economics* **76**, September, 358–65.

Grossman, Herschel I. (1979), 'Why does aggregate employment fluctuate?' *American Economic Review Proceedings* **69**, May, 64–9.

Grossman, Sanford J., and Joseph E. Stiglitz (1976), 'Information and competitive price systems,' *American Economic Review Proceedings* **66**, May, 246–53.

Guckenheimer, J., and P. Holmes (1983), *Nonlinear Oscillations, Dynamical Systems, and Bifurcations of Vector Fields.* New York: Springer–Verlag.

Hadar, J. (1965), 'A note on stock–flow models of consumer behavior,' *Quarterly Journal of Economics* **79**, May, 304–9.

Hahn, Frank H. (1962), 'Real balances and consumption,' *Oxford Economic Papers* **14**, June, 117–23.

Hahn, Frank H. (1965), 'On some problems of proving the existence of an equilibrium in a monetary economy.' In Frank H. Hahn and Frank P.R. Brechling (eds.), *The Theory of Interest Rates.* London: Macmillan.

Hahn, Frank H. (1971), 'Equilibrium with transaction costs,' *Econometrica* **39**, May, 417–39.

Hahn, Frank H. (1978), 'On non–Walrasian equilibria,' *Review of Economic Studies* **45**, February, 1–17.

Hahn, Frank H., and T. Negishi (1962), 'A theorem on non–tâtonnement stability,' *Econometrica* **30**, July, 463–9.

Haltiwanger, John and Michael Waldman (1985), 'Rational expectations and the limits of rationality,' *American Economic Review* **75**, June, 326–40.

Hansen Lars P., and Kenneth J. Singleton (1982), 'Generalized instrumental variables estimation of nonlinear rational expectations models,' *Econometrica* **60**, September, 1269–86.

Hayek, Friedrich A. von (1945), 'The use of knowledge in society,' *American Economic Review* **35**, September, 519–30.

Hellwig, Martin F. (1977), 'A model of borrowing and lending with bankruptcy,' *Econometrica* **45**, November, 1879–1906.

Hicks, Sir John R. (1937), 'Mr Keynes and the "Classics": A suggested interpretation,' *Econometrica* **5**, April, 145–59.

Hicks, Sir John R. (1946), *Value and Capital*, 2nd edn. Oxford: Clarendon.

Hirshleifer, Jack (1971), 'The private and social value of information and the reward to inventive activity,' *American Economic Review* **61**, September, 561–74.

Hosios, Arthur (1986), 'On the efficiency of matching and related models of search and unemployment,' unpublished, University of Toronto, September.

Howitt, Peter W. (1973), 'Studies in the theory of monetary dynamics,' Doctoral dissertation, Northwestern University.

Howitt, Peter W. (1979), 'The role of speculation in competitive price dynamics,' *Review of Economic Studies* **46**, October, 613–29.

Howitt, Peter W. (1982), 'Anti-Inflation policy with a skeptical public.' In Karl Brunner and Allan Meltzer (eds.), *Economic Policy in A World of Change*. Amsterdam: North Holland.

Howitt, Peter W., and R. Preston McAfee (1984a), 'Search, recruiting and the indeterminacy of the natural rate of unemployment,' Economics Department Research Report, No. 8325, University of Western Ontario (revised August).

Howitt, Peter W., and R. Preston McAfee (1984b), 'Stable Low-Level Equilibrium,' unpublished.

Intriligator, Michael (1971), *Mathematical Optimization and Economic Theory*. Englewood Cliffs: Prentice-Hall.

Iwai, Katsuhito (1981), *Disequilibrium Dynamics*. New Haven: Yale University Press.

Ize, Alain (1977), 'Corridor effects in a monetary economy,' unpublished, Stanford University.

Johnson, Harry G. (1971), 'The Keynesian revolution and the monetarist counter-revolution,' *American Economic Review Proceedings* **61**, May, 1–14.

Jones, Robert A. (1976), 'The origin and development of media of exchange,' *Journal of Political Economy* **84**, August, 757–75.

Jones, Robert A., and Joseph Ostroy (1984), 'Flexibility and uncertainty,' *Review of Economic Studies* **51**, January, 13–32.

Kaldor, Nicholas (1934), 'A classificatory note on the determinateness of equilibrium', *Review of Economic Studies* **1**, February, 122–36.

Keynes, J.M. (1972), 'Economic possibilities for our grandchildren,' quoted from *The Collected Writings of John Maynard Keynes*, vol. IX. London:

Macmillan. Originally published in *The Nation and Athenaeum*, October 11 and 18, 1930.

Keynes, J.M. (1936), *The General Theory of Employment, Interest and Money*. London: Macmillan.

Keynes, J.M. (1937), 'The general theory of unemployment,' *Quarterly Journal of Economics* **51**, February, 209–23.

Klamer, Arjo (1984), *Conversations with Economists*. Totowa, N.J.: Rowman and Allanheld.

Kohn, Meir (1981), 'A loanable funds theory of unemployment and monetary disequilibrium,' *American Economic Review* **71**, December, 859–79.

Kydland, F.E. and E.C. Prescott (1982), 'Time to build and aggregate fluctuations,' *Econometrica* **50**, November, 1345–70.

Laidler, David E.W. (1978), 'Money and money income: An essay on the 'transmission mechanism', *Journal of Monetary Economics* **4**, April, 151–91.

Laidler, David E.W. (1981), 'Monetarism: An interpretation and an assessment,' *Economic Journal* **91**, March, 1–28.

Laidler, David E.W. (1982), 'On Say's law, money, and the business cycle.' In *Monetarist Perspectives*. Oxford: Philip Allan.

Laidler, David E.W. (1984), 'The 'buffer stock' notion in monetary economics,' *Conference Proceedings, Supplement to the Economic Journal* **94**, March, 17–34.

Laidler, David E.W. (1988), 'Taking money seriously,' *Canadian Journal of Economics* **21**, November, 687–713.

LaSalle, J. and S. Lefshetz (1961), *Stability by Lyapounov's Direct Method with Applications*. New York: Academic Press.

Leijonhufvud, Axel (1968), *On Keynesian Economics and the Economics of Keynes: A Study in Monetary Theory*. New York: Oxford University Press.

Leijonhufvud, Axel (1973), 'Effective demand failures,' *Swedish Journal of Economics* **75**, March, 27–48.

Leijonhufvud, Axel (1981a), 'The Wicksell connection' In *Information and Coordination*. New York: Oxford University Press.

Leijonhufvud, Axel (1981b), *Information and Coordination*. New York: Oxford University Press.

Lilien, David M. (1982), 'Sectoral shifts and cyclical unemployment,' *Journal of Political Economy* **90**, August, 777–93.

Lipsey, Richard G. (1960), 'The relation between unemployment and the rate of change of money wage rates in the United Kingdom, 1862–1957: A further analysis,' *Economica* **27**, February, 1–31.

Liviatan, N., and P.A. Samuelson (1969), 'Notes on turnpikes: Stable and unstable,' *Journal of Economic Theory* **1**, December, 454–75.

Lloyd, Cliff (1971), 'The microfoundations of monetary theory: Comment,' *Western Economic Journal* **9**, September, 299–303.

Long, J.B. and C.I. Plosser (1983), 'Real business cycles,' *Journal of Political Economy* **91**, February, 39–69.

Lorie, Henri (1977), 'A model of Keynesian dynamics,' *Oxford Economic Papers* **29**, February, 30–47.

Lucas, Robert E. Jr. (1972), 'Expectations and the neutrality of money,' *Journal of Economic Theory* **4**, April, 103–24.

Lucas, Robert E. Jr. (1973), 'Some international evidence on output–inflation tradeoffs,' *American Economic Review* **63**, June, 326–34.

Lucas, Robert E. Jr. (1975), An equilibrium model of the business cycle,' *Journal of Political Economy* **83**, November/December, 1113–44.

Lucas, Robert E. Jr. (1980a), 'Methods and problems in business cycle theory,' *Journal of Money, Credit, and Banking* **12**, November, Part 2, 695–715.

Lucas, Robert E. Jr. (1980b), 'Equilibrium in a pure currency economy,' *Economic Inquiry* **18**, April, 203–20.

Lucas, Robert E. Jr. (1986), 'Adaptive behavior and economic theory,' *Journal of Business* **52**, October, S401–S426.

Lucas, Robert E. Jr., and Edward Prescott (1974), 'Equilibrium search and unemployment,' *Journal of Economic Theory* **7**, February, 188–209.

Lucas, Robert E. Jr., and Thomas J. Sargent (1978), 'After Keynesian macroeconomics.' In Federal Reserve Bank of Boston, *After the Phillips Curve*. Boston, Mass.

Lutz, Friedrich A. and Lloyd W. Mints (eds.) (1951), *Readings in Monetary Theory*. Homewood, Ill.: Irwin.

McCallum, Bennett T. (1976), 'Rational expectations and the natural rate hypothesis: Some consistent estimates,' *Econometrica* **44**, January, 43–52.

McCallum, Bennett T. (1978), 'Price level adjustments and the rational expectations approach to macroeconomic stabilization policy,' *Journal of Money, Credit, and Banking* **10**, November, 418–36.

Malinvaud, Edmond (1977), *The Theory of Unemployment Reconsidered*. Oxford: Blackwell.

Mankiw, G., J. Rotemberg, and L. Summers (1985), 'Intertemporal substitution in macroeconomics,' *Quarterly Journal of Economics* **100**, February, 225–51.

Marcet, Albert, and Thomas J. Sargent (1986), 'Convergence of least squares learning mechanisms in self referential linear stochastic models,' mimeo, The Hoover Institution, July.

Markusen, James R. (1984), 'Micro-foundations of external economies,' unpublished, University of Western Ontario.

Minsky, Hyman (1964), 'Longer waves in financial arrangements: Financial factors in the more severe depressions,' *American Economic Review Proceedings* **54**, May, 324–35.

Minsky, Hyman (1968), 'The Crunch and its aftermath,' *The Banker's Magazine* **205**, February, 78–82, and March, 171–3.

Minsky, Hyman (1969), 'Private sector asset management and the effectiveness of monetary policy: Theory and policy,' *Journal of Finance* **24**, May, 223–38.

Modigliani, Franco (1944), 'Liquidity preference and the theory of interest and money,' *Econometrica* **12**, January, 45–88.

Mortenson, Dale T. (1982a), 'The matching process as a noncooperative bargaining game.' In J.J. McCall (ed.), *The Economics of Information and Uncertainty*. Chicago: University of Chicago Press.

Mortenson, Dale T. (1982b), 'Property rights and efficiency in mating, racing, and related games,' *Amercian Economic Review* **72**, December, 968–79.

Mundell, Robert (1963), 'Inflation and real interest,' *Journal of Political Economy* **71**, June, 280–3.

Mussa, Michael (1984), 'Rational expectations models with a continuum of convergent solutions,' N.B.E.R. Technical Working Paper No. 41, June.

Negishi, Takashi (1962), 'The stability of a competitive equilibrium: A survey article,' *Econometrica* **30**, October, 635–69.

Negishi, Takashi (1976), 'Unemployment, inflation, and the microfoundations of macroeconomics.' In M.J. Artis and A. Nobay (eds.), *Essays in Economic Analysis*. Cambridge: Cambridge University Press.

Newman, Peter (1965), *The Theory of Exchange*. Englewood Cliffs: Prentice-Hall.

Niehans, Jürg (1971), 'Money and barter in general equilibrium with transactions costs,' *American Economic Review* **61**, December, 773–83.

Okun, Arthur M. (1981), *Prices and Quantities: A Macroeconomic Analysis*. Washington: The Brookings Institution.

Olech, C. (1963), 'On the stability of an autonomous system in a plane.' In *Contributions to Differential Equations* **I**, 389–400.

Ostroy, Joseph M. (1973) 'The informational efficiency of monetary exchange,' *American Economic Review* **63**, September, 597–610.

Patinkin, Don (1948), 'Price flexibility and full employment,' *American Economic Review* **38**, September, 543–64.

Patinkin, Don (1951), 'Price flexibility and full employment,' reprinted with alterations in Friedrich A. Lutz and Lloyd W. Mints (eds.), *Readings in Monetary Theory*. Homewood, Ill.: Irwin.

Patinkin, Don (1956), *Money, Interest, and Prices*. Evanston, Ill.: Row Peterson.

Patinkin, Don (1958), 'Liquidity preference and loanable funds: Stock and flow analysis,' *Economica* **25**, November, 300–18.

Patinkin, Don (1965), *Money, Interest, and Prices*. 2nd edn. New York: Harper and Row.

Patinkin, Don (1969), 'The Chicago tradition, the quantity theory, and Friedman,' *Journal of Money, Credit, and Banking* **1**, February, 46–70.

Patinkin, Don (1976), *Keynes' monetary thought: A study of its development*. Durham, N.C.: Duke University Press.

Patinkin, Don (1987), 'Walras's Law.' In John Eatwell, Murray Milgate, and Peter Newnam (eds.), *The New Palgrave: A Dictionary of Economics*, vol IV. London: Macmillan, pp. 863–8.

Patinkin, Don (1988), 'On the *General Theory*,' mimeo, UCLA, December.

Phelps,, Edmund S (1970), 'Money wage dynamics and labor market equilibrium.' In Edmund S. Phelps, Armen A. Alchian, Charles C. Holt, Dale T. Mortenson, G. Christopher Archibald, Robert E. Lucas Jr., Leonard A. Rapping, Sidney G. Winter Jr., John P. Gould, Donald F. Gordon, Allan Hynes, Donald A. Nichols, Paul J. Taubman and Maurice Wilkinson, (eds.) *Microeconomic Foundations of Employment and Inflation Theory*. New York: Norton.

Phelps, Edmund S., et al. (1970), *Microeconomic Foundations of Employment and Inflation Theory*. New York: Norton.

Phelps, Edmund S., and John B. Taylor (1977), 'Stabilizing powers of monetary policy under rational expectations,' *Journal of Political Economy* **85**, February, 163–90.

Pissarides, Christopher (1984), 'Search intensity, job advertising, and efficiency,' *Journal of Labor Economics* **2**, January, 128–43.

Pissarides, Christopher (1985a), 'Short-run equilibrium dynamics of unemployment, vacancies, and real wages,' *American Economic Review* **75**, September, 676–90.

Pissarides, Christopher (1985b), 'Observable shocks and equilibrium cycles in a model of money and growth,' unpublished, London School of Economics, September.

Poole, William (1976), 'Rational expectations in the macro model,' *Brookings Papers on Economic Activity*, no. 2, 463–505.

Prescott, Edward C. (1986), 'Theory ahead of business cycle measurement,' paper presented to U.W.O. conference on Business Cycles – Theory and Evidence, London, Ontario, April.

Purvis, Douglas D. (1978), 'Dynamic models of portfolio behavior: More on pitfalls in financial model building,' *American Economic Review* **68**, June, 403–9.

Quinn, B.G. (1982), 'A note on the existence of strictly stationary solutions to bilinear equations,' *Journal of Time Series Analysis* **3** (4), 249–52.

Rogerson, Richard D. (1984), 'Indivisible labor, lotteries and equilibrium,' ch. of *Topics in the Theory of Labor Markets*, Ph.D dissertation, University of Minnesota.

Romer, Paul (1983), 'Dynamic competitive equilibria with externalities, increasing returns and unbounded growth,' University of Chicago, Ph.D thesis.

Rotemberg, Julio (1984), 'Interpreting the statistical failures of some rational expectations macroeconomic models,' *American Economic Review Proceedings* **74**, May, 188–93.

Rowe, Nicholas (1987), 'Do small menu costs cause bigger and badder fluctuations in monopolistic macroeconomies?' mimeo, Carleton University, December.

Rubinstein, Ariel (1982), 'Perfect equilibrium in a bargaining game,' *Econometrica* **50**, January, 97–110.

Rutledge, John (1974), *A Monetarist Model of Inflationary Expectations*. Toronto: Lexington.

Samuelson, Paul A. (1947), '*Foundations of Economic Analysis*. Cambridge, Mass.: Harvard University Press.

Samuelson, Paul A. (1983), 'Comment.' In David Worswick and James Trevithick (eds.), *Keynes and the Modern World*. Cambridge: Cambridge University Press.

Sargent, Thomas J. (1976), 'A classical macroeconometric model for the United States,' *Journal of Political Economy* **84**, April, 207–37.

Sargent, Thomas, J. (1979), *Macroeconomic Theory*. New York: Academic Press.

Sargent, Thomas J., and Neil Wallace (1975), '"Rational" expectations, the optimal monetary instrument, and the optimal money supply rule,' *Journal of Political Economy* **83**, April, 241–54.

Sargent, Thomas J., and Neil Wallace (1981), 'Some unpleasant monetarist arithmetic,' *Federal Reserve Bank of Minneapolis Quarterly Review* **5**, 1–7.

Scarf, Herbert (1960), 'Some examples of global instability of the competitive equilibrium,' *International Economic Review* **1**, September, 157–72.

Schelling, Thomas C. (1978), *Micromotives and Macrobehavior*. New York: Norton.

Shapiro, Carl, and Joseph E. Stiglitz (1984), 'Equilibrium unemployment as a worker discipline device,' *American Economic Review* **74**, June, 433–44.

Sheshinski, Eytan and Yoram, Weiss (1977), 'Inflation and costs of price adjustment,' *Review of Economic Studies* **44**, October, 287–304.

Shiller, Robert J. (1978), 'Rational expectations and the dynamic structure of macroeconomic models: A critical review,' *Journal of Monetary Economics* **4**, January, 1–44.

Sidrauski, Miguel (1967), 'Rational choice and patterns of growth in a monetary economy,' *American Economic Review Proceedings* **57**, May, 534–44.

Solow, Robert M. (1969), *Price Expectations and the Behavior of the Price Level*. Manchester: Manchester University Press.

Solow, Robert M. (1980), 'On theories of unemployment,' *American Economic Review* **70**, March, 1–11.

Solow, Robert M. (1981), Review of E. Malvinvaud, 'Profitability and Unemployment,' *Journal of Economic Literature* **19**, June, 572–3.

Stiglitz, Joseph E. (1979), 'Equilibrium in product markets with imperfect information,' *American Economic Review Proceedings* **69**, May, 339–45.

Summers, Lawrence H. (1988), 'Should Keynesian economics dispense with the Phillips curve?' In Rod Cross (ed.) *Unemployment, Hysteresis, and the Natural Rate Hypothesis*. Oxford: Blackwell.

Svensson, Lars E.O. (1980), 'Effective demand and stochastic rationing,' *Review of Economic Studies* **47**, January, 339–55.

Taylor, John B. (1975), 'Monetary policy during a transition to rational expectations,' *Journal of Political Economy* **83**, October, 1009–21.

Taylor, John B. (1977), 'Conditions for unique solutions in stochastic macroeconomic models with rational expectations,' *Econometrica* **45**, September, 1377–85.

Taylor, John B (1979), 'Staggered wage setting in a macro model,' *American Economic Review Proceedings* **69**, May, 108–13.

Taylor, John B. (1980), 'Aggregate dynamics and staggered contracts, *Journal of Political Economy* **88**, February, 1–23.

Thom, René (1972), *Stabilité Structurelle et Morphogénèse*. Reading: Benjamin.

Tobin, James (1972), 'Inflation and unemployment,' *American Economic Review* **62**, March, 1–18.

Tobin, James (1975), 'Keynesian models of recession and depression,' *American Economic Review Proceedings* **65**, May, 195–202.

Tobin, James (1980), *Asset Accumulation and Economic Activity*. Chicago: University of Chicago Press.

Tobin, James (1981), 'The monetarist counter-revolution today: An appraisal,'

Economic Journal **91**, March, 29–42.

Topel, Robert, and Laurence Weiss (1985), 'Sectoral uncertainty and unemployment,' unpublished, University of California, San Diego, September.

Townsend, R.M. (1983), 'Forecasting the forecasts of others,' *Journal of Political Economy* **91**, August, 546–88.

Tucker, Donald (1971), 'Macroeconomic models and the demand for money under market disequilibrium,' *Journal of Money, Credit and Banking* **3**, February, 53–83.

Uzawa, Hirofumi (1961), 'The stability of dynamic processes, '*Econometrica* **29**, October, 617–31.

Uzawa, Hirofumi (1962), 'On the stability of Edgeworth's barter process,' *International Economic Review* **3**, May, 218–32.

Varian, Hal (1977), 'Non-Walrasian equilibria,' *Econometrica* **45**, April, 573–90.

Weiss, L., and E.F. Infante (1967), 'Finite time stability uuder perturbing forces and on product spaces.' In J. Hale and J. LaSalle (eds.), *Differential Equations and Dynamical Systems*. New York: Academic Press.

Woglom, Geoffrey (1982), 'Underemployment equilibrium with rational expectations,' *Quarterly Journal of Economics* **97**, February, 89–107.

Woodford, Michael (1987), 'Learning to Believe in Sunspots,' mimeo, University of Chicago, December.

Woodford, Michael (1988), 'Expectations, finance, and aggregate instability.' In Meir Kohn and S.C. Tsiang (eds.), *Finance Constraints, Expectations, and Macroeconomics*. Oxford: Oxford University Press.

Wright, Randall (1986), 'Job search and cyclical unemployment,' *Journal of Political Economy* **94**, February, 38–55.

INDEX